D1191376

CONSCIOUSNESS AND HISTORY:
NATIONALIST CRITICS
OF GREEK SOCIETY
1897-1914

GERASIMOS AUGUSTINOS

EAST EUROPEAN QUARTERLY, BOULDER
DISTRIBUTED BY COLUMBIA UNIVERSITY PRESS
NEW YORK

1977

Burg.
DF
759
.A93

c. 2

Gerasimos Augustinos is Associate Professor
of History at the University of South Carolina

Copyright © 1977 by East European Quarterly
Library of Congress Catalog Card Number 77-071390
ISBN 0-914710-25-7

Printed in the United States of America

MAR 3 1978 IW

To
My Parents
and
Olga

PREFACE

Observers of the modern Greeks have often remarked that this people's past has been as much a burden as an asset. This has been offered as friendly criticism of a society that is seen as having been dominated by a consciousness of its historical past to the detriment of its own contemporary development.

The desire to better understand the nature of this phenomenon led me to consider how the modern Greeks shaped their image of themselves based on the past and what form it took. More importantly, I was concerned with the reaction of certain intellectuals within that society when this well-established image was badly shaken at the turn of the century. Examining the responses of these intellectuals would help to make clearer the significance of the past not only in modern Greece but in any developing society, organized as a nationstate, in the modern world.

While working on this study I received the welcome support of numerous individuals. In Greece Professor K. Th. Dimaras provided guidance through his unparalleled knowledge of modern Greek intellectual history. Dr. Eleftherios Prevelakis and Dr. Domna Dontas were generous in furnishing both advice and needed materials from their respective archives as was the staff of the Gennadius Library. Mr. Philip Dragoumis and Mrs. Sophia Souliote kindly put at my disposal materials from their family archives.

Professors Charles and Barbara Jelavich were unstinting in their encouragement and judicious in their criticism as the manuscript first took shape. I was fortunate also in being able to call upon the extensive bibliographic knowledge of Professor Peter Topping. The manuscript was read at various stages by Professors John Petropulos and Peter Bien and benefited from their careful comments.

The greatest debt that I have can only be partly acknowledged on the dedication page.

TABLE OF CONTENTS

INTRODUCTION

Beginning in the early nineteenth century a series of new nation-states began to emerge one by one in Southeastern Europe. They often made their appearance in spite of the wishes of the great powers that competed for influence in that area and the best efforts of those who would have reformed the "sick man of Europe." The various Christian peoples of the Ottoman Empire were determined to give formal territorial and political definition to a growing awareness that they belonged not to a multi-ethnic state but to a far more inclusive community—the nation. Their loyalty was directed beyond the narrow confines of a family clan or village and away from the institution through which they had traditionally maintained their collective identity—the church. Instead they were asked to look to such factors as language, a common history, and most important of all a common enemy as a means of organizing their lives. The conscious awareness of these factors and the action that resulted from it was nationalism. The goal was to gain territorial independence for the group—i.e., the nation, which was perceived in ethnic terms, and to create a sovereign state.

Historians have long grappled with the complex and vexing phenomenon of nationalism in the modern world. To bring order out of the multitudinous forms in which it has appeared they have resorted to various schemes of classification. This has usually meant attempting to find its origins in a particular place and time and then developing an explanation for its appeal. Most historical theories see nationalism as originating sometime in the late eighteenth or early nineteenth century in Western and Central Europe.[1] In these theories historians have tended to emphasize the ideological content of nationalism. They have attributed its diffusion to imitation or borrowing without really ascertaining why this should be so. The effectiveness of many of these explanations has been further weakened by an implicit moral viewpoint in them. Nationalism has in effect been accused of being an ideology that started out as a liberating force in the modern world but then somehow went astray or that it displayed both humanitarian and tyrannical features depending upon the area in which it developed.

Efforts have also been made to break away from a chronological and spatial framework in dealing with this phenomenon. By concentrating on the movement rather than on the ideological content of nationalism scholars have projected a framework which delineates phases such as "stirrings", "the struggle for independence" and "consolidation" or nation-building.[2] Fruitful as this approach may be, it is too broad in scope to provide anything more than an overview of what is happening. It fails to discern and adequately deal with certain persistent and over-riding concerns in a nationalist movement as opposed to those which pertain to only one phase.

This study is concerned with just such a persistent concern, that of national identity, and those who seek to define and shape it. It is a problem that exists before, during and after a movement for national independence. In dealing with it I have been attracted to the theory which sees the development of nationalism as bound up with the interaction between what we term traditional and modern societies.[3] When intellectuals from traditional cultures have become acquainted with the secular world of the "West" it has often resulted in a crisis of identity for them. To come to terms with these two contradictory and basically incompatible worlds they have resorted to defending their own culture in varying degrees. In doing so they manifested their concern in the form of ethnic nationalism. It is within such a framework that I wish to examine the thought of certain modern Greek intellectuals concerning their nation's identity and to relate this to a very significant period in the history of that state.

Once the stage of political independence was achieved, the new states of Southeastern Europe, including Greece, were eager to cultivate their citizens' loyalty and identification with the nation. This was necessary for the peoples of these newly emerging nations had known little but localistic traditions for centuries and any wider identification, if any, would have been in terms of religion. To encourage loyalty to the new nation it was deemed necessary to define and integrate its culture. If we accept "culture" to mean the attitudes and perceptions that make up the outlook of a society, then a "national culture" may be taken as that which represents values associated with the idea of the nation, which itself is to be understood in ethnic terms.

The Greeks have a word for it. They call their national culture "Hellenism" (*Ellenismos*). This corresponds to the German idea of *Deutschtum* or the Russian *Slavianstvo*. Its growth and elaboration took place simultaneously with the creation and development of the nation-state. Since a Greek state had not existed for centuries, a "national" culture was vitally important in order to weld the disparate elements of the new society together and give meaning to this new political entity. Like most of the peoples of Southeastern Europe whose national consciousness developed during the nineteenth century, the Greeks looked to the past as a model for creating their self-image. The intellectual establishment, the teachers and writers, formulated in successive stages a view of their history that united the contemporary Greeks with the city-states of classical Hellas, the Greek-Christian civilization of the Byzantine Empire, and the Greek culture that had been maintained by the Orthodox Church during the centuries of Ottoman rule in one unbroken chain. This unitary vision of history provided both a proud lineage for a new state just emerged among already established and more powerful nations, and a guide for the nation's future development. The modern Greeks dreamed of creating a state as prestigious as the Byzantine Empire and as cultured as the world of Periclean Athens. That they did not possess the material means to accomplish this ideal, and that the past Greek cultures belonged to a much different political world, was lost among visions of national greatness to come.

As decades passed these views became the firm basis of the country's national culture. Hopes were raised that these well-entrenched beliefs would be fulfilled by the end of the century. Politicians argued hotly that if all the Greeks were brought within the frontiers of an enlarged state, the country would become economically self-sufficient and politically stable. In short it was a dream of salvation by expansion. The dream was called the *Megale Idea* or the Great Idea and it envisioned the taking of Constantinople from the Turks and resurrecting the Byzantine Empire in the form of a great Greek state. This manner of thinking meant that the state, the political formation that provided the government and administered the territory that was Greece, was separable from the nation, the ethnic group that included all those who believed themselves to be Greeks regardless of what state they happened to be living in. The one was not co-equal with the other. Indeed the former was looked upon as existing to promote the welfare of the latter. Under the spell of such ideas the Greeks plunged into a war with the Ottoman Empire in 1897. Defeat for the small kingdom was swift and merciless leaving the nation stunned. Almost a century of nationalist dreams disintegrated before the Turkish onslaught.

The war of 1897 ushered in a decade of political instability and national frustration which culminated in the officers' revolt of 1909 and the coming to power of Eleftherios Venizelos at the request of the military. In a few years the debacle of 1897 was forgotten in the resounding successes of the Balkan wars in 1912 and 1913. As a result of the victories in those wars Greek nationalist aspirations soared once more. The years that make up the period from the Greek-Turkish conflict in 1897 to the outbreak of the Great War were momentous not only politically but culturally as well. Greece experienced a literary renascence that signalled a significant advance in the cultural maturation of the country.

During these years the three individuals discussed here attempted the most conscious critique and re-evaluation of their country's national culture and identity. Kostes Palamas, the first writer examined in this study, was the leading literary figure of the time. His poetry overshadowed all other literary work for this period. Although his writings were not as narrowly nationalist as those of the others, Palamas' intimate and immense knowledge of the Greek past enabled him to create a powerful and original vision of what the nation's culture ought to be in modern times. The second individual dealt with, Perikles Giannopoulos, was significant not because of the popularity or quantity of his writings but rather for the intensity of his nationalism and his efforts to "shake-up" the established nationalist images. Ion Dragoumis, the last writer to be considered, is in a way the most important. He was the leading nationalist and a controversial figure in his time. A diplomat by profession, he also became involved in politics. He was an intellectual who not only wrote but also acted on his ideas.

The socio-political tensions that disturbed the nation in these years had their counterparts in the literary world. I have singled out four issues in particular that caused heated debate at the time and reflected the views of these writers concerning their nation's identity. Our starting point will be the controversy that raged at the time over the form of the language to be used by the nation. Greece is one of the countries that has been plagued by diglossia in its recent history. The Greek language had been developing along two parallel lines since the days of the Byzantine Empire. One form retained many of the characteristics of the classical idiom and was preserved by the church. The other was the outcome of centuries of development as it was spoken by the people. By modern times these two forms diverged significantly from one another. The modern Greeks were faced with this dilemma from the very inception of their state. Instead of solving it, they subordinated the spoken idiom to the purist one. In the early years of this century, however, it erupted as a major issue among the country's educational and literary circles. In the arguments presented by one or the other side were reflected broader views on how the country should be run and to what purpose.

The question of language leads inevitably to a second issue. Since a people's language arises out of their common past how were the modern

Greeks to view what had come before? The passage of centuries had witnessed the rise of several cultures or civilizations that bore the stamp of Hellenism. All had contributed to the creation of a remarkably long and varied tradition upon which modern Greek intellectuals could draw for ideas. The important question, however, was whether or not there was any unity to this past, and if so on what basis. Furthermore, each succeeding civilization developed its own special character with the result that these cultures often represented conflicting and contradictory thought worlds. How each of the individuals discussed here viewed this past will help us understand what they hoped their nation would become in the future.

The nationalist thought of these figures was not just a response to cultural stimuli. They reacted also to the political world about them. Defeat in 1897 only intensified a long and continuous debate over what the nation's foreign policy ought to be and what were its legitimate national interests. During the first years of the twentieth century Greece continued to be at odds with the Ottoman Empire over the fate of Crete. In addition there was the territory to the north of the kingdom which was still a part of Turkey-in-Europe. It was an area inhabited by many peoples including not only Greeks and Turks but Slavs as well. To some Greeks it was a prize that they felt the nation was in danger of losing to other Balkan states. All of this raised questions regarding the proper policies to be pursued and indeed about the very nature of the nation itself.

Probably the most problematic issue that newly emergent nation states have had to face was establishing a satisfactory relationship with the "West." If a nationalist aspired to strengthen the political and economic power of his group, then he inevitably had to come to terms with a civilization that was assuredly the most powerful and dynamic in the nineteenth century. The dilemma was how to maintain the proper balance between borrowing from Europe and retaining one's distinctive identity. Ethnic nationalism presupposes the assertion of uniqueness. To become like another then would be to deny one's identity. In the case of the Greeks this dilemma is even more perplexing. Since European civilization had its foundations in classical Hellas, imitating Europe would have meant merely reaffirming their own heritage for the modern Greeks. Although there is logic to this premise, in reality it did not work out this way. By the end of the nineteenth century people like Dragoumis and Giannopoulos were seriously concerned about their nation's identity vis-a-vis Europe.

As the three individuals whose work we are examining here reached their intellectual maturity in the early years of this century, their country already possessed a significant national tradition of its own making—the war for independence. To it were added the traditions of preceding Greek civilizations as the culture of the new nation developed. Dragoumis,

Palamas and Giannopoulos all shared in this culture as they grew up. How they used it in reacting to the world around them is what we will consider. For these men helped define the intellectual temper in their country during the first two decades of this century.

CHAPTER 1
A NEW STATE AND A NATIONAL CULTURE:
THE NINETEENTH CENTURY

The Making of a New State

The Greeks won their independence from the Ottoman Empire ". . .not as a Western nation with a long history but as a commercial class and a provincial peasantry in a Middle Eastern scheme of society."[1] From these two broad classes a new state was created and a national culture arose.

By the beginning of the nineteenth century the essential elements of pre-independence national consciousness already had taken root.[2] Intellectual sustenance for this consciousness came from the West. The receptors of these stimuli were the members of the Greek commercial and intellectual elite to be found in the islands of the Aegean and Ionian seas, the trading cities of the Ottoman Empire, and especially among the Greek diaspora in Western and Eastern Europe.[3] During this period the West provided the Greeks with two major streams of ideas. Europe was, first of all, the epitome of rational thinking, as represented by the French Enlightenment. Closely tied with this was the importance of the classical world in Western culture. Europeans believed that the ancestors of the modern Greeks possessed those characteristics of perfection in thought, art and literature which were so highly prized at the time. It mattered not if the picture of the classical age that Europeans created for themselves was faulted by time and their own contemporary views. The images were satisfying and the form well set by the time the modern Greeks began to make use of these notions for their own purposes.[4]

Modern Greek national consciousness was stimulated by liberal and secular ideas of government that were given concrete form by the French Revolution. These concepts were transmitted to the theocratic world of the Ottoman Empire to which the Greeks belonged by fellow countrymen who now lived in Europe. By their actions, however, these individuals brought out the inherent contradictions between these two realms. Two notable figures, Rhigas Velestinlis (1757-1798) and Adamantios Koraes (1748-1833), who dedicated themselves to bettering the lot of their people, serve to illustrate this paradox.[5]

Rhigas was born in the small town of Velestino in Thessaly of prosperous parents. After some years he left for the Ottoman capital where he came to live and work for the well known phanariot family of Alexander Ypsilantis. The talented and ambitious young man stayed in Constantinople until 1786 when he managed to secure the position of secretary to the hospodar or governor of Wallachia, Nikolaos Mavrogenes.

During the years before his departure for Vienna in 1790 Rhigas remained immersed in the political and cultural world of the phanariots with its Byzantine associations and contacts with Western culture. His first stay in the Austrian capital was short, lasting only about half a year from mid 1790 to the beginning of 1791. Vienna, however, was another world for Rhigas. Here there were thousands of other Greeks who took advantage of the economic and educational opportunities the empire offered. To the excitement of this large European city there was the added impact of being there while a revolution of major proportions was developing in France and the Austrian emperor and the empress of Russia were waging war against the Ottoman Empire. Under the impress of these events he increased his concern for the condition of fellow Greeks who were the sultan's subjects.

Family business forced Rhigas to return to Wallachia where he stayed for five years. During this time he worked on translations of Montesquieu and other French authors and diligently prepared a series of "maps" that were intended to enlighten the Greeks and strengthen their awareness of their long and rich heritage. Of particular interest is the map of Greece that he published in 1797 upon returning to Vienna. With this map he sought to delineate the areas of the Ottoman Empire which comprised the Greek lands and people. It included not only mainland Greece, but all the territory up to the Danube river as well as the coast of Asia Minor. Places on the map were given both their current appellation and the names they bore in ancient Greek times.

With this map and a revolutionary manifesto that he published shortly thereafter Rhigas presented his plan for a "Hellenic Democracy." In this scheme he combined the eastern imperial traditions that the Greeks were so much a part of with the western ideals of popular sovereignty. His dream was to establish a federation of all the peoples living in the designated area, "regardless of religion or language," to achieve the harmonious cooperation of a free people. As a part of this plan the Greeks would play an important role befitting their economic, religious and intellectual position among the Balkan subjects of the Porte.

Eager to put his ideas into action, this propagandist and fervent supporter of the revolutionary ideals of "liberty, equality, and fraternity" set off at the end of 1797 for the Peloponessos where he hoped to prepare the way for an uprising which would then spread to other major centers of Greek population. Betrayed to the Austrian police, he was arrested by them along with the materials that he was bringing with him and later turned over to the Turkish authorities, who summarily executed him in June, 1798.[6] While Rhigas helped promote the national consciousness of his people through his revolutionary pieces including his famous war hymn to freedom, the *Thourios,* he also left his fellow Greeks with an inherent contradiction in the political goals that he advocated. The major sources of inspiration for his work, the Byzantine tradition, the classical Greek ideals and the modern, Western ideas of revolution were difficult to integrate. The dream of freedom through a national uprising would prove incompatible in the long run with hopes of cooperation among the varied peoples of the Balkans. Rhigas had the best intentions in the schemes and dreams that he promoted with such fervor, but the latent inconsistencies nevertheless remained.[7]

Rhigas' compatriot, Koraes, continued the process of transmitting Western ideas of statehood and nationality to the Greeks. The son of a Smyrna merchant, Koraes was attracted to the world of letters at an early age. In 1772 he left for Amsterdam to look after his father's commercial affairs. Remaining there for six years the young and budding scholar deepened his knowledge of letters as well as his understanding of the humanist spirit. Leaving Amsterdam after his long stay there, Koraes returned to his homeland. He soon concluded, however, that his place was in the West. In 1782 he arrived in Montpellier where he took up the study of medicine. Finally, Koraes settled in Paris in 1788 remaining there until his death. It was here that the erudite philologist began to publish material intended for the enlightenment of his countrymen. He edited the Greek classics in a series called the *Greek Library,* prefacing them with critical introductions, which he hoped would give his countrymen a proper understanding of their classical heritage.

Life in revolutionary and Napoleonic Paris intensified Koraes' concern with the political condition of the Greeks. In a series of pamphlets with titles such as *War Song* (1800), *Trumpet Call to Battle* (1801), and *Dialogue Between Two Greeks Upon Hearing of the Glorious Victories of the Emperor Napoleon* (1805), Koraes sought to prepare his compatriots for the time when they would strike for independence. Seventy-three years old when the Greek War of Independence commenced, he immediately gave his support through memoranda to the Greek National Assemblies offering advice and by his activities on philhellenic committees advocating the Greek cause.

Koraes had long believed that his fellow countrymen had been suffering under a cultural as well as a political tyranny. He included in this not only the centuries of rule by the Ottomans but also the Byzantine inheritance of the Greeks through the Orthodox church and the phanariots. He rejected this part of the Greek past as unenlightened and evil. In its place he advocated the emulation by his people of the West with its dynamic society based on reason, and the classical Greek world with its achievements in literature and the arts.[8]

In his own way each of these two figures provided an important intellectual link with Europe. They supplied their countrymen with a fund of ideas that they could use to assert their identity as a nation in secular terms and to formulate the concepts of a sovereign government. They also stand at an important crossroad in modern Greek intellectual and political history. While contact with the West, both secular and religious, had been maintained for a long time before the nineteenth century by Greek intellectuals, that connection now became all important. Yet the type of thought that Rhigas and Koraes attempted to transmit was in many ways in direct opposition to the thought world that the Greeks had been a part of for so long as subjects of the Ottoman Empire. This resulted in a dualist outlook and gave rise to tension between the Eastern and the Western tendencies in Greek society even as part of that society began a new life as citizens of an independent nation.

The uprising in 1821 did not simply mean the gathering of arms, distribution of literature and the formation of fighting groups. When the standard of revolt was raised in the Peloponnesos the Greeks were upsetting a long-established way of life. In the Ottoman Empire the subject peoples were grouped according to their religion, into a community or millet. Thus all Christians belonged to the same millet, which was placed under the leadership of the Patriarch of Constantinople. While the Church included all Orthodox believers, its use of the Greek language and the staffing of the high clerical positions with Greeks tended to identify it in the mind of the non-Greek Christians with that people. For their part the Greeks saw the Orthodox church and the Patriarch as the one remaining link with the deceased Byzantine Empire. When the revolution erupted the church was placed in a difficult position. The Patriarch of Constantinople still considered himself the leader of all the Orthodox faithful. In this war for national independence, however, there was a dilemma involving a religious concept of belonging, Orthodoxy, and a secular concept of social and political organization, the nation. The Greek world including the Church was forced to choose and to adjust its thinking in the process.[9]

Ethno-religious divisions were not the only difficulty facing the insurgents. The Greek population of the empire was divided both geographically and socially. Three main geographic centers could be distinguished. First, the islands of the Aegean were inhabited by Greeks who made their living either as fishermen or more importantly as merchants. They were the main source of shipping for the Mediterranean and Black Sea trade of the empire. These were the people who provided the "navy" that the insurgents used to carry supplies and blockade the Turks. Names such as Kolokotrones and Mavromichalis identify the revolutionary leaders from the second geographic sector: the mainland. People such as these represented the world of the provincial peasant society found in the Peloponnesos and mainland Greece. They supplied the leadership and the manpower for the forces fighting against the Ottoman armies. The last group was found in the Rumanian Principalities and around Constantinople, in particular the district called the Phanar or lighthouse. Known as Phanariots, they were some of the wealthiest and most powerful families in Greek society. Through their service to the sultans, their influence in the Church, and their business acumen, the Phanariots had a vested interest in the affairs of the empire. When the revolution began and they had to make a choice some of them opted for the insurgents and fought for the national cause. They and the islanders stood in marked contrast to the mainland Greeks. Many of the Phanariots and the islanders, being in closer contact with the West, often knew a foreign language, usually French, wore European attire, and liked to cultivate European mannerisms. The mainland Greeks, on the other hand, generally knew only their local Greek dialect, dressed in the native attire of the area and cared little for the frills of Western civilization.[10]

Despite the difficulties of parochial jealousies, sectional interests and ideological divisions some semblance of a national movement was created. The basis of this movement was an appeal to all Greeks to fight as descendants of the ancient Hellenes. This coincided, first of all, with the views of the European philhellenes, who possessed a preconceived image of the insurgents. Second, the Greek leaders hoped to create at the least a nation-state along the lines that western European countries had already marked out in their own development.

In coming to grips with what it meant to think of themselves as a nation, the Greeks had at their disposal the terms Hellene, *genos,* and *ethnos.* During the last centuries of the Byzantine Empire, following the fall of Constantinople to the crusaders in 1204, the term "Hellene" had begun to be used by Byzantine rulers and intellectuals in referring to themselves and the nature of the empire.[11] This was significant because the Byzantines up until then had used the term *Romaios* designating themselves as citizens of the East Roman empire. The term "Hellene", employed in a pejorative manner, was reserved for non-Christian pagans such as the classical Greeks. The circumstances surrounding the use of the word are bound up with the problems of the Byzantine Empire at that time. It need only be noted here that "Hellene" as an appellative form was used during the *Turkokratia*[12] in conjunction with the other two terms *genos* and *ethnos.*

Both of these two words stem from classical Greek. *Genos,* referring originally to a family, clan or racial group was used by Greeks during the Ottoman era as an expression of their ties to one another and to their past. Because all Christians were grouped together into one millet, the term *genos* served the Greeks as a means of distinguishing themselves from the other Christian peoples of the empire. The word *ethnos* can also be found in Greek texts of the Ottoman period. Through this term the Greeks pointed out their common descent from the classical era.

By the nineteenth century these two terms represented fairly distinct positions. *Genos* expressed the attitudes of those Greeks who had vested interests in the empire such as the Patriarchate and members of the Phanariot class. These individuals viewed themselves as representatives of the Christian and especially the Greek Orthodox members of the empire.[13] The term *ethnos,* which had been used at various times by Greek intellectuals in the preceding centuries, now took on the more modern meaning originating in the West. Greeks of the diaspora and others within the Ottoman Empire began to use the word *ethnos* to express the concepts of a state and a people living within its borders. When the revolution started *ethnos* was the term that best expressed in the view of the revolutionary leaders their desire to create a uniform ethnic, linguistic and territorial entity.[14] "The five Constitutions of the provisional governments during the revolution until . . .1833 used the word *ethnos* which suggests not only the secular connotation of the concept but also its connection with emergent statehood."[15]

Creating a National Culture:
The Problem of Unity and Continuity

The long struggle against the Turks ended favorably in 1830 with the creation of an independent Greek state. In 1833 Otto, son of King Ludwig of Bavaria, arrived in Greece as that state's first monarch. The great powers, England, France and Russia, pledged themselves to overseeing the development of this shaky edifice. King Otho (the Hellenized form of Otto), ruling first through a regency, and then assuming full powers in his person, governed Greece as an autocrat until 1843 and from then until 1862 as a semi-constitutional monarch. Well-meaning in his policies, Otho nevertheless antagonized many people. Most important of all, he was unable to mend the significant social and economic cleavages among his people.[16]

The various interest groups in Greece, the native landowners, islanders and Phanariots, showed their dissatisfaction with the manner in which things were being run through political factions or parties that had arisen by the end of the revolution. Because of the influential role of the great powers in Greek affairs, the parties which developed took their name from the particular power to which they looked for aid and influence.[17] After 1843, when a parliament was instituted, the supporters of these parties vented their partisan passions there as well as through newspapers and even into the streets.[18] Out of this confusing plethora of opinions and voices it was possible to discern only a few issues which might be called national. The most important of these, and at the same time the most volatile, was the Great Idea.[19]

Enduring until after the end of World War I, this concept, called the *Megale Idea* in Greek, encompassed the world of diplomacy through involvement in the Eastern question, was concerned with the nature of the state as it existed in Greece, and affected the thinking of Greece's political leaders as well as the mass psychology of the people. Essentially a form of political romanticism,[20] the Great Idea, in its broadest form, envisioned the recapturing of Constantinople from the Turks and the creation of a large Greek state reminiscent of the Byzantine empire.[21] A missionary element was also present as the first Minister to Greece from the United States, Charles Tuckerman, aptly noted: ". . . the Great Idea means that the Greek mind is to regenerate the East—that it is the destiny of Hellenism to Hellenize the vast stretch of territory which by natural laws the Greeks believe to be theirs . . . ."[22]

It must be remembered that Greece in the first half of the nineteenth century contained only a small portion of the Greek population that was in the Ottoman Empire. Thessaly, Epiros, Crete, Macedonia, the Ionian islands, and parts of Asia Minor were areas where Greeks could be found but which were not a part of the newly created kingdom. The Greeks of the kingdom then, embarked on a policy, the Great Idea, of enlarging their state to include these areas. There were other reasons besides national sentiment that motivated the Greeks. Of the two main centers of Greek society, Athens and Constantinople, the latter was by far the more important from an economic point of view. Much of the trade of the Greek kingdom in the nineteenth century was with the Ottoman Empire. Greeks in the empire invested their capital in Greece which gave them an influential role in the economy of that country.[23] Intellectually, the large number of Phanariot Greeks, who came to Greece during and after the revolution, exercised an important influence on the cultural life of the new state.[24] The ties between the Greeks in the Ottoman Empire and those in the kingdom were thus considerable.

A classic view of the nature of Hellenism was given in 1844 by John Kolettis, leader of the so-called French party and identified in the popular mind as the leading exponent of the Great Idea at the time. A political controversy over who should be considered an "indigenous" Greek as opposed to an "outsider", i.e., one from without the boundaries of the kingdom, led to a heated debate in the National Assembly. An attempt was made to pass a bill aimed at preventing "outside" Greeks from holding office.[25] Kolettis, an outside Greek himself, saw the issue as involving the fate of the entire nation. He envisioned a large state encompassing all of the Greeks in the East.

> But the Greek kingdom is not the whole
> of Greece, but a part of it, the smallest
> and the poorest part of Greece. Autocthon
> [indigenous] then is not only an
> inhabitant of the kingdom, but also one
> from Jannina, Thessaly, Serres, Adrianople,
> Constantinople, Trebizond, Crete, . . . in
> general every inhabitant of land which
> is Greek historically and ethnically . . . .
> The . . . struggle did not begin in 1821;
> it began the day after the fall of Con-
> stantinople; fighters were not simply
> those of 1821; fighters were and are
> always those continuing the struggle
> against the crescent for 400 years . . . .[26]

There were two centers of Hellenism, Athens and Contantinople, and Kolettis touched upon the mission of Hellenic civilization.

> By its geographical position Greece is
> the center of Europe, having on its right
> the East and the left the West, it is
> destined to enlighten the East through
> its rebirth as it illuminated the West
> through its fall.[27]

Greece's role then was to bring the fruits of "civilization" to the East and to encompass within its borders the entire *ethnos*. In essence this meant that Greece would have to expand at the expense of the Ottoman Empire.

By mid-century there were two views among the country's political leaders concerning how the Great Idea was to be implemented. There were those like Kolettis who saw the Great Idea as a panacea for the foreign as well as domestic ills of the nation. To wait for a favorable international climate could mean an irreparable loss for the cause. Otho was prone to follow this line of thinking in his foreign policy whenever the opportunity arose. The opposing view, that of figures like Alexander Mavrokordatos, who was identified with the British party, held that Greece must first prepare herself by meeting her internal economic and administrative problems before embarking on the hazardous path of irredentist expansion.[28] Regardless of the debate over the manner of realizing this goal, the Great Idea was one means of bringing about national unity among the Greeks.

Cultural unification and what is today called nation building was a multi-dimensional process in Greece. A temporal as well as a spatial unity were undertaken. In asserting a national identity the Greeks, following a method that was used by all East European peoples, looked to the past.

The establishment of a continuum with previous Greek civilizations served as a source of pride for the new country and another means of legitimizing their existence as a nation. But these developments took place at a time when the intellectual mood of Europe was changing. This had significant repercussions for the Greeks.

In 1830 the German scholar, Jacob Fallmerayer, published a work which severly challenged the Greeks' claims of common racial descent from the ancient Hellenes. Fallmerayer asserted rather that the modern Greeks were a mixture of the various stocks, particularly Slavic, that had invaded Greece during the middle ages.[29] This struck at the heart of what the Greeks considered to be their national birthright. His theories provoked a furious response as he personally experienced when he visited Athens in 1833.[30] The work of Fallmerayer was but a prelude to the lessening of the classicist movement which diminished as Europe's interest in the Middle Ages grew. By 1840 the romantic movement had come into its own.[31] In Greece it reigned supreme until the end of the nineteenth century. In this atmosphere of romanticism and the Great Idea a Greek historian emerged who made a significant contribution to the idea of the temporal unity of his nation.

Konstantine Paparrigopoulos was an "outside" Greek. Born in Constantinople in 1815, he grew up in the Greek colony at Odessa. Drawn to the new state, he arrived there in 1830. After being dismissed from his post in the Ministry of Justice in 1845 because he was considered an "outsider", Paparrigopoulos took a position in a high school in Athens, where he taught from 1845 to 1851. In the latter year he was able to obtain a position at the university as Acting Professor of History, and after 1855 he became a regular member of the faculty.[32]

His first effort at historical writing came in 1843 with the publication of an essay *On Slavic Settlements in the Peloponnese*.[33] Intended as a rebuttal to Fallmerayer, Paparrigopoulos acknowledged the influx of the Slavs into the Peloponnesos, but attempted to demonstrate that they did not come as subjugators, nor did they destroy the countryside or annihilate the inhabitants; rather they were assimilated by the native Greeks.[34] Important as this piece was, a work of far greater impact and dimensions was still in the early stages of formulation. In 1853 the publication of a prologue heralded the appearance in 1860 of the first volume of his *History of the Hellenic Nation from the Ancient Times Until the Modern*. Completed in five volumes the work quickly became the main authority on Greek history.

Paparrigopoulos perceived the history of the Greek *ethnos* as passing through three stages. In the ancient period the Greeks constructed a base for their life founded on freedom of political and intellectual expression. The middle ages followed (the Byzantine era) and the Greeks became the chief apostles of the Holy Word of God carrying out a mission to all the peoples of Europe. Finally, in the modern world, the Greek nation would be the instigator of ethical and political progress in the East.[35]

Rather than emphasize the ancient periods as he had originally considered doing, Paparrigopoulos, under the impact of the Great Idea and the mounting interest among Europeans in the Middle Ages, shifted the weight of his exposition to bring out the history of the Byzantine era and the period of Ottoman rule.[36] It was his conclusion that the modern Greeks had not taken their political system and culture from either ancient Greece or Byzantium *in toto*. Instead, they had followed the Athenians in constructing a parliamentary government while avoiding the ancients' disunity by using instead the Byzantine monarchical form to complete their political system.[37] In this manner Paparrigopoulos delineated the modern Greek heritage. He created a unity out of the Greek past and, of equal importance, a unity of all the Greek people.

In consonance with an ethnocentric and organic view of themselves the Greeks made use of religion, history and a sense of mission (the Great Idea) in building their nationalist culture. An equally important aspect of such cultures has usually been language. In this instance, however, language has been a thorny problem for the Greeks to this day. The Greek language has had a continuous development since the time of Homer. By the end of the Byzantine era the language had evolved into two distinct and parallel forms. The language of the intellectuals, the Church and the Byzantine court, as it appeared in writing, was an extension of the New Testament Greek or koine. This language form indicates the interest of the ruling elements in Byzantine society in conserving and retaining a rich and lengthy tradition. The intention here was to alter the language as little as possible. Under Ottoman rule this language form was maintained by the Church. Spoken Greek, however, continued to evolve down to the emergence of the modern Greek state. When modern Greek intellectuals sought to employ their language as an integrative force they were faced with the problem of diglossia. At the beginning of the nineteenth century Koraes attempted to surmount this difficulty by taking the spoken Greek and "purifying" it of Turkish influences and dialectical features. This Greek bore the name *katharevousa* (puristic). There were others at this time, however, who felt that the spoken form or demotic was capable of serving as the literary language without major alterations. Dionysios Solomos, the poet of the revolution, believed this and wrote in demotic the poem which became the Greek national anthem. To further complicate matters, a few intellectuals, influenced by Western neo-classicism, and viewing their present language as a debased form of ancient Greek, attempted to revive the classical form as the appropriate national language! The *katharevousa* won the day, though not in the manner that Koraes had envisioned. It was neither the koine of Hellentistic times nor the purified Greek of Koraes. It was a creation of the second quarter of the nineteenth century; an artifical idiom discarding centuries of linguistic evolution in favor of "false archaisms" and "hypercorrect forms." The *katharevousa* was used in government circles, newspapers and at the university. Demotic Greek as a literary form continued on after Solomos, maintained by his followers in the Ionian islands, primarily in the writing of poetry.[38] A semblance of linguistic unity was arrived at in this manner, at least as far as the leading elements in the new kingdom were concerned. The inherent dichotomy remained, nevertheless, since the people continued to use the vernacular at home and in all everyday activities. The language question remained just under the surface ready to erupt once more whenever circumstances in the country were propitious.

A New Generation and Old Issues Reappraised

Irredentist politics continued into the second half of the nineteenth century unabated. During the 1850's Otho and the political leaders continued to pursue the realization of the Great Idea. Greece had not acquired any new territory since its creation in 1830. Politicians were quick to assign to the country's small limits the chief reason for its slow and shaky development.[39] England's support of the territorial integrity of the Ottoman Empire severely cramped any visions of Greek expansion. Russia, as a co-religious nation, seemed a likely candidate to help the Greeks in realizing their dreams. But while the Russians might be willing to tangle with the Turks, they were not about to allow the Greeks to benefit at the expense of the Ottoman Empire.[40]

The clamor for territorial expansion at mid-century was well exemplified in a pamphlet, published anonymously in English in 1853, entitled *Hints on the Solution to the Eastern Question.*[41] The author, Leon Melas, well-known for his literary work, was another "outside" Greek, a native of Constantinople. In the pamphlet Melas painted a somber picture of a declining Turkish Empire. The Ottoman Turks, according to him, had suffered grave setbacks beginning with the Greek revolution and the ". . . deathknell of the Turkish empire has long ago been spreading around its warning and dismal sound . . . ."[42] This led the author to the conclusion that the solution to the Eastern Question ". . . can be no other . . . than THE ERECTION OF A CHRISTIAN GREEK THRONE AT CONSTANTINOPLE."[43] The result of this action would be:

> . . . the maintenance and consolidation of
> European peace and equilibrium; the de-
> velopment and augmentation of the com-
> merce of Western Europe; the liberation
> and happiness of myriads of Christians,
> and consequently the glory of the Western
> powers . . . .[44]

Promising much gain for the West and a "missionary" role for the Greeks in the Ottoman Empire, the pamphlet illustrated the Greeks' desire to emulate their image of themselves as descendants of the classical Hellenes and Byzantines and by implication the inheritors of their civilizations.

The outbreak of hostilities between Russia and Turkey in the fall of 1853 seemed an opportune moment to the Greeks to fulfill their nationalist aims. But efforts to participate on the side of the Russians in the Crimean war were brief and disillusioning. The Turks checked the irregular bands of Greek volunteers sent into Thessaly, Macedonia and Epiros. The English and French quickly landed troops at the port of Piraeus, and it was not until 1857, a year after the war had ended, that the Allies concluded their occupation of Greece.

In the meantime new forces began to develop in the Greek kingdom. A new generation of political leaders began to emerge. They were no less nationalistic than Kolettis had been. Many believed, however, that Greece must be ruled rationally, through an effective constitutional government, which would lead to economic gains as well as diplomatic benefits for the kingdom. Discontent with the Othonian monarchy reached a peak in the fall of 1862 with the outbreak of a rebellion culminating in the fall of the dynasty. Otho, who always wore the Greek national costume and exemplified the desire to enlarge the state, was by now an anachronism. Reared in an age of strong monarchical rule and distrustful of ideas concerning the constitutional rights of men, Otho lacked the necessary vision and flexibility to remain as head of the nation.[45]

The selection of a prince from the Danish royal house, who ascended the throne in 1863 as George I, ushered in a reign that lasted for half a century. Possessing the tact that Otho had lacked, the new monarch weathered many political crises and lived to see his newly adopted country enlarge its frontiers.

From the 1860's to the end of the 1880's the kingdom made real economic progress. There was a marked expansion of shipping and trade. Better communication services, such as the telegraph, were developed, and attempts were made to provide commercial training for students.[46] Concomitant with this change was the growth of the urban middle class. Made up of small artisans and merchants, the rising number of professional people such as doctors, teachers and lawyers, and the increasing bureaucracy, the bourgeiosie became an ever more important group in Greek society. This urban class associated itself with the new state and its nationalist aspirations. Athens was the political, intellectual and social center of life. For these people the kingdom was an end in itself, not a temporary institution and a means to a greater Greek state. We may note here that those who continued to be highly concerned with the affairs of Greeks beyond the borders of the kingdom, were individuals whose families were originally "outside" Greeks. The family of Ion Dragoumis was such a case.

Before the establishment of an independent state, a traveler in the Balkans could visit many centers of Greek culture. Jannina in Epiros, the Ionian islands, Crete and Constantinople all were areas of intellectual creativity. When Athens became the capital of the new nation a significant alteration in the cultural life of the Greek world occurred. Instead of many centers, Athens became the focal point attracting the scattered creative elements to it. With the founding of the university in 1837, Athens began her cultural domination which greatly reduced the importance of the other areas of intellectual activity.

By the third quarter of the nineteenth century important political developments were taking place in the Balkans which significantly affected Greek irredentist plans. Other peoples in the area had intensified their own nationalist efforts, among them the Romanians and Bulgarians. The activities of the Bulgarians heralded a conflict between them and Greek nationalists centered on Macedonia, a region which was then a part of the Ottoman Empire.

In Southeast Europe where strident nationalisms now had developed, where matters were seen as either black or white, Macedonia was a hapless circumstance. It encompasses roughly the area from Lake Ochrid in the west, the Aegean Sea and the Pindus mountains to the South, the river Nestos (Mesta) to the east and the Shar mountains in the north. Macedonia was an ethnically mixed region with large numbers of Turks, Bulgarians, Greeks, Macedonian Slavs, Serbs, and Vlachs residing within it. In past centuries the area had been controlled by Byzantines, Serbs and Bulgarians for various periods of time. Thus, it could be claimed by more than one of the Balkan peoples on historic grounds. From 1767 on, when the Bulgarian archbishopric was abolished by the Turks, the Greek Orthodox Church dominated the religious and educational life of the Christian peoples of this region.[47]

The existing order of things was challenged by the Bulgarians, who sought to give expression to their national consciousness by throwing off the political rule of the Turks as well as the ecclesiastical and cultural control of the Greeks. An important goal of the Bulgarian nationalists was the re-establishment of their own national church. Approaches to the Greek Orthodox Patriarchate in Constantinople had been made by Bulgarians as far back as 1840, in an effort to regain the use of their national language in the churches and the appointment of Bulgarian priests and bishops. The Patriarchate had resisted these demands, seeing them as a threat to its ecclesiastical economic interests within the Empire. The Turks, however, were not slow to grasp that it would be to their benefit if these demands were met. In 1870 the issue was taken in hand by the Ottoman government and the sultan issued a firman (decree) establishing a Bulgarian Exarchate in Constantinople and a Bulgarian Orthodox church.

At the conclusion of the Russo-Turkish war of 1877-78, the Russians by the Treaty of San Stefano attempted to secure their national interests in the Balkans by creating a large Bulgarian state. The treaty, had it gone into effect, would have created a Bulgarian state that would have included most of Macedonia. The other great powers of Europe were unwilling to see this take place. Thus in 1878, at the Congress of Berlin, a much smaller Bulgarian principality, not including Macedonia, was established as an autonomous state. Nevertheless, Bulgarian nationalists now had a state and a national church at their disposal in their desire to create a "great" Bulgaria.

The Exarchate had been given authority to expand into areas of the empire beyond the territory designated as the Principality in 1878. In the firman of 1870, Article X allowed the Exarchate to establish a diocese wherever two-thirds of a community desired to belong to this Church. Since nationality in the empire was determined by religion, the implications of this decree were readily apparent. The Bulgarians were quick to take advantage of this and soon a series of churches, schools and dormitories sprang up in Macedonia. The Society of Saints Cyril and Methodius was established to aid in the movement. The Turks hoped to use this as a means of playing off one Christian party against the other in their effort to keep control of Macedonia.[48]

The Greeks as well as Serbs reacted, as might be expected, by stepping up their own nationalist efforts. After 1885 the Turks allowed the Serbs to increase their activity through their organization, the Society of Saint Sava. The Greeks in the area, having a large number of primary and secondary schools at their disposal already, responded by using the influence of the Patriarchate to offset Bulgarian propaganda. While the fate of Crete still held the attention of the Greeks, Macedonia began to attract more interest. A few individuals, such as the father of Ion Dragoumis, Stefanos, were willing to seek money and arms in support of Greek efforts in Macedonia.[49]

A new factor in Greek nationalist culture had now appeared; the fear of a Slavic threat from the north. Neokles Kazazis, a university professor and a leading figure in nationalist circles for decades, already in 1879 was writing that:

> . . . a predominance of the Hellenic element
> in the East had in nowise for its object
> to satisfy the ambitious tendencies of a
> race. Modern civilization is in danger of
> being overrun by the furious waves which

> threaten to carry away everything in the
> Russian empire. [Kazazis saw the two forces
> of "Panslavist Caesarism" and "Nihilism"
> battling for the life of the Russian empire.]
> The Cossack in the East, at Constantinople or
> near it, signifies nothing else but an entire
> and immediate overturning of the European
> equilibrium and of modern civilization.[50]

Events were dramatically changing the political conditions in the Balkans. The Greek *Megale Idea* was now one of many "Great Ideas." In an area where boundaries had been fluid for centuries, nationalism was forcing a more rigid political pattern on peoples. There were of course moderates both in and out of government who sought what they considered to be a just solution to Greek nationalist interests.[51] Nevertheless, the rise of Slavophobia in the country only served to complicate matters for the political leadership of the kingdom. With regard to both nationalist feeling among the people and the formulation of foreign policies by the government, the issue was no longer the simple one that it might have seemed a half century before. The goal of the Great Idea, to encompass all the Greeks within one state, a pan-movement of a sort, now had to accept another orientation. Unity of the nation was linked with preservation from outside threats, military and racial.

The development of an urban society in Greece and the concomitant changes in literary tastes as well as the size of the reading public by the third quarter of the 19th century provided the backdrop for the re-emergence of the "language Question."

As noted previously, the *katharevousa* was established as the language of government, education and the newspapers. The puristic form, however, besides being difficult to use properly even by the well-educated, was associated with the traditional social elite of Greece. As the country's urban population grew there were demands for a literature that would reflect its outlook and needs.[52]

The increased interest in folklore that developed in Europe had made a great impact on the intellectuals of the newly emerging nations including Greece. If folktales, folksongs and popular poetry were the expression of the culture of a people, then this collective culture was the embodiment of the nation. So argued the supporters of these concepts. To some Greeks then, the vehicle of popular culture, the demotic, was the language form that fully expressed the culture of their modern nation.

"Language and motherland are the same. To fight for one's country or for one's national language, there is but one struggle."[53] This statement by Giannes Psicharis, one of the leading figures in the demotic movement, illustrates the close connection of language to politics in a nationalist culture. Already one aspect of the culture of the new state, the *katharevousa*, was being called into question by those who considered it narrow and artificial.

Ironically, Psicharis spent most of his life outside of Greece. Born in Odessa in 1854 he left at the age of fifteen for Paris to continue his studies. He remained there for the rest of his life, teaching Greek at an institution of higher learning. From his study of the language Psicharis became convinced that demotic was the "national" language of Greece. He possessed both a competency in philology and the qualities of leadership that enabled him to assume command of the demotic movement. His manifesto appeared in 1881 in the form of a travel account entitled *My Journey*. Ostensibly a narrative of a journey that Psicharis made to the Near East, the work was a carefully written demotic piece with frequent excursions into the problems of the modern Greek language. Psicharis was interested in establishing a grammar for the demotic and he wrote several volumes developing his ideas. Other authors, living in Greece, including Ion Dragoumis and Kostes Palamas, eventually took exception to this linguistic legislating that Psicharis practiced. But his importance to this movement was summed up well by Palamas, who wrote of him:

> . . . in the work of Psicharis you do not
> recognize where scholarship begins and
> leaves off and where imagination comes
> in. He, Psicharis, is neither a dream—
> weaving idealist, nor a realistic
> painter of nature. He is an apostle of
> an idea, and along with it, he wants to
> implant within us a consciousness. . . .[54]

"A nation," Psicharis commented, "in order to become a nation needs two things; its frontiers must be expanded and it must produce its own literature."[55] At the beginning of the twentieth century nationalists, such as Dragoumis, who wrote in the demotic, attempted to do both. The argument of the demoticists, that the language form they supported was the language of all the Greeks, complemented the expansionist thrust of the Great Idea.

End of A Century: the Greek-Turkish War of 1897

By 1890 the economic spurt that had taken place in the 1870's and the 1880's had come to an end. The Greek debt had risen steadily. While English and French capital was entering the country most of the revenues were used to take the interest due on the foreign and domestic loans. The financial situation reached a crisis in 1893 when the government was forced to declare the country bankrupt. Trade had fallen off markedly and there was overpopulation on the land, causing the first in a series of emigrations by Greeks.[56] The kingdom could ill-afford any irredentist schemes to gain new territory.

The lure of national expansion remained, nevertheless. In 1896 the Cretans, as unhappy as ever with Turkish rule, rebelled once more. Theodore Deligiannes was prime minister at the time. A skillful politician, he followed in the lively tradition of Kolettis, espousing the idea of an enlarged Greece. Though not as foolhardy as his opponents made him out to be, Deligiannes was forced to respond to the crisis. A number of ships under the command of Prince George and an armed force headed by a Colonel Vassos were sent to the "great island."

By now the great powers had been thoroughly aroused, but they were not united on what action to take. The English, with divided opinion on the question, could not work effectively to calm down the tense situation. Germany and Russia, in agreement that Crete should not be united with Greece, could not get the English to react quickly enough.

At home the king and his prime minister were in a difficult position. In 1894 a secret organization called the *Ethnike Etairia* (National Society) had been formed. Made up mainly of junior officers in the army, its avowed aim was the realization of the Great Idea. Through an intelligent recruitment policy it had managed to enlist the support of many important civilians in and out of government. While many joined the organization to see the Great Idea become a reality, the National Society was also secretly anti-dynastic. Thus when the latest uprising on Crete occurred the king and the government were faced with a group avowedly patriotic and opposed to the monarch in addition.[57]

Regardless of the role of the National Society in pushing Greece into a war for which she was not prepared, popular opinion had been worked up into a frenzy of war-fever, which the king could not refuse if he wished to maintain his throne. Deligiannes found himself faced with a reckless opposition in parliament goading him on. In March of 1897 irregular Greek bands crossed the northern frontiers of Greece. When nothing was done to pull them back, the Turkish army attacked. The conflict that followed lasted approximately a month, ending with a complete defeat of the Greek army. Upon the frantic request of the Greeks, the powers once again intervened and arranged a settlement. Greece lost some minor areas in Thessaly to the Turks, was forced to pay an indemnity, and was required to allow an International Customs Commission to supervise the handling of port revenues to enable the Greeks to pay off their debts. Crete gained autonomous rule, with Prince George of Greece as the first governor.[58]

The material cost of the war to Greece was not great. But after almost a century of visions of an enlarged Greece, the defeat was a stunning blow to the country. The culture of this state was by now heavily invested with romantic nationalist concepts. Seeking an identity as a nation had led the Greeks, first of all, to an emotional and overriding attachment to the past, especially the classical era. At the same time consciousness of ethnicity as separate from statehood imbued modern Greek culture with an irredentist notion of political expansion. This culture included both elitist as well as popular elements. As we have noted, the changing nature of Greek society by the last quarter of the nineteenth century did affect the culture of the country as evidenced in the language issue and the emergence of a semblance of two-party politics. Similarly, the new political conditions in the Balkans and the Near East demanded that the Greeks make necessary alterations in their foreign policy. The war of 1897 put an immediate and heavy strain on Greece's nationalist culture. It forced issues to the forefront that had been gestating for some time. Developments in Greece after 1897 must be seen as reactions to both the war itself and the underlying forces of change in that society.

The Greco-Turkish war lasted only a few weeks. Yet this event marked the beginning of a period, lasting several years, of political instability and national frustration. The war itself was not the cause of all the problems that confronted the country, but it served to focus attention on the condition of the kingdom. The political, military, and economic weaknesses of the country crystallized with a shattering abruptness in the minds of many Greeks during those few weeks in 1897. During the following decade heavy criticism was directed at the country's leading institutions. The monarchy, parliament, the army, and the educational system all came under attack. Those taking part in these debates ranged from individuals who accepted the established traditions of the country to socialists who were emerging as critics of the entire society. Before taking up the ideas of Palamas, Dragoumis and Giannopoulos individually, it is necessary to place these men in the context of the society that they lived in and reacted to.

National Frustration

The psychological impact of the defeat on the Greeks would not have been as great had they gone to war with any sense of balance. Instead, they plunged into hostilities infused with nationalist visions that had been nurtured for almost a century. Defeat is never easy to contend with. A government could be blamed or the army, but for many Greek writers there was an uncomfortable feeling that the entire nation shared the responsibility for the defeat.

The attitude of the Athenian daily, *Akropolis,* published by Vlasis Gavrilides, was characteristic. Gavrilides, who remained an ardent advocate of Greek expansion, quickly printed several editorials concerning the defeat. In a column entitled "Those Responsible," *Akropolis* stated that the Greeks' egotism prevented them from admitting that they had been beaten by a superior force. Instead, they searched for traitors among themselves. Traitors there were, editorialized the paper, but more than the Greeks believed existed. *Akropolis* castigated the incompetence of the politicians as well as the military. This was the chief reason for the disaster.[1] The people themselves, however, could not escape the onus of complicity in the defeat. They had been living in a world of dreams and now they needed to awake and face reality.[2] The paper stated its feelings by asking rhetorically:

Are there still people who argue seriously that we were not
engaged in a nationalist war. . . ? Are there still people
who think . . . that if we had made a *nationalist* . . . war we
would have been victorious. Truly the war which took place
was not *Nationalist,* because it proved to be most anti-nationalist.
But thoughts like these which prove us to be more than incorri-
gible are even more anti-nationalist.[3]

By blaming all the Greeks the guilt feelings that people like Gavrilides
must have had could be lessened. The humiliation was not only in the
military defeat of the country, but in seeing their self-deceptions
mercilessly exposed. It was assumed that this guilt had to be borne by
the entire nation. Confessions such as the editorials of Gavrilides
rendered a cathartic service without really altering the basic beliefs in the
body politic.

Aggressive conservative nationalists like Neokles Kazazis now were
forced to defend their actions. As we have already seen, Kazazis had
been harping for many years on the need by the Greeks to assert themselves in areas like Macedonia. President of *Ellenismos,* a society devoted
to nationalist causes, Kazazis grappled with the meaning of the 1897
defeat in the first issue of the society's journal which appeared in 1898.[4]
Kazazis attributed the loss of the war to an excess of imagination on the
part of the Greeks which prevented them from realistically estimating
their strengths and weaknesses and pursuing clear objectives. This,
however, was no cause for despondency as far as Kazazis was concerned.
Instead clear heads needed to prevail.

Resorting to the past the university professor had nothing but compli-
ments for the generation that fought the war of independence. The same
was not said of their successors. In Kazazis' estimation they had created
an ideal, presumably the Great Idea, without fully appreciating the
sacrifices needed to realize it. Defeat by the Turks, therefore, was the
lesson that resulted from this carelessness. Rectifying this problem was a
matter of greater preparation by the government, the military and society
at large. To achieve this there had to be a national education, though what
this meant was not at all clear, which the society hoped to encourage
through its journal. Significantly, Kazazis asserted that it ". . .was the
state that had been defeated and not the nation, and this because of its
defective organization and functioning; as for the nation, its forces
emerged sound and undamaged."[5] Essentially what the directors of
Ellenismos were saying was that the nation and its goal were sound, but
that the country's leaders were at fault. The political and social culture
that had developed during the nineteenth century and had obviously
shaped Kazazis' values was not brought into question. Individuals of this
type could not cut the ground from beneath them. They therefore could
see no reason for nor would they coutenance any real changes.

The debate over the country's future continued into the new century. In the manner of newspapers that conduct surveys to ascertain public opinion on particular issues, the magazine *To Periodikon Mas* (Our Periodical) in 1901 asked for the views of various writers concerning the ideals of the nation with particular reference to the Great Idea.[6]

The unidentified author who promoted the survey conceived of the question in historical terms. He harked back to the formative era of the modern Greek state, arguing that the ideals of the eighteenth century were "freedom" and "civilization." The Greek Revolution thus was seen as the result of these concepts being put into practice. The sense of the author's argument was that the Greeks of 1821 were attuned to the ideas of their time and acted on them. His contemporaries seemed to be "strangers" to the goals "imposed" on them by the spirit of *their* time. The author then asked that the writers of the day discover the way by which all of the ". . . oppressed children of the great Greece" might be brought together.[7] The author felt that art was the means by which the country's future ideals would be found. He used the example of the poet of the revolution, Solomos. The great writer of that era had created a poetic image of a ". . . beautiful, strong, and independent Greece."[8] The author of the survey obviously hoped for the appearance of a writer who would perform the same service for the country in the twentieth century.

The responses ranged from the complacent to the cynical. The views of the historian Paul Karolides provide a point of reference. An immensely knowledgeable man, Karolides, a professor at the university, typified the traditional outlook concerning Greek affairs. In a reassuring tone the professor argued that the proper ideal was ". . . the great national idea . . . " which has as an objective the ". . . freedom and political unity of the entire Hellenic nation." This ideal was the same in his own day, Karolides stated, as it was before the creation of the Greek state. "Before the great revolution and for decades after it, this idea, drawing inspiration only from the past, had as its guidelines for national and political unity Byzantine Hellenism and Byzantine traditions."[9] Modern Hellenism, as far as Karolides was concerned looked upon Byzantium as its ". . . religious and at the same time national center."[10] The Great Idea of course was the personification of this tradition. At present, Karolides concluded, Hellenism had to persevere in claiming its "national and historical rights," and he cited Macedonia as a place where the national idea was in danger. Unwittingly Karolides formulated exactly what many of the younger generation of intellectuals were against: a superficial and by that time thoroughly commonplace conception of the country's nationalist goals.[11]

Several of those who responded were not concerned with any lack of ideals. Rather they complained that there was little or no effort being made to realize those ideals. "The Greek people act as individuals and dream as a nation."[12] There was nothing wrong with the concept of the Great Idea. The problem was that it had become mere rhetoric. Demetrios Tangopoulos, soon to publish the demoticist periodical *O Noumas,* sarcastically observed that the war of 1897 had shown how worn out the Great Idea had become from too much "use", i.e., too much rhetoric. The consensus was that national ideals were very important to the country, but most significantly, these men, who made a living by writing, stressed the importance of action.[13]

While most of the responses did little to answer the questions originally posed by the periodical, that of Kostes Palamas was easily the most idealistic as well as the most intellectual. The other writers approached the problem by accepting the nationalist goals but criticizing the efforts made to realize them. Palamas, on the other hand, attempted a different approach. He argued that the ideals of nations were created by great people, the heroes of action and thought. Ideals stemmed from the creative world of art. Palamas conceived of them as entities in their own right, which people must be capable of appreciating. The poet explained that he had first become aware of the Great Idea as a youngster in his own home when his family spoke of it as the future "resurrection" of the nation. The ideal had become more familiar to him when he attended school and learned the various national legends concerning the Byzantine Empire. But when he saw it expressed in real life, Palamas stated, it seemed a "crippled" and "ugly" thing. Presumably he referred to the period which ended with the 1897 war. The poet argued that the ideals of a nation were cheapened when they became a commonplace entity mouthed by all the people. High ideals could not survive in the "miserable reality of life." They must remain at a lofty height. In art they would find such a place. So it was with the Great Idea. Palamas believed that a national ideal possessed a life of its own independent of the masses of the people. He insisted that it remain in the realm of spirit. This would protect the ideal and allow it to retain its allure for the people.[14]

The defeat of 1897 had made a marked impression. Most of the intellectuals whose opinion appeared in that article continued to accept the premise of the Great Idea. It was their confidence in its being carried out that was shaken.

Political Instability and Social Conservatism

Political and social conditions in the country were not altered significantly by the war of 1897. Society retained its basically traditional and nationalist orientation. Yet there were good reasons for the dissatisfaction that characterized the writings of numerous individuals, nationalists as well as socialists. To begin with political life in the early years of the twentieth century was marked by petty factionalism. This was nothing new. But it was setback from the preceding twenty years when Charilaos Trikoupis had been on the scene. An admirer of the English political system, he had managed to build a party during that period that was more than just a personal faction. With Theodore Deligiannes as the opposing political leader, Trikoupis had promoted a form of two-party government in Greece. Retiring from political life in 1895, he died the following year. His efforts at building a viable party were successful to the extent that the party stayed together after his death. In November, 1898, George Theotokes, was elected by the party as its leader.[15] Theotokes, however, was not equal to his predecessor in ability. The party soon lost much of the discipline and unity it had possessed.

With the passing of Trikoupis, Deligiannes became the acknowledged senior politician of the country. He used his considerable oratorical abilities to win elections but failed to provide the country with the type of sound leadership that it needed. Deligiannes' political career was ended by an assassin in 1905.[16] His party immediately split into factions thus adding to the political instability of the country.

Two-party government was disrupted during these years, making it necessary for political leaders to rely on coalitions in the formation of ministries. This facilitated the growth in importance of small parties like that of Alexander Zaimes. A nephew of Deligiannes, he built a party of about thirty followers in parliament. Because of the prevailing political fragmentation he was able to hold the balance of power in new governments several times. In addition, the question of local against national interests was ever present. A product of the social and political conditions that had existed from pre-revolutionary times, the parochial outlook of politicians survived into the twentieth century. An English observer, well acquainted with Greek affairs at the time, wrote that the decline of strong party leaders during these years only increased the influence of local politicians. The "magnate" of each local district was often the determining factor in the election of deputies to parliament.[17]

The monarchy, which had served as an important stabilizing factor for decades under the careful rule of George I, found itself in a difficult position during these years. Since it was closely connected with the army, where the king's sons held high positions of responsibility, it could not escape the onus of defeat. The crown prince, Constantine, was heavily criticized for his failure in leadership during the war. Calls for army reform were coupled with expressions of anti-dynastic sentiment.

The major institutions in the country, the church, the university and the public school system remained permeated with a strong conservative nationalist spirit. At the university of Athens, under the tutelage of professors such as Neokles Kazazis, who was also president of the nationalist society, *Ellenismos,* and George Mistriotes, the arch defender of the purist form of Greek, the Great Idea continued to be propagated among the future professional people of the country. Students came from all areas where Greek communities existed outside the kingdom. Among these young people nationalist sentiment found its most enthusiastic supporters:

> For every Greek from beyond the present frontiers of the
> kingdom who has studied at Athens goes back to his native town
> or village imbued with the "Great Greek Idea", of which he
> thenceforth becomes a missionary. It is among these Athenian
> graduates, the doctors and lawyers of "unredeemed Greece", that
> the flame of patriotism burns most brightly . . . . [18]

Within Greece the process of indoctrination began at the primary level. Maps used in schools showed the area between the Danube river and the Aegean sea as the "Hellenic" not the Balkan peninsula.[19] The language of instruction was the puristic form of Greek. Emphasis was on the distant past with reading or rather memorizing of classical texts. History began with ancient Greece but stopped before reaching the reign of King Otho.[20] Since a formal education was within reach of only a small percentage of the population, the educational pattern tended to reinforce itself because it was mainly the more prosperous elements of society that could afford the leisure to obtain a full education.

While the shock of defeat in 1897 forced many members of the intellectual and political establishment out of their complacency, it did not bring any real change in their attitudes and outlook. They continued to have faith in the validity of their urban, upper middle class values—sobriety, undiluted nationalism, civic consciousness, and a belief in the importance of education. George Drosines, a well known poet at the time but of limited talent worked diligently to propagate these values. Only a year after the war he was busy presenting his nostrums for the country's social and political ills. Writing in the first issue of a journal dedicated to "National Education," Drosines soothingly explained that:

> By strengthening the customs and the virtuous traditions
> of our fathers within the family, by perfecting our schools
> as much as possible, by keeping an eye on the healthy develop-
> ment of our society, we too will succeed, perhaps slowly but
> surely, to make Greece a nation of socially and politically
> enlightened citizens, a nation securing its existence not on
> a crumbling materialist basis but on a granite-like foundation
> of moral and spiritual superiority.[21]

In 1899 Drosines along with other concerned individuals including Demetrios Bikelas founded an organization that was intended to realize the ideas that Drosines strongly supported. Presided over by Bikelas with Drosines as secretary, the Society for the Spread of Useful Books endeavored to supply suitable reading material for the people in the countryside. The society or *Syllogos,* as it was called, and its activities were imbued with the values of its members who were merchants, businessmen, professionals and teachers. Numerous titles were published covering everything from beekeeping to world history. The little red books were sold at a small price, which was within the means of most everyone. The importance of these works to the reading public in the provinces is noteworthy since they were practically the only books to be found in village bookshops along with translations of "bad French novels" as one traveler observed.[22] The language of these books was not the demotic that most people learned from childhood, but rather the *katharevousa.*[23] Those who directed the society were interested in enlightening their countrymen but obviously along lines that reflected their outlook and position in life.

The importance of tradition in this culture at the time may be judged from the "Gospel riots", an episode that possessed both political and social implications. Religion, language and politics were intertwined in this event that occurred in Athens late in 1901. The *Evangeliaka,* as the incident is known in Greek history, began with the altruistic desire of some individuals to make the Bible accessible to those whose education did not permit them to read it in the koine Greek. At the urging of Queen Olga of Greece the New Testament was translated into a mixture of puristic and demotic. The queen believed that her less well-educated subjects would be better Christians if they could read the Bible for themselves. This particular translation, completed in 1900, was presented to the theological review board of the Orthodox church.[24] What must have been an unusual step at the time might not have caused any trouble had it not been for the appearance of yet another translation of the Gospels a short while thereafter. In 1901 the Athenian daily *Akropolis* began to publish a translation done in the demotic by Alexander Pallis. This translation set off a furor among students at the university that ended in bloodshed on the streets of Athens. Those who supported tradition, especially theology students, felt that a sacrilege had been committed and the Greek language degraded. The incident grew in severity when opponents of this demotic translation attacked the earlier translation that the queen had commissioned. A sinister Russian and Slavic plot was believed to lie behind this version. Because the queen was of Russian origin there were immediate accusations of Russian "rubles" involved that would benefit no one except the Slavs in Macedonia![25] When the disturbances began to get out of hand the government was forced to step in. A political crisis of major proportions resulted.

In November, 1901, the students, who had sought support from other segments of the population, decided to take to the streets to vent their anger. Riots broke out on November 8, and the government was forced to call out army troops. The rioters were finally subdued but not before blood had been spilled. The Theotokes government, which was in power at the time, fell as a result of these disturbances.[26] Incidents such as this continued to disturb Greek public life during this period.[27] Those opposed to change often found themselves on the same side as those who were against the government that happened to be in power at the time.

It was in such a milieu that the country's intellectuals, the majority of whom lived in Athens, worked. In a few instances, as in the case of the socialists, there were attempts to challenge the social system as it existed. Most of the artists and writers merely exemplified in different ways the prevailing views of the time. The individuals to be discussed here belonged to neither group. They reacted to the political and intellectual conditions that we have looked at by calling for a critical examination of their national culture without, however, wanting to throw it over.

Revival of the Nation: The Demoticist Movement

The romantic movement, which dominated much of Greek literary production in the nineteenth century, reigned supreme until at least the 1870's when new currents made their appearance, partly as a reaction to romanticism. At the end of the century the works of European authors such as Ibsen, Nietzsche, d'Annunzio, and the French symbolists were being read and appreciated by Athenians.

Intellectual life in the country matured in many ways during the last decades of the century. Besides being willing to experiment with new concepts, Greek writers progressed towards creating a more unified body of national literature. Several authors now argued that foreign ideas and fashions were fine as long as they did not stifle the production of a native literature. There was a desire expressed that literature with a Greek spirit in it be created. The periodical *Techne* (Art) exemplified this mood. The magazine lasted only one year after the appearance of its first issue in November, 1898. Nevertheless, during its brief life the magazine dedicated itself to publishing literature with varied themes but with the idea that it would be based on Greek life.[28]

Europe itself contributed to the Greeks' understanding of their history and culture during these years. The history of Byzantine literature by the German philologist Karl Krumbacher was translated into Greek and published in Athens between 1897 and 1900. In a series of studies published at this time the French scholar, Gustav Schlumberger, did much to acquaint the modern Greeks with the Byzantine aspect of their past.[29]

Most important was the unification of the nation's culture through the use of one form of Greek. Literary works during the first half of the nineteenth century were written in the *katharevousa* with very few exceptions. In the later decades a few poets, including Palamas, began to write in the demotic. When Psicharis launched his demoticist crusade in the late 1880's the movement to use demotic in all forms of literature gained momentum. By the end of the century practically all significant poets were writing in this form and an increasing number of prose authors had turned to it also. The generation of demoticists that began to publish around the beginning of the twentieth century fought to secure the acceptance of that idiom and to bring a linguistic unity to Greek literary work. Demoticism was the answer for those such as Palamas and Dragoumis who were seeking a Greek way.

In an article on the Gospel riots written for a French publication, Psicharis noted that the ". . .language question comprises everything, country, religion, the whole national heritage."[30] The statement reflects the concern with which demoticists viewed this issue, and it indicates the broad area of public life that they aspired to influence. The scope and outlook of the movement were national. By the twentieth century both nationalists and socialists supported the demoticist cause. Each used the movement for his own particular purpose so that there often were conflicting opinions on means and ends. All agreed, however, on its importance to the nation.[31]

Due to the absence of a definitive grammar for the demotic and the existence of a variety of local idioms, numerous variations of this language form appeared in the writings of its exponents. Attempts by Psicharis to provide a linguistic basis for a demotic grammar resulted, as we have noted already, in a reaction against this by other demoticists. They resented his attempts at linguistic legislating, arguing that this was an arbitrary effort of one individual. Because he lived and wrote in Paris he was considered an "outsider" unfamiliar with the Greek scene. Authors like Dragoumis acknowledged Psicharis' importance to the movement, but felt that he could not himself produce the demotic literature for Greece that he called for.[32] The demoticists also had to contend with their determined opponents. Supporters of the *katharevousa* labeled them "vulgarists" and "long hairs" (*malliaroi*) seeking to identify the demoticists with those who lacked culture and refinement. The demoticists defended themselves by constantly trying to prove that their form of the language had just as long a tradition as the puristic.[33]

Probably the ablest exposition of demoticism at the time was the book *Glossa Kai Zoe* (Language and Life) by Elisaios Giannides, a high school teacher of mathematics. First published in 1908, it went through several editions and did much to popularize the movement.[34] Written with clarity and vigor the work attempted to show that demotic Greek was the "natural" language of the nation. Giannides argued that a language is the creation of a people. When it became their literary language it was then their national language. To account for the diglossia in the Greek language, Giannides proposed a "natural law" of language. A division could occur, he argued, between the written and spoken language of the "mind" and the language of the "heart." In this case the former must always give way to the latter because this was the language of the people.[35] The language question was posed by Giannides as a conflict between what a child learned at home and what he was taught in school. Giannides, who understood the social value of language, pointed out that the Greeks learned the *katharevousa* because they felt that it was the language of the "educated" and "gentlemanly." It was ingrained in their minds that knowledge of the puristic made it possible to share in the achievements of their classical ancestors, which then made Greece more respected in the eyes of classical-oriented Europe.[36] Giannides argued that these were fallacies which obstructed real progress for the nation. A language in his view was the instrument by which all the people were educated in the affairs of the nation. His objection to the *katharevousa* was that it served only a segment of the people. What was ". . . that cohesive force," he asked rhetorically, "which will unite all of Hellenism into one firm mass and will make it think with one soul?"[37] Giannides asserted that the demotic was the only real choice for a national language. Nationalist and social aspects of the language question intermingled in this work. Underlying everything, however, was the notion that demoticism would provide the country with a truly national and unified culture.

During these years several demoticists felt that greater efforts were needed in order to make a direct impact on society. They therefore formed several organizations through which they hoped to accomplish their purpose. Their divergent values and views are evident in the history of these organizations. In 1907, a small group of these individuals founded the National Language Society. Its members included the entire ideological range from nationalists like Ion Dragoumis to socialists such as Kostas Hatzopoulos.[38] The aim of the society was to promote the use of the demotic in all areas of life. The group did not achieve any real success primarily because of disagreement over the means to be used. Some like Psicharis believed in the immediate implementation of a grammar in order to standardize the demotic. Others, including Dragoumis, felt that it was more important to disseminate the demotic without concern about correctness of form.[39] Demotic was a "weapon" to be used in areas like Macedonia where people had little education and nationalism was to be promoted.[40]

In 1910, a new organization was established with the intention of seeking changes in the educational system of the country, in what seemed to be a new and favorable political atmosphere.[41] The Educational Society, as it was called, continued to function until after World War I. Its membership consisted of demoticists of various socio-political persuasions.

Dragoumis was a member for some time. Urban and middle class in origin, its members believed that the educational system was not serving the needs of the nation. They proposed to aid in the reform of the system on the basis of ". . . ideas taken from Greek life."[42] While their planned reforms had social overtones, their objectives were nationalist in essence:

> Genuine modern Greek reality and ideals are manifested in the
> neohellenic tradition, folk songs, folk tales, legends, pro-
> verbs, customs and the varied ways of life . . . and above all
> in the living language and creative literature. This unadulter-
> ated modern Greek world must become the basis of our education.[43]

The Society was not, however, chauvinist. Its members tried to place Greek civilization in the perspective of world civilization as a whole.[44] Their aim, was to cultivate the demotic tradition, which they considered the foundation of modern Greek culture.

The main outlet for the views of the demoticists during these years was the periodical *O Noumas*. It made its appearance in January, 1903, as a journal of political satire written in a mixed purist-demotic. Within a few months it broadened its scope to include articles on all subjects and became a staunch supporter of the demotic cause.[45] *O Noumas* stated in its first issue that it desired to examine conditions in the country in a new light with the hope that others would act to bring about changes. Its raison d'être was in part a reaction to the defeat of 1897. It condemned what it called a "war of words" in that year. Distrust of politicians was evident in its columns. Characteristically, and with a flair for the dramatic, the periodical stated that it was born from the trials of Greece, a true *Romios*.[46] *O Noumas* rendered an invaluable service to the cause of the demoticists by opening its columns to them regardless of their political and social views. Palamas, Dragoumis and Giannopoulos all published material in *O Noumas*. In its pages the literary, educational, nationalist and socialist ideas of the time were presented and debated.[47]

Demoticism was looked upon as a fresh approach to Greek affairs by its supporters because it was deemed capable of being adapted to many different programs. Ion Dragoumis asserted confidently that ". . . the people who will take a leading part in the nation in this generation—that is, the generation after 1897—will all be avowed demoticists or willing to accept the demotic language."[48] He represented the thinking of those who believed that the country had formulated its "ideals", that is, its national culture, improperly, in a context that was "artificial." Demoticism in their view offered a needed alternative. It was a language form that was spoken by all the Greeks, including those "unredeemed," and they associated their culture with it.[49]

Demoticism was even more important at this time to people like Dragoumis who felt that the conduct of the country was listless and its political leadership irresolute. In their view demoticism represented a movement that would stimulate a change. It provided links with both the past and modernity, which made it suitable for the future. Dragoumis saw in it the ". . . motivation and source of creative life . . ." throughout Greek history.[50]

But demoticism also presented a dilemma. It originated in a pre-modern era of empires. It belonged to a pattern of life that was eastern and parochial. Modern Greece on the other hand was coming of age at a time when the nation-state was becoming the dominant form of government in Europe with its attendant demands for unity and discipline from those within its borders. The West not the East exercised an increasing influence on the Greeks' way of life. The world of both the Hellene and the *Romios* existed in Greece. Nationalists who believed in demoticism were not faced with the task of simply doing away with one tradition and replacing it with another. They needed to reconcile their traditions to what was taking place around them.

It was natural that demoticists would wish to reform the country's educational system. We have already noted how this resulted in the formation of societies with precisely that purpose in mind. Demotic Greek was supported as the language of instruction. There was also the problem of deciding what the content of the material to be taught would be. Through their ideas on Greek education demoticists revealed their own diverse values.

The views of the demoticist author, Penelope Delta, whose children's books are still in print, typify the attitudes of some of this group. Born in Alexandria, Delta came from a well-to-do family. The education of children keenly interested her, and she criticized those of her class that provided their children with a European education.[51] Delta was concerned that these children grew up lacking the proper national ideals. While she understood education in the broad sense of the ancient Greek *paideia* or the German *Bildung,* she felt that a national as well as a moral issue was involved. Children who grew up without understanding what they owed to their homeland were poorly educated as far as Delta was concerned.[52] Delta believed that through the demotic tradition patriotism could be instilled in children. The moral issue was there also. Children that learned ". . . respect, dignity (and) pride," or what she called "character" would grow up to be worthy citizens.[53] Demoticism, in Delta's opinion, was a stimulating "national" approach to education. It is evident, however, that her values remained those of the upper middle class to which she belonged.

Delta's bourgeois approach to education was not the only demoticist response. Alexander Delmouzos, a socialist, argued that demoticism was relevant to all members of society and that it would benefit the common people particularly. Ideological views had not yet hardened to the point where cooperation was not possible between socialists and nationalists. Each used demoticism to suit his own needs. The socialists, however, were more perceptive in their understanding of this movement. They considered it bourgeois in content and outlook. Academic discussions concerning the language question, the creation of demotic poetry and novels, and the support of demotic as an educational vehicle were seen by socialists as serving a basically nationalist rather than a social purpose.[54] Demoticism, nevertheless, appealed to them. They had no ideological reservations in adapting a tradition that had originated in a non-industrial era and among peasants for use among the urban working class, which they considered the prime social sector for their attention.

Greek socialists varied in their estimation of fellow, non-socialist demoticists. George Skliros, whose pamphlet *Our Social Question* caused a strong reaction among nationalistically-minded demoticists, viewed the movement as beneficial to social progress in the country. He considered the demoticists the "healthiest" of the bourgeoisie, because they possessed knowledge, enthusiasm and awareness. The failing of these middle class individuals was their lack of proper tactics. They concentrated on others of their own class rather than working with the lower classes. Skliros argued that demoticists wanted improvement in the country but without altering the social structure.[55] Other socialists were much more critical of the demoticists. They desired a clear demarcation between those demoticists who were concerned with nationalist matters and those interested in social problems.[56]

Whatever the political tendencies of those involved, it is clear that they supported the demoticist cause because it was a "Greek way" for them. To the socialists this meant a vehicle through which the people would become better educated. This could then lead to other social changes in the country. While the nationalists also believed that a demotic education was the means by which to improve their society, their end of course was national unity through a more appealing tradition. It must be remembered that during the early years of the twentieth century the movement was basically in the hands of an intellectual elite. Its importance increased, however, as larger numbers of Greeks became active in their country's affairs, especially with the Balkan wars and World War I. As the temper of the time was basically nationalist, demoticism fitted admirably into this atmosphere.

The "Generation of 1897": Palamas, Giannopoulos, Dragoumis

Approximately a decade separated each of these men in age. Palamas was born in 1859, Giannopoulos in 1869, and the youngest, Dragoumis, in 1878. Seniority, however, belonged to Palamas for more than age alone. By 1900 his stature as a writer was already assured. Dragoumis and Giannopoulos made themselves known in the years after the turn of the century. The first decade was significant to all of them, however, for they created their most important works during these years.

These three individuals had both negative and positive aspects in common. Pertinent to the views of all of them was the belief that the nation's values, both cultural and political, had come close to bankruptcy. Palamas, Dragoumis and Giannopoulos grew up in the latter part of the nineteenth century, absorbing and identifying with the nationalist culture that was so much a part of the kingdom. They were all old enough to share in the feeling of humiliation at the defeat of 1897. In this sense it may be said that they are part of the same generation. Their concern with the condition of their nation was abundantly apparent in their literary work during the next few years.

There was also a positive unity in the writings of these men who possessed such differing personalities and intellectual vision. All three figures cultivated a sense of individualism vis-a-vis the society around them. Palamas and Giannopoulos were primarily men of letters. Dragoumis not only wrote, but he became involved in the world of diplomacy and politics. All three attempted to express in their writings the unity they believed constituted Greek civilization. Palamas had by far the broadest vision. He discerned that it was in the realm of art (*techne*) that the unifying and creative forces for all of Greek history were to be found. Hellenic civilization advanced by constantly striving to be creative in the world of art. Giannopoulos sought the timeless constant in nature, in the physical world of Hellenism; the sky, earth and water remained for him the seminal creative forces through history. Dragoumis believed that the demotic tradition taken in a broad cultural context was the fundamental factor in the life of the nation. He pictured it as the living force in whatever form it took throughout the millenia of several Greek civilizations.

There was a natural affinity between Palamas and Dragoumis. The latter admired the spirit and thought of the former. In an autographed copy of his book, *The Blood of Martyrs and Heroes,* which he presented to Palamas, Dragoumis wrote: ". . . to the only Greek whose opinion of this book interests the author."[57] Palamas, in Dragoumis' estimation, had captured the essence of Hellenism, especially in his *Dodecalogue of the Gypsy.* Dragoumis and Giannopoulos were close friends for many years until the suicide of the later. The young Dragoumis applauded the fervor of Giannopoulos' writings.[58] Palamas, on the other hand, took exception to Giannopoulos' totally negative attitude regarding European culture. He felt that even though Giannopoulos was motivated by laudable nationalist sentiment, his ideas about the nature of Greek civilization were mistaken.[59] Dragoumis and Palamas wrote in the demotic while Giannopoulos used an unorthodox mixture of a puristic heavily laced with demoticisms.

Despite numerous differences in style and personality the common nationalist motivation of all three men made kindred spirits of them. In the decade and a half following the Greco-Turkish conflict of 1897, these individuals became the most conscious exponents of a Hellenism that rejected a synthesis based on the use of the *katharevousa*, the supremacy of classical Greece and the emulation of the West in favor of a nationalism that included less reliance on Europe as a standard, more emphasis on the Greek world, both temporal and physical, and in the case of Palamas and Dragoumis the acceptance of demoticism. The Great Idea as a political ideal remained, but not without a close examination, expecially from Dragoumis. On this basis they set the tone of nationalist thought and action that prevailed in Greece down to the end of the Great War.

The integrative process that had gone on in Greek national culture during the first half of the nineteenth century had resulted in an uncritical acceptance of the supremacy of classical Hellenism and the expectation that the kingdom would expand by emulation of the Byzantine imperial past. Romanticism, through the use of the *katharevousa* in literature and the promotion of the Great Idea in politics, held an unquestioned primacy in the country. Even Kostes Palamas, whose literary career has been aptly characterized as "overshadowing" the Greek literary scene in the first two decades of this century, was only gradually able to free himself from these entrenched values and assumptions. At the approach of war in 1897 he reflected the nationalist enthusiasm that seized the country, just as he later mirrored the shock of those who saw complacently held values harshly tested and found wanting as a result of the defeat that followed. It was Palamas, however, who after that year grappled with the problem of a national identity, and sought to resolve the inherent contradictions and divisions through his literary visions.

Kostes Palamas (1859-1943) outlived the other two figures in this study by many years. Born in the Peloponnesos at Patras, he was preceded by a worthy intellectual lineage. Both his grandfather and great-grandfather were active in the creative world of their time. When Kostes was but seven years old his father, an official of the judiciary, died and he went to live in Mesolonghi with an uncle. This small town across the gulf from Patras still lived with the memory of Lord Byron and the heroic seige of the revolutionary period. The young boy grew up in an atmosphere of patriotism and a belief in the Great Idea.[1] Introduced to literature at an early age, Palamas quickly developed a love for books.

In 1875 he left for Athens to study at the University. Palamas arrived in the capital at a significant moment in the cultural development of the country. The heyday of romanticism and the *katharevousa* was just about at an end. Their influence in the arts, especially literature, had peaked and Athens was witnessing the first stirrings of new currents. The unification of the Ionian islands with Greece led to the infusion of a strong local culture that had preserved and promoted the demotic tradition in literature. The basic divisions in the nation's culture, apparent from the beginning, were still there. The *katharevousa* remained, however, and continued to exercise a powerful influence on fledgling writers like Palamas. His first literary efforts were written in this idiom. But the young author from the provinces was not satisfied by what the *katharevousa* offered, and he recognized the tension that resulted from Greece's two conflicting traditions. Gradually he began to turn away from the *katharevousa* and by 1886 had published poetry written in the demotic. From these first halting steps his output of poetic works grew steadily and along with it his stature as an artist. In 1895 he received the honor of composing a hymn for the forthcoming revival of the Olympic games. Two years later he was appointed Secretary of the University of Athens, a post he would hold continuously with but a small break until 1928. By the end of the century Palamas had been recognized as one of the country's leading poets. And his most creative work was still to come.[2]

The intellectual giant of his time was not physically imposing. Possessing a slim build he always dressed neatly and with taste. He kept his hair short and sported a well-trimmed beard that became sprinkled with grey as the years passed. A quiet man he preferred the world of his book-lined study. Palamas was the only one of the three writers to marry and have a family. In 1898, however, he experienced personal tragedy with the death of his youngest child, a boy named Alkes. By the turn of the century Palamas still had more than half his life to live. At the time of his death in 1943 he was looked upon by the Greeks as their national poet.

Nationalist Enthusiasm and Individual Disillusionment

Like many of his contemporaries Palamas reacted with enthusiasm to the challenges, both political and cultural, that confronted the country after 1880. The desire to expand the boundaries of the nation and the demand for a more relevant literature by the post-revolutionary generation were reflected in the essays that Palamas wrote for Athenian dailies. In an article written in 1896, the poet argued that his countrymen needed to make their patriotism the basis for all their conscious endeavors. Had not the time come he asked rhetorically, ". . . for us to perceive the idea of the Homeland more deeply, organically, and purely, relating it to all areas of our spiritual and social actions?"[3] Palamas harked back to the days of 1821 noting that the words and ideas of the revolutionaries were of equal importance with their deeds. There was no better example of this than the writings of Dionysios Solomos, which Palamas admired and enthusiastically championed. In his view, an intimate relationship existed between a poet and his nation. The latter was a living source from which the former could draw inspiration. Conversely, the poet, through his literary activity, encouraged the maintenance of national traditions.[4]

Inflamed and urged on by the happenings on the island of Crete no doubt, Palamas published in February, 1897, an article entitled "National Renaissance." Written in the *katharevousa* this piece illustrated the poet's most fervent hope that there indeed had been a change in the nation.

From a servile state insulted and suffering in the past, Greece was now ready to fight for its rights.[5] Palamas loudly proclaimed that the nation does

> . . . not turn away from the struggle, it challenges the
> unjust oppressor not to argue but to fight, it protects
> against obstinacy of the powerful, it wants to make it
> understood that it lives and thinks, that it is capable
> of redeeming the land which belongs to it. . . through
> armed action. . . . [6]

In succeeding articles, all preceding the war, Palamas made use of the historical past, as if he were mesmerized by it, to support his nationalist contentions.[7] He pictured his nation as being challenged once more as it had so often in the past. Battle lines were clearly drawn: Hellenism, "hero and martyr," against the "franco-Turkish" opponents, apparently a combination of the Ottoman Empire and the European powers, which Palamas depicted as the "transgressor" and "tyrant."[8] With nationalist fever now gripping the country, many, including Palamas, believed that the time had come for Greece to complete the long dreamed of task of uniting the "unredeemed brethren." Although he did not actually take part in the fighting, the poet shared the enthusiastic expectations of the rest of the nation.

While the war was fought on the northern frontiers of Greece, the effects of the defeat were soon visible on the streets of Athens. Thousands of refugees streamed south from the plains of Thessaly to the relative safety of the capital. Palamas observed them as they arrived in the city and wrote of their plight, graphically depicting their wretched circumstances.[9] Watching the harsh consequences of the war, the poet concluded that the country would have to bear a heavy burden before there could be any hope of regeneration.

> There are those who think that the absolution of our sins
> lies still far away. . . . But before we are born into a new
> life we must wear the martyr's crown; and this will not happen
> until we see Turkish hordes encamped under the shadow of the
> Acropolis. It is only through this ultimate ordeal that the
> inconceivable vision of rebirth would take on flesh and bones and
> that the light of day would emerge out of the darkness of national
> despair.[10]

In the fall of 1897, a severely disillusioned Palamas lamented, in deliberately Biblical allusions, the misfortune that had overtaken the country. The nation had been martyred, but worst of all, it seemed to the poet that there was no one to be found who was capable of gathering up the shattered remnants and beginning the process of rebuilding.[11]

In the aftermath of the war, as the shock of defeat gripped the country, Palamas vented his wrath at those he presumed were the culprits of the nation's humiliation. It seemed to the poet that a penchant for the past was one of the country's greatest sins. The modern day Greeks could not deal effectively with the reality that was the contemporary world because they had steeped themselves uncritically in the unreality of past Hellenic civilizations. Obviously, on this matter he was as guilty as anyone else! Nevertheless, what concerned Palamas was the lack of individuals in the country who were in touch with the times and could provide needed leadership. As he expressed it, Europe had produced a Darwin and a Moltke; the Greeks had countered with an Aristotle and an Onesandrus.[12] The world of reason and *Realpolitik* had made their impression even on the small Greek nation. Palamas was incensed at the politicians who, he believed, pandered to the emotions of the people by proclaiming that the country was destined to recapture the political grandeur of Byzantium and the artistic achievement of classical Greece. The result, in his view, was the destruction of true patriotism and the growth of chauvinist feelings. Only when politicians acted like statesmen rather than demagogues did he feel that the nation would be able to manage its affairs intelligently.[13] To one who felt as deeply as he did about the modern Greeks' heritage there seemed to have been a gross abuse of the past by the men who guided the nation's affairs.

Palamas drew the conclusion, accepted eagerly by so many of his contemporaries, that the country, including the military, was ailing from a lack of "discipline" and national unity. In Palamas' words, there was ". . .no understanding, no national, proper relationship between the State and the nation, the government and the people. . . ."[14] The poet relied on the notion that a society organized as a polity consisted of two distinct elements, the state and the people. The success of the polity depended on how well the needs of the state were reconciled with the needs of the individual. Obviously, the poet felt that in the case of his own country these two elements were at odds with each other and in times of crisis the nation could not work effectively as a unit to overcome adversity.[15]

The Poet and Society

While the nation was not lacking for a long and notable cultural heritage, Palamas was concerned that its ideals no longer corresponded with reality. In consonance with his own intellectual proclivities, he noted the importance of spiritual vigor for the well-being of the country. If a nation's intellectuals were responsible for its spiritual condition then it was necessary to admit to their share in the difficulties that Greece now found itself in.

Living as a young boy in Mesolonghi Palamas was moved by the historical atmosphere of the town and saw it as the ". . . embodiment of the Great Idea."[16] His patriotism developed simultaneously with his writing of poetry and, as he himself noted, it always remained intellectual in substance. "My patriotic impetuousness is always inseparable from an intellectual disposition which itself stands as its own purpose, and it is never an instrument for something else. . . ."[17] Earlier poems formed the springboard for later creations that expressed his love of country.[18] Palamas observed that he never sat down deliberately to compose patriotic poems. He believed that this form of writing was merely a type of "sophisticated politicizing," political rhetoric smoothed out by the "rhythm" of poetry.[19] If a poem were good or beautiful, in the platonic sense, it would be worthy of the nation, for it was the nation's culture that helped give birth to it.[20]

Palamas began the final year of the nineteenth century with the wish that the nation would come under the leadership of a few "strong" and "free" individuals, who would guide the country along an enlightened path in all areas of endeavor.[21] Palamas was a steadfast adherent of the Nietzschean view, that society benefitted most through the work of the exceptional individual. But how did the poet fit into the scheme of things? Palamas forcefully expressed his position in a poem written at the time of the 1897 defeat entitled "Offering" (*Afieroma*). The thematic unity of the piece is based on an antithesis, a form of development the poet favored. On the one hand Greece is presented as being in a state of upheaval, "desolate" and "shattered." At the same time Palamas depicts the poet who has withdrawn into his own world, cultivating his art. The poet does not wish to be a part of the chaos that swirls around him, but hopes instead to remain detached from worldly affairs. He has vowed that his endeavors on behalf of his nation will occur in the realm of art. His dream is to forge an image of his homeland which will not portray the suffering and humiliation that it has experienced. Instead a new image, corresponding not to the visible reality surrounding the poet, will serve as a means of inducing a new spirit among the people. In this manner the poet will be a true patriot for he has the ability to rise above the transitory nature of the world around him and create something lasting for his country.[22]

Poets have often considered themselves as apart from the society they live in. During the heyday of the romantic era an individual might assert this stance by claiming a heightened sensitivity and power of feeling that would set him above other individuals. This sense of being apart from the rest of humanity continued as a factor in the intellectual currents of the nineteenth century varying according to the individual's wish to emphasize the importance of intellect or that of emotion as the critical factor that set him off from others. In Palamas' case the world of intellect certainly was of paramount importance in his view of himself as the exceptional individual.

The poet's contribution then to the national culture of his country depended upon his conception of the relation between him and society. Palamas believed that there were times when the poet found himself not in accord with his nation. There would in effect be an open conflict between him and the community.

> Not only is he badly thought of and misunderstood, but because he is a poet, because he has the heightened consciousness of a truth which has not yet arrived to enlighten the others around him . . . , there are times when the poet is considered an enemy of the state and is assailed.[23]

If such an instance arose should the poet withdraw from society or play the role of a martyr? Palamas felt that the poet ought to consider his social mission, and remaining steadfast, carry out his role as the bearer of new ideas. The poet, by nature an idealist, ought to be imbued with a deep consciousness of the role he must exercise.[24] Like the symbolist poets, with whom he felt an affinity and whose movement he even helped introduce into Greece, Palamas envisioned himself in the role of a prophet. Through a heightened intellectual awareness the poet would herald what he believed were the coming "truths" about his society.[25]

While Palamas accepted the idea of a national mission in a poet's work, he remained convinced that a truly great poet could not be narrowly national in his creative efforts. A writer needed a work without being hemmed in by rigid territorial frontiers. Palamas felt that neither poets nor politicians could shape their love of country in accordance with the boundaries of their nation or the area under the influence of its arms. Small nations should not make for narrow visions on the part of their intellectuals. The well-being of a country depended not on aggressive points of view but rather on broadly conceived ideas. As he stated ". . . homeless ideas create homelands."[26]

Goethe was no less a German poet, as far as Palamas was concerned, simply because he wrote *Faust*. Palamas never consciously circumscribed himself by labeling his work simply as "Greek" poetry. While a sense of belonging to a society was important to him, Palamas adhered to the idea that through his sources of inspiration he could create works that were in the deepest sense Hellenic, without a conscious effort on his part to do so.

Art was a dynamic force that was capable of having as much impact on a nation as politics or war. Ideas, in Palamas' estimation, whether from outside a state or generated from within, were a form of progressive activity. The artist himself was the instigator of the ideas as expressed through his work.[27] Creative individuals, an obvious elite in society, provided the leadership needed to organize and guide a nation. Intellectual activity then was a form of action, and in Palamas' view, intellectual change preceded social transformation. Because of this he felt that there ought to be few restrictions on the work of artists. Like politicians, however, intellectuals needed to be aware of their potential power and exercise responsibility in their actions.[28]

A man given more to contemplation rather than action, Palamas devoted his life to managing the administrative affairs of the university and producing a considerable body of writing. Yet he was not afraid to involve himself in the controversies of that era. His active support of the demoticist cause was a direct outgrowth of a commitment to use this language form in his own creations.

As Palamas himself noted, his conversion to demotic came in stages or "crises."[29] In his first excursions into literary creativity Palamas accepted the lead of the literary establishment in Athens and produced poetry written in the "purified" Greek. As noted above by the 1880's the young poet had become dissatisfied with being tied to the "badly enthroned queen," *katharevousa.* He experimented with the demotic and in 1886 a collection of poems written in that idiom and entitled *Songs of My Homeland* appeared. It was some time before Palamas was able to break away from using the puristic form in prose work. Palamas quarrelled not with the written literary language, so much a part of the Greek cultural tradition, but with the "scholastic" and archaizing excesses that had occurred in the nineteenth century.[30]

Palamas' willingness to use the demotic in prose as well as poetry undoubtedly was bolstered when he read the "revolutionary book" of the Greek philologist and son-in-law of Renan, Psicharis.[31] Asked to review the work by an editor friend, Palamas was moved by both the logic and the activist tone of *My Journey.* It provided Palamas with philogical and moral support in his desire to use demotic exclusively as the language of creativity. Yet while he admired the scholarship and tenaciousness behind Psicharis' demoticist crusade, Palamas could not follow the philologist into every grammatical position that his cause took him. As a poet Palamas felt that he could not allow himself to be guided by scientific thought in what he wrote. He believed instead that a writer had to be faithful to his own creative impulses. A literary language was neither the unaltered spoken idiom of the people nor something conjured up by grammarians. In a manner reminiscent of Koraes, Palamas implied in his writings that a language was the product of both natural development, i.e., as it was shaped by a people through time, and creative human intellect.[32] Palamas' demoticism, in other words, was the result of his shaping of spoken Greek through literary inspiration. It amounted then to a compromise between the demand that the spoken language be accepted as is and the desire by people like Psicharis to legislate a formal grammar.

The sparring of those caught up in the language question became a pitched battle in the first years of this century as we have noted already. Athens shook with the fierce linguistic controversies associated with the *Evangeliaka* and the *Orestia*. Palamas expressed his commitment, already sharpened by the events of the preceding years, through the numerous articles that he published in *O Noumas* supporting demoticism by example and argument.

The appearance of Palamas' two major poetic works *The Dodecalogue of the Gypsy* and *The King's Flute* in 1907 and 1910 respectively was of major significance in establishing Palamas' stature as the leading poet of that generation as well as the validity of demotic as the linguistic vehicle for modern Greek literature. In *The King's Flute* Palamas treated with scorn those who insisted on maintaining the artificiality of the *katharevousa* and refused to acknowledge nothing but classical Greek culture as worthy of emulation. Through the figure of the Emperor Basil the poet attacks these individuals:

> And the unwise wisdom of the learned men
> is my enemy,
> all the assassins of life and the stranglers of
> the truth.
> A bad seed, grammarians, orators, philosophers,
> with blown up words and empty heads,
> spinners of trifles and chanters of nonsense!

The works of these people inspire nothing but distaste:

> And your rhymes and mud-pies and all your
> writings
> . . . .
> are nothing before the scorned,
> the unwritten, evening song which the shepherd
> begins as he descends from the green
> mountainside . . . .

It is the language of the people that Palamas supports through his poetry as expounded by the emperor:

> The language which thunders in my speech is the
> language
> of the working man, of manliness and of
> the upright,
> . . .

> because in the language of the common
> man whenever they allow it to blossom,
> the holy Spirit breathes,
> leading hands and thoughts to great deeds.[33]

Palamas believed that the demotic was the national language because it was the idiom of the people and at the same time it was capable of serving the nation's literary needs.

The language question was still a volatile issue when the Cretan politician, Eleftherios Venizelos, became prime minister and set about to reform the constitution in 1911. In the spring of that year Palamas found himself in deep trouble with the members of parliament. An article that the poet published in *O Noumas* in February brought on the wrath of both church and state. The article was a response to remarks by the patriarch of Constantinople deprecating the literary ability of demoticists. Palamas' defense of the demotic cause led to heated debate in parliament and among establishment literary circles about the propriety of a public official supporting such a movement. Forced by criticism from literary and educational conservatives to act, the government accused Palamas of going beyond the limits of his position and demanded that he "defend" himself.[34] Palamas replied to these accusations in a letter to the Ministry of Public Education and Church Affairs.[35] He argued that the demotic question was now not simply a linguistic one but an issue that concerned the political and social life of the nation. Responding to its detractors the poet asserted that demoticism had the support of several important scholars and that it was not the lowly product of anti-national elements in the country. Finally Palamas pointed out that because an intellectual was a public official it did not mean that he had to give up either his honor or his conscience.[36] All of this was carefully phrased in flawless *katharevousa!* But it did the poet little good for he was given a month's suspension from his post as Secretary of the National University.[37]

The demoticist cause in general did not fare any better at the hands of the "reform" parliament. At the urging of linguistic conservatives it added an article to the constitution which specifically stated that the official language of the state was that in which the laws of the land were written—namely the *katharevousa*.[38] The war and the Venizelist movement of 1917 did finally bring about a change in the policy of the state but there was no clear cut victory for the demoticists' program. Nevertheless, by his actions Palamas showed that he was willing to stand up for what he believed. It meant having an impact, no matter how little, on society and those men who were actively shaping it. Conflict in the world of ideas, of course, was where Palamas felt most at home. Yet the dialectic of this conflict brought him inevitably into interaction with society.

Critic of the Nation

By the end of the first decade of this century Palamas had published two works that represent his most creative effort, and which for many of his contemporaries symbolized the hope for a refreshing look at their society and its culture. The two works, "epiclyrical" poems, were inter-related in the poet's thinking and followed one another in an intellectual progression. They established the author as the leading literary figure of those years. Palamas poured many things into these poems; a self-criticism; his views on the role of the artist in society; the importance of art to any civilization, and what is most relevant to this study, a critique of contemporary Greek culture as well as a reaffirmation of his belief in the nation.

The *Dodecalogue of the Gypsy* appeared in 1907, the culmination of several years of thought and writing. Palamas had begun to compose it in 1899, and several chapters appeared separately in *O Noumas* from 1903 onwards.[39] The author himself noted that there were many factors involved in the creation of this work.[40] Among them were the impact of the debacle of 1897 and the popularity of Nietzsche's thought at the time.

The Byzantine Empire as it neared the end of its long history is the setting for the *Dodecalogue.** It is about to fall to the Ottoman Turks, who are just over the horizon. The Gypsy is the central figure and the vehicle for the poet's ideas. Palamas expressed the conflict within himself through the character of the Gypsy. As the poet stated:

> I used the Gipsy as a pretext and an occasion to express
> through him, through a type congenial to my soul, my
> intellectual aspirations. To repeat, I also, however
> weak may be my voice, the emotion of Man in the face
> of certain problems of life, his submission or his resis-
> tance; the feelings of the citizen and the thinker when
> confronted with certain episodes of the history of his
> nation.[41]

The Gypsy is a figure who does not consider himself a part of society. He embodies the spirit of independence and resistance to the conformist demands of the community. Yet the Gypsy has been shaped by that same society, which has left an ineradicable mark on his personality. He cannot deny that imprint, but he knows that he posseses knowledge and will that set him apart from other men.[42] Thus the Gypsy finds himself in a dual struggle. He must grapple with the pressures of the community to conform to its social contours and his consciousness of other worlds that pull him away. The character of the Gypsy represents a literary expression of the intellectual condition of Palamas during these early years of the new century.

The poem will be referred to by this abbreviated form of the title from here on.

Palamas did not envision the Gypsy as the symbol of the national revival that Greece needed. The Byzantine emperor, Basil, the chief character in *The King's Flute,* was a more appropriate figure for that role. The Gypsy is really a figure who is essentially above society. In the second canto the Gypsy seeks to participate in the community by contributing his share of useful labor.[43] He tries his hand at being a blacksmith, and later attempts to build fine structures. Predictably, he fails at these tasks. Even his venture at being a musician is unsuccessful for the Gypsy finds that playing for hire only alienates him from nature. To confine himself within society is hopeless. His world is not that of the people. This only suffocates his creative spirit.[44] But the conflict within the Gypsy and through him the poet, implies a concern with the condition of society around him. The Gypsy was a figure conceived by Palamas as capable of rewarding and creative efforts. But what limited him and what mattered to the poet was the restraining force of unchanging traditions that suppressed creative impulses.

Modern Greece's cultural heritage was of course drawn from both classical and Christian sources. How ought the modern Greeks to approach these two well-springs of their culture? Ought one to claim pre-eminence over the other. This concerned Palamas for the problem had obviously affected the work and the outlook of his contemporaries in literature. In the fifth Canto the Gypsy speaks of a procession of scholars which he meets at the outskirts of the City, bearing the treasure of the ancient Greek philosophers' works. These men, whom Palamas labeled the "ancients," had come to Constantinople to find a secure atmosphere in which to carry on their studies. Now that the "City" is threatened by the Turks they are fleeing to the West, in the hope of preserving and propagating the classical tradition.[45] To all of this the Gypsy bluntly asserts that their time has passed. New eras are coming that do not need to imitate the past. "Men may bow, bound to the idols of past Hellas and its shades. Hellas, though, is one and vanished—Mourn her, mourn her evermore!"[46] The Gypsy is not obsequious to the past, but rather takes only the vital essence of it.

> Hellas leaves me all undazzled,
> And I have never been drunk
> On the incense of past glory
> Or past creed
>
> When I chance to find a parchment,
> I set fire to it to gain
> Warmth or light.
> Unconcerned, my hearth I kindle
> Amid any ruined pile,
> Monastery or stately palace
> School or temple site[47]

It is the "flame" that offers whatever is necessary and worthy from the classical world. Of the ancient world the Gypsy says:

> Whether light you be or music,
> You are but of a lost past
> The last toll.
> O you awe-inspiring phantoms,
> Know in me the Whole and the True
> For I am that pair united:
> Flesh and Soul![48]

The Byzantines had "solved" the inherent contradiction between the worlds of classical paganism and Christian thought by developing their own Christian theology, which incorporated elements of classical Greek philosophy. It was the modern Greeks who had reopened the problem by insisting on giving primacy to the classical thought world in imitation of the West. Palamas felt that they had taken the form but not the spirit of that world.

But what of the other major tradition? The Christian inheritance was of equal significance with that of pagan classical Greece. Palamas considered the issue and expressed it in terms of a confrontation between supporters of the two positions on the outskirts of the City as witnessed by the Gypsy. A group of Christian monks have gathered to burn the books of the pagan philosophers as a number of pagans look on. *Romiosyne,* the medieval Greek-Christian world, is in danger of collapse argue the Christians. It must therefore be protected as much as possible. The pagans respond asserting that their world was created in classical times and must be kept alive for future generations.[49] In the Gypsy's view, however, both groups are mistaken in their assumptions. The two traditions, in conflict with one another, can offer little in the form that they have come to take. "All, all are nothing; all of nothing spun; Illusions every one!"[50] The Gypsy implies that something new must arise from these two worlds. They cannot destroy one another. Ancient Greek culture will journey to the West and there will spring up anew. The dichotomy can only be resolved through a blending of the two traditions. This will result in a synthesis that will be the basis for a new culture.[51]

Yet this synthesis was not what was really important. It had already been achieved to a large extent in the culture of Byzantium. Rather, it was the poet's belief that the people, the modern Greeks themselves, were the deciding factor in any new civilization that might emerge.

> A self-reliant folk that knows no books,
> That has no idols of the polytheists,
> And whose high strongholds are its only schools;
> It has a mind, a power and a will,
> Its men look like the statues of the gods
> And live by their own ballad's valliant rules.

> The cowards of the lowlands fear them,
> They speak of them by denigrating names
> And call them brigands, Klephts and traitors.
> The despots and the tyrants hate them;
> Among bowed heads they dare to stand upright,
> Among faint hearts they are the liberators.
>   . . .
> Call them pagans, they are Nature's chosen;
> Call them Christians, for they worship Christ—[52]

Simply imitating the past then was not the answer. This resulted only in the shadow of a new civilization. Only when the past was combined with a creative spirit could the modern Greeks expect a culture of any consequence. The reasoning behind these thoughts is readily apparent. Palamas, the artist who desired vitality in culture, felt that in a like manner a civilization could not flourish if it depended on an arrid imitation and preservation of traditional forms.

Civilizations and their cultures, if they are to possess vigor, must depend on the presence of creative individuals. But this is not enough if a society dissipates its energy in self-indulgence. To illustrate what he thought were the consequences of such a situation, Palamas depicted the Byzantine capital during the waning years of the empire. Constantinople in the eighth canto, entitled the *Prophecy,* is in the midst of a May Day celebration. The "City" has never been more splendid or the inhabitants more festive. But an ominous dark cloud hangs threatening on the horizon. The Turks are coming.[53] Yet it is apparent that this is not the real problem. Already the damage has been done by the internal forces of decay and all that Byzantium can do now is await the approaching conquerors.

What has sapped the vitality of that society? The poet shows us a populace and their emperor who care not for the fate of their civilization. Worst of all is the fact that the elite of that society, symbolized here by the frontier guards of the empire, the Akrites, is powerless to act, for it is held in contempt by the rest of the people. Byzantium's impending demise is vividly portrayed as a failure of will. In the Hippodrome, where preparations for chariot races are in progress, the prophet looks about him and sees:

> Disregarded and rejected,
> A small group of veterans
>   . . .
> These the Acrites, and they were
> Scattered here and there and scorned,
> Remnants of the Frontier Guards,
> Last of the Picked fighting-men.[54]

The emperor presents an equally sorry picture.

> But the Prophet did not see
> The hieratic countenance
> Of the Emperor appear
> On his high tribunal-stand.
> He beheld the King instead
> With the clowns and with the dwarfs,
>   . . .
> With the Circus charioteers
> And the other Circus heroes.
> For he is their boon-companion,[55]

When the signal fires warn of the approach of the Turks, the emperor refuses to cut short the festivities and prepare for war. The Akrites vent their rage at the impotence of the populace in the face of danger.

> Brainless, sightless and unhearing,
> Mob of toadies, on you woe!
>   . . .
> All by drunkenness are driven
> To the tavern and the ring;
> All of them, the Harlot City
> And the roisterer, her King;
>
> Till, entangled in the bridle
> Of the royal charioteer,
> Everything of worth is toppled,
> And the Turkish hordes are here![56]

The image of a decayed society, disintegrating from within could not be more devastating. Indeed this period in Byzantine history is hardly edifying. From the time when the Byzantines regained their capital in 1261 from the Latins the political power of the empire was but a shadow of what it had been in earlier days. The fate of the eastern Mediterranean was in the hands of other states. The central authority of the empire was powerless to control the largely independent outlying regions in Anatolia. From the mid-fourteenth century on Byzantium was caught between the growing power of the Ottoman Turks and the "national" states of the Balkans. Constantinople itself had suffered heavy depredations during the Latin occupation. While these facts would tend to confirm Palamas' concept of this era, his account, nevertheless, was overdrawn and simplistic. The dissolution of the Byzantine Empire was the result of many causes and not simply a failure of "nerve."

Amid the political and social disintegration of the last two centuries in the empire's history there occurred, surprisingly, a literary and artistic renaissance. This was exemplified by the mosaics in the narthex of the church of the Saviour in Chora donated by Theodore Metochites and the writings of the neo-Platonist philosopher Gemisthos Plethon. Palamas did not deal with this significant phenomenon, however. As we shall see below he viewed the development of societies in organic and cyclical terms. His intent then was to depict a civilization that had exhausted itself. In this view he was supported by contemporary Byzantine observers who saw their state as an organism which had worn itself out.

Palamas summoned up an image in this episode from the *Dodecalogue* that he must have hoped his countrymen, whose state had recently suffered a humiliating defeat, would identify with. In a passage bitter with disillusionment he summed up his own feelings about the Greek kingdom.

> "O City, famous among famous cities,
> The day is coming and with it the hour
> When you shall fall. And over you shall Fame
> Sound her last trumpet call
> To every quarter and in every hall.
> Your greatness is in ruins; gone your power!
> . . .
> And your orphaned soul, O City,
> Damned by your iniquity,
> Shall leave your corpse beneath the earth
> And roam in search of a new birth.
> . . .
> And the time shall come at last,
> In an hour of ill-omen,
> When your wandering soul, O City,
> Shall settle over there, far, far away,
> In that glorious land of old,
> In the sunshine and the gladness of an April day.
> And then shall issue from the earth
> An insult to the sun on high,
> Though claiming from your womb its birth,
> A mockery, a freak, a lie,
> A Kingdom, a calamity! . . . .
> . . .
> It shall exist with all your vices
> And nothing of your grandeur and renown;[57]

Yet the vision was not one born of total despair. Since Palamas believed that history was cyclical, consequently a nation could regenerate itself. There was hope for the revival of Hellenic civilization.[58]

The poet's real concern in the *Dodecalogue* was not the nation, but the need for a personal ordering of his priorities. However, by resolving the questions within himself the poet was indirectly contributing to the revitalization of the nation. Palamas found the answer in the very creativity of his work. The finding of a violin by the Gypsy symbolizes this solution.

> For the vast universe entire
> From an encounter springs

> Like that of bow and strings;
> And all things great and beautiful
> Here on this earth below
> In the red fury of the battle's fire
> Are fashioned; and they know
> The victor for their sire.[59]

An individual's work, whether physical or mental, had to be active and dynamic. Speaking through the Gypsy, the poet envisioned his efforts as directed towards not only the creation of art but providing the people with "new" and often "unwelcome" ideas as well.[60]

Through the nurturing of "Love", the "Fatherland" and the "Immortals," that is, those who created the culture of the ancient world, the poet fulfilled his highest callings. Promoting these forces would then aid in bringing about a new era in man's history. In this ideal, as Palamas perceived it, the nation had an important role to exercise.

> Just so long as among countries
> There are lands of better choice
> Which can beckon to the spirit
> With a fairer hand and voice;
>
> Just so long as in one bee-hive
> Honey flows and not in all,
> And so long as every Nation
> Knows a cramping frontier-wall;
>
> Just so long as Love is nourished
> Upon hatred, war and fear,
> And the Gates of Eden guarded
> By the sword and by the spear
>
> Just so long as Heaven's sunbeams
> Warm not all. Earth's souls the same,
> Then to fatherlands, for so long,
> Glory; glory and acclaim![61]

Nations were certainly here to stay, in Palamas' view, as something of a mixed blessing. While allowing for the necessity of these entities the poet, nevertheless, asserted his belief in a higher ideal, that of the creativity of art. The Muses, personifications of creativity, were the prime generators of civilizations.[62]

Although the *Dodecalogue of the Gypsy* was not a nationalist paean, its thrust was unmistakable. Palamas presented a sweeping critique of the nation's cultural milieu at the time. Written in the demotic, the poem made an undisputable contribution to the advancement of the movement. Through this work Palamas expressed both his love and frustration with his nation. From the point of view of this study it is important to note that the *Dodecalogue of the Gypsy* was seen by many at the time as both a moving attempt at national criticism and an effort to re-formulate the basis of modern Greek culture.

Renewed Confidence in the Nation

While the *Dodecalogue* unfolded in the poet's mind during what were certainly critical years in the country's history, reflecting to some extent the uncertainty of the time, *The King's Flute* presents us with a markedly different mood. Conceived a few years later than the *Dodecalogue* and published in 1910, it testifies to a resurgence of nationalist sentiment in the kingdom.

In time of creation the two "epic-lyrical" works overlap to some extent. The introductory canto entitled "The Son of the Widow" first appeared in 1886 under the title "The Macedonian King."[63] Despite the temporal overlap, the two works are in striking contrast to one another. In both poems the Byzantine Empire provides the setting. Yet the mood and the chief character of *The King's Flute* differ noticeably from the earlier poem. Palamas himself considered the *Dodecalogue of the Gypsy* as the "propylaea" through which one entered *The King's Flute*.

There is even less of a plot or story in the case of the second work. The poem begins at the time when Michael Paleologos, Emperor of Nicaea, was besieging Frankish-held Constantinople in the thirteenth century seeking to reunite the Byzantine Empire.[64] A few of the Emperor's soldiers, resting in an abandoned monastery, discover a skeleton in an opened grave with a flute stuck in its mouth. From the inscription on the tomb they quickly realize that these are the remains of the Emperor Basil, nicknamed the Bulgar-slayer, who ruled in the late tenth and early eleventh centuries. When they attempt to remove the flute it comes to life, speaking and singing. Through this mystical symbol the poet unfolds his story. Basil's genealogy and his feats are described in the second and third cantos, providing a vivid portrait of the medieval Greek world. In the following cantos the emperor begins a journey from Constantinople to Athens with his army in order to worship the Virgin in her christened temple, the Parthenon. All the Greek lands through which the emperor passes on his journey are named and praised in turn. The seventh and eighth cantos relate the passing of the pagan cults in Athens and the arrival of the Christian world with its veneration of the Virgin. Palamas draws an evocative picture of the emperor and his supplication to the Virgin. The poet characterizes him as a form of super-man. The emperor's past is recounted in the ninth and tenth cantos. In the eleventh *Word* the poet depicts the destiny of the *genos* in a prophetic vision of the fate of medieval Hellenism and the coming of a new materialistic civilization. The tale is now completed and in the last canto we return to the original setting of the poem. Now the flute falls silent and the skeleton turns to dust when touched. Palamas affirms his belief in the indestructibility of the *genos* throughout the centuries and then compares his work to the Homeric epics with the conviction that his poem has encompassed a wider vision in its conception.

A clear indication of the tone that is to be found in the poem is provided by the setting itself. Palamas, as we have already noted, showed a discerning interest in the history of Byzantium. His poems *Songs of My Homeland,* published at the end of the past century, already contain themes taken from that period of history. His choice of Byzantium during the time of Basil II was in accordance with the mood of the work. The period between 867 and 1025 is known as the Macedonian era in the empire's history, taking its name from the ruling house of that time. One authority has characterized this as politically the most brilliant era in the history of the empire.[65] Separatist movements in Asia-Minor were suppressed and Byzantine influence in Syria was strengthened. More significant for the poet was the fact that Bulgaria was transformed from a rival state into a Byzantine province through the military successes of the Macedonian dynasty. The high point, militarily speaking, was reached under the reign of Basil, who ruled from 976 until 1025. During the tenth century the Bulgarians, under the able leadership of their Tsars Simeon and later Samuel, had created an empire that was a serious challenge to the Byzantines for several years. Not until the beginning of eleventh century, when Basil was emperor, was the empire able to defeat the Bulgarians. Basil's great victory came in the year 1014, when he defeated the army of Tsar Samuel. Tradition has it that the emperor had 14,000 Bulgarian soldiers, who had been taken prisoner, blinded and then sent back to Samuel, who subsequently died of shock when he beheld the catastrophe that had befallen his forces.[66] This deed later earned Basil the epithet "Bulgar-slayer."

Palamas chose this era as the setting for the poem having in mind obviously the vigorous character of Basil and the political and cultural greatness of the period. If the work was a reaffirmation of his faith in the nation, one might ask why he did not turn to the thirteenth century and the Empire of Nicaea for his setting. During the years between 1204 and 1261 when the Latins held Constantinople Byzantine political and religious influence was reduced to the small state of Nicaea in Asia Minor. Faced with foreign occupation of their capital and the assertion of ecclesiastical independence by the Serbs and Bulgarians in the Balkans the Byzantines deliberately focused on their classical heritage. "Hellene," a term customarily used to refer to a pagan, now found favor with the Byzantines of Nicaea becoming synonymous with the word *Romaios* by which they normally referred to themselves. In recent years some scholars have argued that this era was the seedbed for a modern Greek national consciousness.[67]

Whatever the merits of this argument, the era in question did not serve Palamas' interests. In the *Dodecalogue of the Gypsy* he looked at the past in order to criticize the present. In *The King's Flute* his intent was to praise the *entire* Greek past and to integrate it both chronologically and spatially. What better way than to choose an era when the Byzantine Empire was at its zenith. *The King's Flute* is a testament to the power of the Great Idea.

By recounting the areas of the empire from which Greeks who fought in the Byzantine armies came, Palamas produced a panorama of what he considered to be the totality of the Greek people. Each region inhabited by Greeks was described and the people praised.[68] Macedonia, where the Greeks were involved in a struggle with their Bulgarian neighbors in the early years of this century, received as might be expected, a prominent place. The poet described it as an area that was ". . . the Slav's dream and the *Romios'* glory."[69] There was no mistaking where his sympathies lay, for he asserted that the "Macedonians," i.e., Greeks, had held firm and had acted as a barrier against the Slavs.[70]

To further the image of the Greeks as a vigorous people with a unified tradition the poet used the device of the Emperor Basil's journey from Constantinople to Athens to recall heroic episodes in their past. Thermopylae and the Three Hundred are mentioned as well as the successes of Nicephoros and Basil over the Bulgarians.[71]

National greatness was not necessarily associated with military might and territorial expansion, however. To Palamas a great nation was above all the product of a culturally creative people. In *The King's Flute* the poet emphasized those elements in the Greek past that would provide examples of the creative power of the nation. Thus Palamas showed an affinity for those lands that had been closely identified with artistic creativity from ancient times. Thrace, the home of Orpheus, was singled out in the *Dodecalogue of the Gypsy*. In *The King's Flute* Thessaly, home of the Olympian gods and the Parnassian muses, received similar attention.[72]

Mount Parnassos had been the symbol of poetic inspiration since classical times. Palamas, himself a lyric poet, esteemed this tradition. His vision extended beyond this, however, and the mountain emerges in *The King's Flute* as the symbol of the generative powers within the nation. By referring to the double name that the mountain possessed the poet posed a dynamic interaction of forces. Parnassos, the classical appellation for the mountain, represented the culture of the ancient world. Liakoura, the name for the mountain in modern Greek, provided the interacting element symbolizing vitality and creativity. Through the former name which is masculine in gender and the latter, which is feminine, Palamas constructed that dialectic formula that he felt was so necessary for the maintenance of cultural vigor.[73] He had already emphatically asserted in the *Dodecalogue of the Gypsy* that the ancient

world had passed and that it could not be revived. Yet through the dualism
of Parnassos-Liakoura a living tradition could be continued and sustained
in modern Greek culture. The mountain was always recreating something
new out of itself. In a like manner the nation could also continue to be
creative by combining the enduring traditions of the past with the vitalistic forces of the present.[74] Finally, the mountain symbolized for the
poet a haven for the strong-willed and those "exiles of the world." Creative
individuals were necessarily part of a select group. Parnassos represented
the ideal that they should strive to reach.

> And they came towards the liberator to find
> a place to breathe,
> And to retain their honor, and to remain free,
>
> . . .
>
> Because in the towns are the evil and the slack,
> and in the countryside the slaves.[75]

The mountain symbolized both the poet's vision of Hellenic culture and
his concept of the artist's role in society.

The theme of the unity of Greek culture through the centuries
continues throughout the poem. While there were some like Giannopoulos,
who as we shall see, believed that the transition from the ancient to the
medieval Greek world had been accomplished to the detriment of the
former, Palamas stressed the idea that Hellenism contained both classical
and Christian elements, the one complementing the other. The poet had
emphasized this notion already in the *Dodecalogue of the Gypsy* and he
continued and developed the theme in *The King's Flute*.[76]

In dealing with the Greek world in the middle ages the natural tendency
would be to concentrate on Constantinople, the capital of the Byzantine
Empire. Palamas, however, chose to dwell upon Athens as he elaborated
his ideas concerning the character of that era. This city with its famous
Academy continued to be the spiritual center of the pagan world for
centuries after the end of the classical era. The Academy itself lasted
until the sixth century, when it was finally closed by the Emperor
Justinian. After this Athens declined as an important cultural center
emerging in the nineteenth century as a small town of about ten thousand
inhabitants. Yet there remains to this day in that city a monumental
symbol of the ancient world, the Parthenon.

Athens fascinated Palamas. It represented both the artistic achievement of ancient Greece as well as the Christian world that succeeded it.
As the poet celebrated the city:

> Is it you [Athens] who wears the Rock [Acropolis]
> as a crown?

> Is it you Rock that holds the temple [Parthenon],
> crown of crowns?
> . . . .
> And so with you, You would not allow
> yourself, temple,
> to live elsewhere but where you first took root
> You the blossom and Athens the vase.
> . . . .
> With you begins the rejuvenation of the world,
> With you the rejuvenation of the world is completed.[77]

The "crowning" temple was of course the home of Athena, goddess of wisdom. Symbolizing the achievements of the classical age the Parthenon now becomes the setting for the arrival of a new goddess and a new era.[78] The pagan philosophers must pass giving way to Christianity and the Virgin; but the temple remains. Through the figure of the Emperor Basil Palamas establishes the underlying constancy from one civilization to another. In Constantinople the Virgin is the protectress of the city and known by the name Vlacherniotissa, from the principal shrine where she is worshipped. Basil, not content to worship the Virgin in the City, seeks an appropriate place among the Christian centers of the East, and is finally drawn to Athens. The Virgin, enthroned in her church in the ancient Parthenon, has taken on the attributes of the ancient pagan goddess: wisdom and a love of battle. This then is the deity that attracts the emperor.[79] The poet speaks of the Parthenon as it has been changed by succeeding religions and conquerors. Each new ruler has destroyed the former statues and replaced them with his own. Apollo's likeness on the Acropolis has given way to Constantine's bust. The temple then reflects whatever will befall the *genos*. By surviving all the upheavals it exemplifies the fate that marks the nation's history.[80] In this manner Palamas expressed his belief that flux and change must occur in history, while at the same time there remained a fundamental unity in a people's history based on the enduring elements from the past. Athens symbolized for Palamas that enduring unity as Constantinople could not.

The Need for Vigorous Leadership

A favorite device that Palamas employed in both of the epic poems was the presentation of ideas through the prophetic vision of one of the characters. The Gypsy performed this function in the *Dodecalogue of the Gypsy* and the poet used the character of the Emperor Basil in *The King's Flute* to the same end. Palamas had in mind here the use of the past for the betterment of the nation in the future.

In the eleventh canto of *The King's Flute,* Basil awakens from a prophetic dream that he has had. In the dream an angel, bearing within itself three distinct forms, appears before Basil. At one time it is an angel of God, at another the "archangel of the abyss," and finally the image of the sleeping emperor himself.[81] The reason for this triple image becomes apparent as the emperor recounts the dream that he has seen. At the beginning there is a panorama of the City in all its splendor. Its reputation and power are recognized both in the East and the West. Over this magnificent civilization stands the Greek as "captain" with Byzantium as the "support." But this is not to last. The second stage of the vision unfolds. Evil days are approaching and even Basil with all his military prowess cannot change what is to come. The empire, the *genos,* church, even the people are all in danger.[82] Basil appeals for aid to the Virgin Vlacherniotessa, protectress of the City, but it is of no use. The imminent downfall of the City is proclaimed in vivid physical terms of cloudbursts, cataracts, volcanoes spewing forth, earthquakes, and plagues.[83] *Romiosyne,* the civilization of Byzantium, is fated to travel to the West where it will sell itself, giving its culture and art of warfare to others.[84] Palamas then speaks of the coming of a new civilization, Europe, and the consequences for his own day. The vision ends, however, on an optimistic note when the third image, that of the emperor himself appears.

In the prologue to the poem Palamas voiced his despair at the condition of the nation: "All the creative lights in the land are extinguished."[85] It was at moments such as these, both past and present, that the need for a strong leader was greatest. As Palamas wrote of the emperor and the Akrites:

> And when a warring king of the City
> Amidst   the disintegration of society and the chaos
> . . . .
> rediscovered, reseized and returned to life
> the warrior class of the world queen Rome
> and bequeathed it to Romania that
> she might become the ruler of Europe,
> Africa and Asia.[86]

The message that the poet wished to convey was clear; his countrymen needed a fighting leader and they themselves had to assume a more militant stand towards life. Basil, as Palamas portrays him, is both a creator and a destroyer. His faith lies in his own power and those mystical forces outside of man. The emperor is a true Hellenic figure, placing his faith in a high ideal; in this instance it is the worship of the Virgin. Greece's failures, in Palamas' thinking, no doubt were due as much to the lack of proper ideals as to economic and military weaknesses.[87]

The figure of the emperor, a form of medieval super-man, exemplified the poet's concern with the need for steadfastness on the part of the nation. As we have noted, towards the end of *The King's Flute* Palamas recounts the fate that will befall medieval Hellenism. After doing so, however, the poet ends on an optimistic note by reintroducing the figure

of Basil as the eternal protector of the Greeks. In the poet's words the
emperor states:

> I said; wherever Greece struggles and
> the Romaic spirit blows
> wherever the race is a martyr and the
> *genos* has vitality
> forever and ever, always, unto ages of ages everywhere
> . . . .
> on Byzantine thrones and in Attic ruins
> and with royal purple and a klephtic cloak
> . . . .
> I will be the spirit, I will be the soul,
> I will breathe full of life.[88]

Many of the traits that made up the personality of the Gypsy can be
found in the figure of the emperor: a strong will, a sense of apartness
from the people, dedication to a personal vision, and the possession of
both creative and destructive impulses. But there is also a significant
difference between the two characters. Palamas created in Basil the
embodiment of a hero-figure. Furthermore the poet certainly understood the nationalist overtones inherent in his portrayal of the emperor.
Palamas, like others at the time, had experienced the quickening of the
nationalist impulse that was stirring the country at the time. *The King's
Flute* was but the outpouring of a renewed national enthusiasm on the
part of the poet.

The Greek World and the West

With the end of the medieval world and the collapse of the Byzantine
Empire a new era dawned in European history. In the West powerful,
centralized states were slowly emerging in the form of the nation state.
Palamas recognized the necessity of these developments and unlike
Dragoumis, who distrusted what modern Europe stood for, the poet
understood and appreciated the significance of that world and what it
had to offer. He accepted both nation states *and* European civilization
as critical forces in the modern world. He recognized in these factors a
hierarchy, however. No matter how important nations were, European
civilization, nevertheless, stood above them.[89]

The development of these forces in the modern world had initiated
powerful and disturbing trends. The old gods had disappeared and a new
and more powerful one had arisen. Mammon, as Palamas saw it, symbolizing the desire for riches and power, now claimed the allegiance of many.[90]
It was the destiny of nations, Palamas asserted, to struggle continuously
for power in aid of this god, using war and force as their means.[91] The
outcome of this conflict was already apparent to the poet. Palamas would

have agreed with Nietzsche who noted that there would be ". . . deep 'rumblings' in the stomach of the next century . . . ."[92] There is vivid presentation of this Armageddon in *The King's Flute*. The people, "tightly bound in chains" by the "ogre" Mammon will rise up against this hard master following the lead of socialism, the "lion of poverty."[93] Even the nations themselves would not be spared.

> The Lion of poverty comes, bearing a pitcher
> and a sword,
> . . . .
> the inheritor comes at the end of the ages
> holding pitcher and sword, to slaughter the
> Nations![94]

Although there is a social romantic theme in this, Palamas never really placed himself in the socialist camp or any other for that matter. His loyalty was to the world of the artist, while his politics remained on a decidedly lower level of commitment.

Whatever the role of nations and material interests in the modern world, Palamas remained convinced that there were even stronger forces that were the prime factors in mankind's destiny. These were associated with the flow of history. Individuals, nations, and movements might achieve many things, but Palamas placed these factors in the "sea of eternity," noting that all creations were at best temporary.[95]

> The rivers of progress flow into the sea of eternity
> and are lost, but the sea remains and it drinks
> everything with all its stirring and then swallows it.
>
> And all the risings and destruction, rich, poor,
> all are thrown on the scales; the scales
> go up and down.[96]

Events occurred in time, became part of history and gradually a pattern emerged. The "pattern" might be a nation, a civilization or an empire. In time the pattern would have to change and give way to a new one. History then was cyclical, though not necessarily repetitious or recurrent. To use but one example from *The King's Flute*, Athens had blossomed at one time as a culture, but then a new world, Europe, arose and the earlier civilization was gone forever. There was no point in seeking to recapture it. Rather, the idea was to seek the proper moment when a new culture might be created on the traces of the past.[97] Within this pattern of development the exceptional individual had a role to play. Palamas was neither a historical determinist nor a subscriber to the "great man" theory as an explanation for the unfolding of human events. He visualized instead an intimate relationship between men and their times. The two forces each influenced the other, and both in turn affected the development of the world.[98] This, as he indicated in *The King's Flute,* meant that his own nation had the opportunity to create a vigorous culture in the future, provided that there was a proper understanding of Greece's past and a realistic appraisal of her position in the modern world.[99]

The dominant theme that emerges from *The King's Flute* is the interest of the poet in the destiny of his nation and thus his efforts to create a suitable image out of the Greek's past. Through a Byzantine setting Palamas was able to construct a unified tapestry out of the many threads of Greek history. Critics have already noted how the poet linked the pagan era of classical Greece to the Christian world through the culture of Byzantium, which in turn contained within it the seeds of modern Greek culture. His work, however, is not just the reassertion of a continuity that had been traced out several decades before by the historian Paparrigopoulos.[100] Palamas exalted the Greek past as spirit and dynamism with the idea that the nation would be inspired to emulate it in the future. But in the process he remade the past. The Emperor Basil was no longer an historical character but a legendary figure who performed the union of the two worlds, the Hellenic and the Byzantine. Yet in reality the Byzantines did not look to the classical era for their identity. Rather they saw themselves as *Romaoi,* citizens of the Eastern Roman Empire, the chosen people of God. The interaction that Palamas conjured up in *The King's Flute* was the result of a need felt by the modern Greeks and not by the Byzantines. The poet used the past in order to serve the demands of modern nationalism.

The Poet and the Nation

In the fall of 1897 Palamas had penned an article which eloquently expressed the depression that gripped the country at the time. Comparing the Greece of his own day with the Hellenic world in the first centuries after Christ, he argued that the nation was in a state of decay and disarray similar to that which typified the Greek world of that earlier era. His objection was that the country was not taking the demands for reform and regeneration seriously. Consequently nothing worthwhile was happening to bring about the needed transformation of Greece.[101] This mood of distaste for the condition of society about him, the need to order his own priorities in life and a universal appetite for new ideas were the main sources for his prodigious creative efforts during the following decade.

Palamas can be considered an activist in the sense that he was convinced that the artist, in his own case a poet, could and ought to have an impact on his society through his works. The poet abjured involvement in political controversies, however, and throughout his life refused to associate himself directly with such affairs. Yet the intellectual history of the country during the first decade of the twentieth century has been aptly described as that of "Palamas and his epoch."[102] The poet was pre-eminent during this period in his ability to grasp the varied European intellectual currents and to fuse them with native traditions producing a literature that possessed an unmistakable national character.[103] He did not fear the impact of the West but instead welcomed it. The tension that Greece's historical and geographic legacy posed for Dragoumis and Giannopoulos was not felt by Palamas. Like Dragoumis the poet's world was Greek, historical and dynamic. But he felt no compulsion to isolate it. Nor did he have any difficulty in dealing with its geographic extensiveness. His Hellenism was contained within the realm of ideas, and here he believed it properly belonged. As he stated in the preface to the *Dodecalogue of the Gypsy:*

> When great national ideals live and bloom
> in everyone's home, the poet can build them
> palaces; when they are declining and
> everyone is denying them, the poet takes
> them into his hut and gives them shelter.[104]

Palamas was able to syncretize the highly developed but antithetical worlds of classical Hellenism and medieval Byzantinism with the popular culture of modern Greece. The resulting image was historically distorted but none the less highly satisfying to the nationalist impulse in the country.

The country had been independent less than a century when Perikles Giannopoulos began to publish his pamphlets and articles. Greece at the end of the nineteenth century, the Greece of his day, seemed to him befuddled and purposeless. He felt that the country's politicians and intellectuals had lost touch with their people and had failed to provide the proper leadership for the country.[1] His writings reflected the frustrations and prejudices of those who believed that somehow the state had been betrayed from within. But in Giannopoulos' case his works also reveal a man who was unsure of himself and uncomfortable with his milieu, and who tried to give meaning to his life through his writings. Even when he thought that he had found it, however, the satisfaction with the results can only have been partial.

Patras was the birthplace not only of Palamas but of Giannopoulos as well. He grew up there, the son of a doctor from Mesolonghi. On his mother's side the family believed that it could trace its line back to Byzantine times. After finishing the gymnasium in Patras Giannopoulos went to Athens to enroll in the School of Medicine. He did not remain there long. Like Palamas, who had begun his studies in law but then had changed to philology, Giannopoulos came to the conclusion that medicine was not for him. He found literary life far more attractive, and like so many others he set out for Paris drawn to the mecca of the European cultural world. There, Giannopoulos apparently lived the type of life that he later came to condemn so vigorously. In Paris he met and became friends with Jean Moreas, a fellow Greek who was one of the exponents of the symbolist movement which was at its peak at the time. The role of the *bohème* appealed to Giannopoulos who dabbled in writing poetry.

In the early 1890's, however, he returned once more to Athens continuing for some time the style of life that he had followed in France. After publishing a few poems done in the symbolist manner Giannopoulos turned from what was patently an unproductive literary exercise to his native world, which now absorbed his attention and drew both his wrath and his praise. The dashing boulevardier, with well trimmed mustache and fine clothes in the best European style, became a lover of everything that was Greek. From an admirer of modern European culture and cosmopolitanism Giannopoulos now turned into a fervid detractor of that civilization. He styled himself a gadfly who would show the young Greek intellectuals the value of relying on their native culture and physical surroundings for inspiration.[2]

As Giannopoulos wrote several years later, 1897 was the nadir of Greek life in the nineteenth century. If the revolution of 1821 had been a time of heroism and glory Greece in 1897 was a shameful relic of that heritage, a nation of ". . . Lawyers, Bureaucrats and Politicians."[3] Administrative or political changes could not remedy the problem. A failure of spirit was at the heart of the matter in Giannopoulos' view and he charged this failure to the intellectuals.[4] The defeat that the country suffered had an impact on his thought but it was not the decisive factor. The young man, now in his late twenties by the end of the century, was impelled by personal disatisfaction and disorientation as much as by the current conditions in the country in taking on his new role of savior of the nation's culture.

Attack on the Present

The Greek revolution, as all revolutions do, quickly became institutionalized and sanctified in the Greek mind. Producing its share of legends and heroes, it symbolized for the Greeks their rebirth as a nation. By the end of the century and especially after the ill-fated war of 1897, there was a widespread feeling, in which Giannopoulos shared, that the promise of the revolution had not been fulfilled. It had achieved the liberation of only a small piece of territory from the Turks and even this was immediately subjected to the influence of the European powers. Giannopoulos felt that a new civilization, a "blossoming of Hellenism," as he put it, did not materialize out of the revolution. The struggle for independence, in his view, had been a partial success at best.[5]

In his criticism of modern Greece Giannopoulos continued in one respect a current that had existed in Europe since the days of the Enlightenment and had been accepted by Greek intellectuals of that time including Koraes. According to this view, Greece's Byzantine legacy was as objectionable as the centuries of Turkish rule. From the perspective of the early twentieth century Giannopoulos challenged the idea of the birth of a modern Greek national culture in 1821 as a myth.[6] In his mind there had been no break with the past. He argued that Byzantium had not been destroyed on the walls of Constantinople in 1453. Byzantine Hellenism had lingered on into the nineteenth century as manifested in the activities of the Phanariots, the writings of the Greek intellectuals of the Ottoman period, and the Orthodox church itself.[7] The modern Greeks had been heavily influenced by what Giannopoulos considered a deleterious spirit. This implied that the Turks were not solely to blame for the sad state of affairs that had befallen the Greeks since the middle ages. Echoing the prejudices of the Enlightenment Giannopoulos argued that Greek culture was held down by the unenlightened and superstitious forces of religion and its sterile intellectualism.

Giannopoulos' disillusionment with modern Greece was not based solely on what he felt were nefarious social and cultural holdovers from the preceding centuries. The new state seemed to him to possess elements which fostered mistaken and even harmful attitudes in society. Hesitating on an outright and clear attack on the political life of the nation, Gianno-poulos turned his wrath on those in society whom he termed "klephts." These were not simply figures from the revolutionary era, but rather characters who were to be found in his own day. The klepht, as Gianno-poulos pictured him, was like an Achilles, an undisciplined warrior who was not one to muse about philosophy or nationality. In his estimation this was not someone who could possess the qualities needed to unite and lead the Greeks.[8] Giannopoulos identified the klepht with the historical figures of the revolution: the military chieftains from the mainland who thought in terms of a small state and understood little of the heritage of Hellenism especially the classical era.[9] He felt that these individuals took the narrow approach with regard to the Great Idea being "Helladic" rather than "Hellenic" in their outlook.[10]

Giannopoulos did not restrict himself to the period of the revolution but applied this term uncritically to any political leader of his own time who seemed to him to reflect this outlook.[11] His labeling of Theodore Deligiannes, who, as we have seen, was closely associated with the Great Idea, gives us a better understanding of his approach and motivations.[12] Giannopoulos expressed little admiration for men with military or political talent if they did not possess the proper cultural accouterments. Unlike Dragoumis and Barrès who considered themselves political realists, Giannopoulos' political views were imbued with a cultural elitism that left them bordering on the point of naïveté.

But statecraft and diplomacy were peripheral to Giannopoulos. What concerned him most was the fact that the revolution was by nature an im-proper breeding ground for the type of society that he desired. As he stated:

> Klephtism is the religion of the Greece of the
> Revolution. The obsession with one era. The
> belief that all the necessary raw material for
> life is found in that era. Admiration for the
> common man, the klepht, the man of the Revolution,
> the contemporary peasant, his language and folk
> songs. The belief that the Byzantine, Roman and
> Alexandrian eras are one and the same ultimate
> downfall. The belief that the perfect era of
> antiquity is the same in relation to us as
> mythology to reality.[13]

In contrast to his contemporaries Dragoumis and Palamas, Giannopoulos was hostile to the notion of a national culture based on the common man.

Rejecting the merits of the peasant society that made up much of the modern Greek nation and the efforts of writers like Eftaliotes who wrote about it, Giannopoulos opted for the self-satisfying "reality" of a culture that would somehow match the acme represented by classical Athens. He derived no satisfaction from associating with and trying to uplift the peasant masses. Where Dragoumis and Palamas saw primitive but creative energy Giannopoulos smelled provincialism and vapidity. His ego could not be sustained by a culture that drew its inspiration from the unlettered. Yet there was ambiguity and contradiction in Giannopoulos' views regarding this matter. He demanded, as we shall see, that the Greeks base their culture on their own world to which demoticism certainly belonged. What he expected were peaks of high creativity not valleys of picturesque but low culture.

Since he inveighed so mightily against the culture of the masses then one ought reasonably to expect that he would have felt at home among those who appreciated the classical Greek world and its achievements. Here, however, Giannopoulos found himself on common ground with Dragoumis and Palamas in their vehement dissatisfaction with the manner in which educated Greeks understood that bygone era. As Giannopoulos forcefully noted:

> Archaism or Classicism is the religion of
> antiquity. The belief that all the necessary
> raw material for the life of every Greek
> civilization of whatever era is [to be found]
> there. The total contempt for every con-
> temporary reality and any other tendency.[14]

Individuals like the university professor George Mistriotes, of whom we have already spoken,* aroused the ire of all three figures discussed here because of their use of classicism as a means of maintaining a cultural status quo. This exasperated Giannopoulos. In his estimation it was not the "archaists'" love of ancient Greece that was at fault but their perception of that period. Giannopoulos felt that these individuals looked at the literary and cultural achievements of Periclean Athens as impossible to match much less surpass. Like the battle between the Ancients and the Moderns in the eighteenth century this attitude meant that the modern Greeks could only model themselves on that past and seek to emulate it. While Giannopoulos relied on a cultural traditionalism as the basis of his concept of Hellenism, he nevertheless tried to introduce a factor that would allow the modern Greeks to achieve what their ancient

---

*See chapter 2.

predecessors had accomplished through dynamism, vitality and creativity, which in his estimation was a high and dynamic culture.

Giannopoulos believed that neither the "klephts" nor the "archaists" had the correct understanding of the needs of the nation. In fact he felt that the intellectual clash that took place between the two groups only divided the country. The "klephts" for their part rather than producing a modern Hellenism engendered a "hatred of Greece" (*misellenismos*) through their activities. This left the country adrift, cut off from her roots in the past, a people without a real tradition.[15] The "archaists" on the other hand only proffered a sterile copy of the classical world. Giannopoulos sarcastically characterized the "archaists" as men whose minds were filled with antiquity, while the minds of the "klephts" contained nothing. The former worshipped the "zenith" of Greek culture, that of Periclean Athens, the latter idolized the "nadir" of Hellenism, modern Greece.[16] Sensitized to the divergent and contradictory cultural currents that were part of the Greece of his day, Giannopoulos posited stark polarities in order to assert the need for unity and cultural creativity. However, his understanding of Greek society and its problems was simplistic. This was reflected in the schematic view that he produced which did not go to the heart of the issues involved. His image of contemporary Greece certainly was a product of both his psychological needs and intellectual preferences. The would be European aesthete turned to a nationalist culture to serve both the self and his desire to be creative.

The Uses and Abuses of the Past

In Giannopoulos' consideration of the nature of the modern Greeks and their culture the past figured prominently. To begin with he felt that the past served as a mirror in which a people could see itself reflected and thereby gain self-awareness. It was needed in order for the people to see ". . . the forms which they created in all the manifestations of life, and . . . to use them as raw material to transform them and to create new forms from their innermost being."[17] He projected an almost Nietzschean supra-historical sense of the past. As he put it, the ". . . entire past coexists with the present and contains all the seeds of the future."[18] History was not to be studied, memorized or understood. If this was done it would only weigh a people down. Men needed to be aware of the past only as an incentive to be creative in their own time.

Despite his intention to "use" the past Giannopoulos was not free of it. He turned to it for a sense of belonging and intellectual grounding. His passion for classical Greece was unbounded. He saw in this era a standard of creativity that had not been equaled by anyone since. The ". . . two prophetic books," for the Greeks, "the two genuine Bibles of the race . . ." were in his view the *Iliad* and the *Odyssey*.[19] Homer had captured the nature and characteristics of the Greeks for all time. In Odysseus, Giannopoulos discerned the essence of the Greek; a man born to wander, restless for adventure and new worlds. Thus in his own day when the Greeks emigrated to such far off places as America, India, and Africa they represented not a new development, but a tradition that had been established centuries before. The most important aspect of this tradition was that these people never forgot their homeland. They sought always to return even after decades of absence. In this way Giannopoulos explained away a harsh fact of life in his own day: that the country could not support its people. From his point of view the nation was not to blame for it was in the very nature of the Greeks to desire to travel.

Unlike Barrès, who preferred Sparta to Athens, Giannopoulos insisted that the city of Pericles was the essential force in that ancient culture. It was a "workshop," a school of politics, military affairs, letters, philosophy and science. "It [was] a school for the *Creation of Men,* and for the Creation of nations."[20] * He felt that the Athenians had mastered the basic problems that confront all societies. Through the works of Plato and Aristotle, and the sculpture of Phidias, the Athenians had created the image of the ideal man in their culture.[21] Greece in classical times could hardly be the model for a nation, since its unity and the loyalty of the ancient Greek remained confined to the polis. Giannopoulos, therefore, stressed the role of individuals and their value in stimulating ferment in society. He emphasized that the culture of ancient Greece was the creation of men and of a place and that this process could be repeated in the future given the re-appearance of the proper conditions.

> With the creation and completion of the Greek Ideal, the purpose of Athens concludes here, for a long series of centuries.
>
> Until the time comes once more and the need for us to return to the center of the heart of the Greek Earth, which is Athens. . .[22]

Giannopoulos believed in a cyclical approach to history, which allowed for recurrence and repetition. But if classical Greek culture was the product of individuals, then there would have to be the presumption that culture could be passed on only through people. By stressing the significance of geography and nature, however, Giannopoulos succeeded

---

* *Giannopoulos' Greek will be discussed below. It must be noted here, however, that he tried to create both a visual as well as a literary impact by his writing. Therefore the punctuation and style have been left as they were in the original.*

only in further confusing the problem. His views encompassed both racial as well as geographic factors with a haziness that suited him but did little to distinguish the actual forces that generate and transmit a culture.

Although classical Athenian culture was brilliant it was also lamentably localized for Giannopoulos' nationalist taste. He became an ardent advocate in his works of the idea, already pronounced in modern Greek nationalist culture, of a mission for Hellenism. In an effusion of cultural chauvinism Giannopoulos trumpeted the virtues of Alexander the Great, whom he saw as a figure who united the Greeks and spread their civilization.[23]

The advent of the Hellenistic era raises important issues, however. Classical Greek culture now interacted with other traditions and was altered in the process of diffusion. Giannopoulos accepted the notion that a new form of Hellenism had arisen. A new world emerged ". . . trans-formed into a religious theater, containing all the ancient celebrations at the same time . . . and bearing the famous, genuine Greek stamp. . . ."[24] His Hellenism then was dynamic, capable of geographic and cultural meandering yet remaining constant at its very core. Why this would be so and how it could be achieved Giannopoulos preferred to leave aside trusting instead in the intuitive faith of those who believed as he did.

The rise of Christianity was of course the most important force to confront the pagan classical world. Both in spirit and content it provided a real alternative to classical Hellenism. Giannopoulos, like Palamas, was greatly interested in the interaction of the two forces. Yet unlike the older man, he was temperamentally and intellectually drawn to passing judgment on the new movement.

Giannopoulos' estimation of the New Testament religion was abundantly clear in his brash assertion that:

> . . . not We [the Greeks] but that New
> Religion would have been anonymously lost
> in the sewers of Rome and other cities, if
> We did not catch it and raise it up. That
> it gave us absolutely nothing which we lacked,
> but that we made it and gave it everything.[25]

He maintained this view, not because of Christianity per se, but because it was an other-wordly religion and, more importantly, something that he deemed alien to classical culture. No religion of this type, in his estimation, given its nature was able ". . . to create men, to educate Peoples, and to form Nations."[26] The Christian religion, with its emphasis on an after-life and its denial of earthly things, was antithetical to the worldly and humanistic orientation, which was what Giannopoulos admired most about classical culture. To this neo-pagan, Christianity was a foreign element, an "Hebraic virus," which had insinuated itself into classical Greek culture and thus had to be combatted.[27]

As far as Giannopoulos was concerned the only form of encounter between classical Hellenism and Christianity would be one of confrontation. Arguing in biological terms he saw the former as an organic entity capable of dealing with foreign elements by either assimilating them or totally rejecting them. In the instance of Christianity Hellenism had merely changed its form but had nevertheless retained its essence. As Giannopoulos phrased it, the classical pagan goddess Athena now took on a new "costume," Byzantinism, and exchanged the sword for a cross, becoming the revered Virgin.[28] The emphasis, however, was on a *Hellenic* Christianity. In Nietzschean terms the Greeks were reprimanded for calling themselves simply Christians and thus being nothing but a part of a large "herd of humanity." They needed instead to identify themselves by what they really were, "users of Christianity" (*Christianopoioi*).

> If you cannot feel that you are Greeks
> except from within the bedcover of Christ-
> ianity then to hell with such Hellenism.
> Because then your Hellenism is dead.[29]

The synthesis of pagan Greek culture and Christianity that took place in the East and found expression as the culture of Byzantium was just as repugnant to Giannopoulos as it had been to Koraes. While the disciple of the Enlightenment opposed this world as being antithetical to reason and justice Giannopoulos disliked Byzantium's reliance on a weak and egalitarian religion. He refused to see in this synthesis the fruitful interaction of mutually accomodating traditions that so fascinated Palamas. The image of Phanariot and patriarchal intrigue in more modern times was sufficient as we shall see to convince Giannopoulos that the culture of Constantinople was basically harmful to the Greeks.

The political importance of this empire was not denied, however. All three figures with whom we are dealing considered this period in one way or another as essential to understanding the modern Greeks. Even Giannopoulos accepted its role as a link between the ancient and modern periods.[30] Characteristically in discussing Byzantium's significance he altered things to suit his needs. Of the three traditions that were synthesized and became Byzantine civilization, Roman law, pagan Greek culture and the Christian religion, Giannopoulos rejected the last and reinterpreted the first. For him the double headed eagle symbolized the combining of classical Greek culture with a mighty Greek state headed by a powerful emperor. Thus Hellenism was still able to exert, in his opinion, a powerful influence during the millenium of the empire's history. What awaited the Greeks after 1453, however, were centuries of steady decline.[31] with more than enough villains as far as Giannopoulos could see.

What neither the Bulgarians[32] nor the Franks[33] had been able to do for so many centuries the Turks succeeded in accomplishing in a relatively short period of time. While Christians at the time saw in this event the withdrawal of the protecting hand of God from his "chosen people," Giannopoulos insisted that "independently of the fate of mankind" the Greeks had become exhausted. The two supports of their civilization, culture and the state, were now reduced to one, the Turks having done away with the state.[34]

The centuries of Ottoman rule are considered by Greeks to this day as an era of darkness and slavery. The villain of this era is of course the Turk who imposed the Ottoman "yoke." While this has been the standard rationalization by the Greeks for the instability and difficulties that have marked their history in modern times, Giannopoulos' indictment included the Greeks themselves as culprits. He drew a much more somber picture of the times and asserted that his countrymen had borne a far heavier burden than they realized. We have already noted that the affairs of the subject peoples of the empire were to a large extent in the hands of their respective religious officials. In the instance of the Greeks the Orthodox church had been delegated these wide-ranging powers by the sultan. Rejecting the notion that the church had served as a mediating body helping the Greeks to maintain a basic identity and awareness, Giannopoulos charged that it had used the privileges granted to it to create a "monocracy of Christianity," and in effect had abetted the Turks in keeping the Greeks in a state of subjection.[35] As he saw it, the ". . . only difference between a Turk and a monk is that one wears a black and the other a red fez."[36] He boldly asserted that Orthodoxy had been befuddled by monasticism to the extent that the church claimed to represent all the Christian peoples of the empire. In the eyes of Giannopoulos this was a grievous error. Only a *Greek* Orthodox church could work wholeheartedly for the interests of the Hellenes.

Oblivious to the fact that the Ottoman Empire was based on a theocratic government and all subjects, both rulers and ruled, were distinguished on the basis of religion, Giannopoulos introduced his own criterion. Influenced by the current political conditions in the Balkans, the self-proclaimed promoter of national awareness saw the entire problem as a matter of race. The Greeks could not count on their fellow Orthodox since they were Slavs and even less on their fellow Christians in the West. With obvious reference to the nationalist strife over Macedonia, Giannopoulos argued paradoxically that only if the Greek nation were powerful would a feeling of brotherhood between it and the other Balkan peoples result. It was his firm conviction that a potential adversary respected only strength.[37] As we have seen, in the first half of the nineteenth century Greek intellectuals reacted strongly against assertions that they were not really the actual descendents of the ancient Hellenes.

In the course of defending themselves they asserted both a cultural and a racial continuity. In addition to this Giannopoulos now used race as a means of asserting exclusivity and national unity for the Greeks. The historical vision of Hellenism had narrowed dramatically in this individual's conception of it.

Giannopoulos was disturbed not only by the transformation of Hellenic culture, which he viewed as a negative development, but also by the changes that had affected the Greeks as a people. Projecting present conditions into the past, he saw the era of Ottoman rule leading to the breakdown of cohesiveness and solidarity among the Greeks. To speak of national unity at that time was historically inaccurate but Giannopoulos was using the past for purposes of the present. The solidarity that he so desired was more social than geographic. As an example he cited the fact that after the fall of Constantinople many of the Byzantine intellectuals had fled to the West.[38]

Ottoman conquest had not simply instigated divisions among the Greeks. Rather, it had created the conditions for the emergence of types that Giannopoulos felt were now the bane of the country. These he stereotyped as the merchant, the monk and the teacher. As Giannopoulos pictured him, the merchant was someone who believed that his people were politically and culturally in difficult straits and therefore the best thing to do was to confine one's efforts to amassing wealth. Then and only then would the Greeks be able to demand their rights. The monk in turn pleaded that the nation was suffering for its sins. Finally, the teacher offered only language and grammar to his people, and this really for the benefit of the West.[39] It was these people who had produced the *Romios,* the modern Greek who sat in the cafes of Athens fingering his conversation beads and uttering the ideas that the three figures had fashioned for him.

Although he posed these types as existing in the historical past, what moved him to do so was the conviction that the Greece of his own day was dominated by people such as these. In reality then he was attacking the bourgeois culture that represented and dominated Greek society at the time. This society seemed to him as distant in spirit from that ancient ideal that he so admired as it was in actual time. A neo-romantic in outlook, Giannopoulos wished to overthrow the present, which he considered mediocre, languid and unexciting. In its place he hoped to see a culture that would not be a copy of that of classical Greece, but instead one that would possess its vitality and élan. He understood that this era was far removed from his own and that the modern Greeks were not closely related to it. What made it appealing to him was its freshness and vigor. Indeed the essence of Giannopoulos' version of Greek history was an attempt to show how time had destroyed this vigorous spirit. It was this vitality that Giannopoulos desired to see spring forth in his own time.

To promote this idea he conceived of the past in terms of race and nature rather than as an intellectual legacy. For him Hellenism was above all the possession of a particular people living in a definite physical space. The modern Greeks had removed themselves from it by adulterating their civilization, but they were still surrounded by the same natural environment and they could revitalize their culture. Europeans on the other hand could never recreate the spirit of the ancients because they lived in a different natural world.

Greece Without the West

As we have seen already Giannopoulos had willingly joined those who streamed to Paris in search of culture and of themselves. After a few years there he had returned to Greece and was soon calling Europe a "sickly, raving, and rotten blossom."[40] Contrary to the attitude of many westward looking intellectuals, Giannopoulos felt that there was little that his countrymen could learn from Europe.[41] Even the most creative works of Western genius seemed to him marked with "crudeness." His conception of Europe, however, was heavily determined by geography. The northern and therefore climatically harsher areas rather than the Mediterranean littoral of the Continent were associated in his mind with "Europe." In a crude form of environmental determinism Giannopoulos argued that the heavy and wet climate of the north led to the creation of art opposed to the tenor and line of the Greeks' accomplishments in that realm.[42] The West did not possess the environmental "raw material" needed to produce a great art and literature.

> The Civilization of Peoples is a matter of
> Nature and Time. We, [the Greeks] the Indians,
> the Japanese, are the Civilized. The Franks
> are crude and incapable of civilization. There-
> fore if the Japanese desire to wake up in 20
> years . . . they will surpass them and rub their faces
> in the dirt.[43]

It is obvious that the esteem and honor in which Greek intellectuals of the early nineteenth century had held the West had radically changed. But then so had Europe. The *ancien regime* was of course gone and Giannopoulos was one of those who found little to praise in what had come after.

Taking up a familiar lament voiced by the weak in a world preoccupied with a concern with power, Giannopoulos felt that his nation was in a humiliating condition. When an independent Greek state had finally emerged it could not compare with the economically and militarily powerful nations of Europe. The period of Ottoman rule was blamed for much of what had befallen the nation. But what awaited small countries like

Greece was even worse in his estimation. Now they were faced with a colossal world, which could impose its economic, political and intellectual will on them. As Giannopoulos graphically noted: ". . . all the Small States [were used] as latrines for [the West's] commercial and industrial constipation. . . ."[44] Rather than the West turning to the Greek world for enlightenment, the Greeks were forced to look to Europe. The West had become their overlord.

Giannopoulos was of course particularly concerned with Europe's impact on the culture of his nation. In metaphorical terms he noted that Aphrodite had abandoned the beauties of Greece and had become enamored of the "moldy," "rotten" and "dark" West, preferring the "coal-filled air of London."[45] His countrymen, symbolized by the figure of Aphrodite, had lost the sense of their own nature through imitating and emulating the West.[46] The problem was even compounded when Europeans visited Greece. They would come and make use of the vast artistic treasures of Hellas for their own intellectual needs while the Greeks themselves failed to exploit this reservoir of Hellenism.[47]

The thrust of Giannopoulos' argument was that it was his fellow nationals who looked to the West for everything from wisdom to wearing apparel, who were the real problem. They were attacked by him as *xenomaniacs,* worshippers of everything foreign, who represented a dual evil. In the first place, they regarded everything Greek as backward. Second, they desired to imitate and copy everything and anything the West had to offer. With some truth Giannopoulos charged that the military organization of the armed forces, the laws of the land, the educational system, art, architecture, indeed an entire way of life had been brought to Greece by either these people or foreigners.[48]

Giannopoulos feared that this problem had reached endemic proportions in his own day. Writing in 1903 he claimed that:

> The Greek is passing through the most
> unnatural era in his history; for the
> first time he is faced with living, thinking
> and working unnaturally. His body, soul
> and spirit find themselves in a sickly,
> feverish condition.[49]

He saw not the malaise of a civilization that had lived too well and was now degenerating, but a society which had not yet been allowed to assert its own values. The West was a threat to modern Greece not only because of its political and economic power, but also because of its cosmopolitanism. In Giannopoulos' estimation this spirit, which he considered detrimental to a nation's life, had permeated the ranks of the country's intellectuals.[50] As is the case with most nationalists, Giannopoulos focused his attentions on the younger generation of artists and writers. He accused them of thwarting the advance of the nation's culture by doing nothing but copy German and Italian works of art. The cause of what he felt was a nefarious trend was two-fold. An archaic educational system, in the dual sense of what it taught and how it was run and which could easily be blamed on the Germans, and the obsession with foreign goods and ideas conspired to mislead the young.

It was Giannopoulos' belief that Greece was not troubled by the cultural exhaustion that was seen to afflict other European countries. Instead it was the problem of a misguided and wrongly educated society. Greece's intellectuals had to be made to realize that they were the "strongest, socially progressive force," the most "valuable asset of their nation," and that they needed a nationalist not a cosmopolitan basis for their work.[51]

The charges made by Giannopoulos were not new. From the time of Otho, Greece's first monarch, voices had been raised in protest against European political influences in the country. The actions of the great powers during the 1896 Cretan revolt and the ensuing Greek-Turkish war only served to confirm the fears of people like Giannopoulos. It was ironic, however, that the person who would have been the accused just a few years before was now the accuser. It was only after he himself played the *xenomaniac* and was not able to find a personally satisfying life that he returned and became a convert to nationalist rootedness. The allure of the West, as Giannopoulos personally experienced, was still powerful. But now there were Europeans who questioned their civilization and it was their ideas that Giannopoulos found attractive. If Europeans no longer accepted uncritically the premise of their culture's superiority over others, then why should others? Giannopoulos represents the coming together of two currents: the anti-rationalist impulse to be found in western Europe combined with the intensified and cruder nationalism that now existed throughout all of Europe. Giannopoulos' virulent anti-Westernism merged fin de siècle elitist and vitalistic theories with particularistic concerns about the nation.

Aesthetics and Society

In his pamphlet, *The New Spirit,* Giannopoulos prophesied the coming of a revolution which would "save the Greeks from themselves."[52] His zeal for revolution, however, remained, for the most part, within the bounds of culture. In consonance with his criticism of Greek society he demanded that the country's intellectuals reject all foreign influences and the sterile imitation of any one era in the nation's past.[53] Apparently Giannopoulos believed that this spiritual revolution would affect the political sector of the nation bringing improvement there also. He voiced the modern Greek's never-ending dissatisfaction with the government but he did not enter into any real discussion of politics. In a rather imprecise

manner Giannopoulos expressed the notion that his countrymen ought
to put their house in order, run their state intelligently and free themselves from the unattainable grandiose dreams that they had been bound
to in the nineteenth century.[54] With respect to the Great Idea, about
which he wrote very little, he seems to have favored an enlarged Greek
state believing, however, that this would never be accomplished unless a
basic change in the outlook and culture of the country took place first.

Giannopoulos' vision of culture had its intellectual roots in the late
eighteenth century thought of the German philosopher Kant and his
successors. "IDEAS are not VAPOR. IDEAS are GREAT FORCES.
They create THINGS which are tangible, alive, beautiful, high brave."[55]
In his view ideas were not simply mental expressions of the material
world. Emotion and ideas were inextricably bound together. He spoke
of this combination as the "raw material" that he worked with. Contemporary ideas in Greece, Giannopoulos asserted, were "muddied" and
"darkened" and as a result produced "words" not "deeds." These needed
to be cleared out and the life of the nation should be founded on what
he called "Hellenic ideas." The sweeping and often vague character of his
statements leave one with the impression that it was not the content of
what he said that was important but the manner in which he stated it.
Thus he repeated over and over again the need for Greek intellectuals
to remain free of ties to any one faction or party and to expel foreign
ideas from their culture.[56] He caricatured Europeans, especially Germans,
with unbounded pleasure. That he owed a heavy intellectual debt to
them, particularly to the German idealist philosphers, did not trouble
him for a moment.

Man's ideal, proclaimed Giannopoulos, was to search for the "Beautiful."
Having begun on that fairly broad premise, he then stated as almost a
categorical imperative that this could not be attained outside the confines
of the nation. Art was a national creation. A D'Annunzio without Italy
or a Wagner without Germany were inconceivable. That an Italy or a
Germany without these two figures was conceivable was not the issue.
Men needed to be creative and nations existed as shelters and incubators.
The concept of the "Beautiful" meant not a universal, "objective" ideal,
but rather a narrow, hedonistic and subjective goal. In a theosophic
manner Giannopoulos depicted this through the symbolism of three
female figures. Ancient Greek civilization had been embodied in the
goddess of wisdom Athena. Following this era Byzantium had turned to
the Virgin Mary. Now modern Greece had to find a new ideal and this
ought to be none other than Aphrodite, goddess of the Beautiful.[57]
Giannopoulos wanted neither the rational culture of the drab bourgeoisie
nor the mystical, other-worldliness, and egalitarianism of Christianity.
His culture must appeal to the aesthetic sensibilities and he sought it
through a form of environmental and geographic determinism.

"The basis of Greek Aesthetics is the GREEK EARTH. Every land creates a person in its own image and likeness."[58] Giannopoulos cherished the belief, which was popular in the eighteenth century, that the environment imposed a way of life and a perceptual framework on a people. They in turn through interaction with that environment expressed its nature in their art. In the case of Greece then, Giannopoulos asserted that a truly Hellenic culture could arise only if the nation's artists had an intimate understanding of their country's landscape. He purported to see a unity in the sky, earth, trees, water and flowers around Attica which he labeled the "Greek Line." It was obviously something that existed independent of time.

The demand for unity in Greek culture based on geography and environment reflected Giannopoulos' dislike for cross-cultural interaction. He held classical Greek culture, which was locally generated, in high esteem, subordinating to it those of Byzantium and the Hellenistic era which were the products of fruitful contacts between diverse cultures. Giannopoulos saw no line of creativity continuing through time. His vitalistic conception of culture was cyclical and organic.

Cultural prescriptions for the nation were matched by vehement proscriptions against those whom Giannopoulos considered "anti-Greek." There was no chance in his view for the "Greek Line" to emerge if Westernism and its purported promoters, the *xenomaniacs,* were not eliminated. His anti-egalitarian conception of society placed the burden of guilt on the intellectual elite for misguiding the "masses." He demanded that these people be curbed. To do so Giannopoulos was willing to see the press exercise a form of censorship and exclude from publication literature which was in any way cosmopolitan. Furthermore, he wanted the press to undertake the task of instilling a nationalist culture in the people.[59] That some individuals wished to indulge in European culture was acceptable to Giannopoulos as long as they were isolated from the rest of the nation.[60] Yet in the same breath he lamented the fact that the study of history in Greece was in a deplorable state for lack of a scientific spirit. If the nation were to understand what course it had to take historians were needed who could properly study the modern era.[61] What he really hoped for was the arrival of someone to speculate on the past and prophesy the future. Giannopoulos feared the power of the rational spirit in the West, yet he was unwilling to use anything but irrational methods to combat it.[62]

Like other contemporaries throughout Europe, Giannopoulos displayed an ambivalent attitude towards intellectuals. "We intellectuals" (*ideologi*), he asserted in an egoist tone, "are the spiritual fathers of the people. We hold in our hands their soul, their heart, and their spirit."[63] Foreshadowing Julian Benda, Giannopoulos complained that many of these people had betrayed themselves and their responsibility to society by becoming enmeshed in the governmental bureaucracy. In doing so they subjected themselves to exploitation by politicians, who, heedless of the national interests of the country, urged the introduction of Western ideas. The result was that even the two "temples" of the intellectuals, the University and the Polytechnic, did not shape their products correctly so that they would not fall prey to "Europeanism." He hoped, therefore, that those who were so important in forming the character of the country would be inspired by the proper national sources.[64]

Giannopoulos' strident warning that interaction between Greece and Europe be kept to a minimum and the insistence on a thoroughly nationalist culture for the country reveal a basic uncertainty about himself and his nation. Despite the bombast and overt sarcasm, the tenor of his arguments indicates an underlying fear that Hellenism was not capable of maintaining that much desired independence vis-a-vis Europe. Asserting the need for a "Greek Line" was reasonable if it helped focus the creative efforts of the country's artist and writers. But at the same time the receptivity to Western trends and ideas that had existed a century before among Greek intellectuals was now gone, and in Giannopoulos' case, replaced by cultural insecurity and anxiety. To overcome this he offered nationalist aesthetics and xenophobia.

A Saving Mission

Giannopoulos wrote that every ". . . people of every age feels the need of kneeling and binding itself to something."[65] But if Hellenism were to survive and flourish in the modern world there had to be a change in the social and political conditions of the nation.[66] It was his self-imposed mission to make his countrymen understand this. Where others discerned tradition, old and new, Giannopoulos saw only sterile forms from the past. His proclaimed goal was to destroy what he believed were the false idols that the nation worshipped.

Giannopoulos' first efforts were a series of articles, the majority of which appeared in 1903 and 1904 just as the language question erupted into a major controversy. In 1906 his first pamphlet appeared entitled *The New Spirit.* Characteristic of all his work, this was not a reasoned and reasonable piece. Rather it was a broadside which attacked the values and life of modern Greek society as false, decayed and anti-national. This was followed in 1907 by another pamphlet, *Appeal to the Panhellenic Public,* in which he continued his declared task of demolishing whatever erroneous notions he felt the Greeks had about themselves. His trenchant criticism was combined as we have seen with appeals for a dynamic national culture.

The form of Greek that he used gives us a clear indication of how Giannopoulos thought. He wrote mainly in the puristic, but peppered it with a liberal dose of demotic and occasionally even dipped into slang.

As he himself stated he wrote consciously ". . . entirely in an unrestrained language grammatically loose, for which a true forbearance is asked for its distortion and barbarism . . . ."[67] This he deemed necessary in order to show his disdain for the language question, which he felt divided the nation, and to aid in his scheme of overthrowing outdated values. Giannopoulos wanted to literally startle and catch the reader's eye. He made liberal use of capitals, italics and any other printed form that he could think of. Language ". . . just as everything else must be pulverized and become RAW MATERIAL first in order to recreate a NEW TRUE FORM afterwards, consisting of everything that comprises it and us."[68]

This corresponds with his view of history and how it was created. Reminiscent of the "great man" theory, Giannopoulos believed that history was like "dough," and that a forceful individual or a people could shape it in whatever manner they desired. But while the role of the individual was important and this view of history allowed for cycles of creativity and decline, Giannopoulos was still committed to a form of cultural traditionalism in his appreciation of the past. He was greatly disturbed by the feeling that Europeans had done great harm to his nation's history by breaking it up into various eras and studying them apart from one another. This, he argued, placed the Greeks' past in improper perspective and caused a distorted image of Hellenic civilization. Giannopoulos believed in what Claude Levi-Strauss has called "cumulative history," the idea that one's civilization is significant because its past development has been productive and influential, though not necessarily continuous, as seen by the observer.[69] Paparrigopoulos sought, as we have seen, a synthesis: bringing together and unifying Greek history. Giannopoulos was concerned not so much with the continuum but with what he called ". . . the total Greek phenomenon. . . ."[70] What he sought for his Hellenism were roots as well as an organic unity.

Like those who believe in "cumulative history" Giannopoulos was certain that Hellenism was destined for a greater role than being simply the culture of the modern Greeks. He upheld the notion, already part of Greece's nationalist culture, that his country was in a special position, both geographically and intellectually, to be a mediating force between East and West.[71] One suspects, however, that this vision was more egoist than humanist in inspiration.

By thinking and writing as he did, Giannopoulos found few genuine supporters. The demoticists were put off by his unorthodox (for them) language as well as by his attacks on their views. Critical intellectuals like Palamas saw the inconsistencies in his work and the vagueness of his ideas.[72] His prescriptions and proscriptions for the nation's artists and writers amounted to a cultural autarky that few found intellectually acceptable.

Perhaps sensing that he had not been successful in his saving mission Giannopoulos decided to take his own life. He committed suicide by drowning in the waters near Piraeus. By this act he gained at last the attention that he had sought in life through this writings. A flood of articles appeared at the time lauding the fervor of his beliefs. His iconoclastic attitude towards Hellenism, and the intense expression of national consciousness in his writings are indicative of this era of ferment in modern Greek history.

Beyond the exaggerations and cyncicism in his work, Giannopoulos strove to promote an era of creative activity in Greece. He did not pedantically glorify the past. His was an attempt at freeing the nation from what he perceived was a narrow and distorted view of its culture. Like Dragoumis he reacted against the generation of politicians and intellectuals whose smugness had brought on defeats such as 1897. Giannopoulos, however, in rejecting the culture of his own day sought the saving answer in a civilization long past. His Hellenism was compounded of cultural insularity, a reliance on exceptional individuals and a turning to nature for inspiration. Intended to clear away any unrealistic views the Greeks may have had of themselves, Giannopoulos' Hellenism was the embodiment of neo-romantic anti-rationalism. It reflected both the alterations in values that had occurred in Europe and a dilemma that confronted the newly emergent nations of Europe. A century before material progress and enlightenment was considered the means by which all nations ought to develop. Giannopoulos symbolizes the loss of confidence in this outlook. Since the nation had not achieved success by these means other alternatives were needed. Asserting a unique cultural identity he placed the nation outside the confines of comparison with other states. What Giannopoulos had done was to update the way in which those like Koraes had seen the benefits of the past. While there was no escaping the long shadow of the West, it was the *attempt* to do so that mattered most to Giannopoulos.

During the years examined in this study it was Ion Dragoumis who provided the best expression of a modern Greek national identity. When the clash between Greece and the Ottoman Empire occurred he was not quite twenty years old. Of the three individuals who are discussed here he was the most representative of what may be called the "generation of 1897." While Palamas and Giannopoulos were primarily men of letters, Dragoumis combined in his life both thought and action. In him the vitalistic and anti-positivist ideas then current in Europe found a forceful exponent in Greece.

Ion Dragoumis' life (1878-1920) ended abruptly when he was but forty-two years old.[1] Within that period he was at various times a diplomat, author, soldier and politician. Dragoumis came from a family that had been associated with the history of the modern Greek state from its very beginning. The family originated in western Macedonia tracing its lineage back to the time of Scanderbeg in the fifteenth century. Eventually some of them found their way to Constantinople where they settled. When the Greek revolt broke out in 1821 the Dragoumis' immediately supported it, wisely fleeing Constantinople at the same time. Dragoumis' grandfather, Nicholas, was at one time a secretary to John Capodistrias, the first president of the new state. Later Nicholas served as foreign minister during the reign of King Otho. His *Historical Reminiscences* are still an important source for the early history of the kingdom. Stefanos, Ion's father, continued the family's involvement in the public affairs of the country. A follower of Trikoupis, he was a member of parliament for many years. As late as 1907 he founded his own political group, the Japan faction, and in 1910 headed the caretaker government that held elections for the reform parliament called by Venizelos. Stefanos, like his father before him, found time to pursue literary interests and he produced among other things a study of the *Chronicle of the Morea*. There was a natural patriotic atmosphere in the Dragoumis household which was intensified by the family's special interests in areas inhabited by Greeks outside the country's frontiers. Stefanos Dragoumis was a consistent promoter of the Greek nationalist movement in Macedonia for decades. This was the world that Ion inherited and grew up in.

Dragoumis was just nineteen and studying law at the university when war broke out between Greece and Turkey. He immediately joined the army as a volunteer but the war ended before he saw action. The defeat made a strong impression on the young man. Like Palamas he too saw a great contrast between 1821 and 1897.[2] He ascribed this to the Greeks' tendency to accustom themselves to a "deplorable" way of thinking. The real issue, in his view, was the nature of the actions that resulted from these thoughts. Dragoumis asserted that the Greeks had followed a policy of seeking small "crumbs" of the Ottoman Empire, and hoping at the same time that the Greeks within the empire could fend for themselves. Thought and action combined to produce the conditions that culminated in the defeat of 1897.[3] In his mind this defeat was the catalyst that gave rise to the "ferment" among the younger generation. They reacted against the ideas and politics of their elders by working for the Greek cause in Macedonia a few years later.[4] Dragoumis was of course coming of age during a period of greatly intensified tension in the Balkans as the Ottoman Empire shrank and new states arose. The 1897 defeat must certainly have shocked the sensibilities of this eager young nationalist.

The disappointment with his country's loss of the war was only part of the disorientation that Dragoumis experienced at this time. In the next few years he went through a period of introspection in which he questioned his purpose in life and his relation to the rest of the world. During this time he completed his studies at the university. Upon graduation he half-heartedly considered the problem of a career and finally settled on that of a diplomat. He was accepted into the service and received his first assignment to a consulate in Macedonia in December, 1902. During the next two years he gained a first hand acquaintance with the region and worked clandestinely in support of the Greek nationalist effort in the area. He discussed his experiences in Macedonia and made an appeal to fellow countrymen to direct their efforts there in a book, *The Blood of Martyrs and Heroes,* published in 1907.

In that same year Dragoumis was posted as a secretary to the embassy in Constantinople. Here once again he engaged in the same sort of extra-diplomatic nationalist activity that he had practiced in Macedonia. He worked with a friend, Athanasios Souliotes, whom he had met in Thessaloniki while serving in Macedonia. The Young Turk revolution of 1908 brought new opportunities to the nationalities in the Ottoman Empire. Dragoumis hoped that the Greeks in the empire would gain a more important role in the affairs of that state. In 1911 he published another book entitled *Those Who Are Alive,* based on his activities in Constantinople. The appeal of his books stemmed from the author's constant searching of the self, his striving to find meaning in life, and the nationalist tenor of his writing. They were written in a clear and vigorous demotic of which he was an ardent advocate.

Dragoumis took an active part in the Balkan wars, personally helping to arrange the handing over of Thessaloniki to the Greeks by the Turks. Greece's victories, however, did not alter his disagreement with the

policies of premier Venizelos. He was still in the diplomatic service when
the Great War broke out, but he resigned to run for parliament in 1915,
winning a seat as a representative from Florina in Greek Macedonia.

The growing division between King Constantine and his prime
minister found Dragoumis on the side of the royalists. He participated
in the publication of a new journal, the *Political Review* in 1916. When
King Constantine was forced out by the Entente powers, who supported
Venizelos, Dragoumis was sent into exile in 1917. He returned in 1919,
a time when Greece's political atmosphere was still very much unsettled.
A clear indication of how strong feelings were was the attempt made on
the life of Venizelos on August 12, 1920, while he was attending the
peace conference in Paris. There was a swift reaction to this attack in
Greece. Venizelos' supporters quickly carried out reprisals and the very
next day in Athens Dragoumis was picked up by members of the Security
Division and was shot in the street. A man who often expressed a dislike
of politics, Dragoumis became the victim of a political assassination.

The Individual and His Nation: From Egoism to Rootedness

In 1902 Dragoumis, who was now twenty-four years old, wrote a work
which bears the title: *The Footpath (To Monopati).*[5] As much a self-
analysis as an autobiography, it revealed the psychological needs and
intellectual predilections of the young man. In the book he remarked
that he sought to discuss questions of a serious nature with friends his
own age only to find that they shared little common interest in these
problems. He addressed letters to "no one" giving vent to his distaste
for the ideas and values in Greek society that he felt were meaningless.
As the title of the work implies, Dragoumis was deeply concerned with
ordering his life and finding a purpose to fulfill it. What strikes the reader
in this and in his other writings is the constant questioning of his values
and aims. This irresolution marked his life even when he seemed to have
reassured himself through his nationalist orientation.[6]

At this time Dragoumis believed that the primary question in his life
was the nature of the self and its relation to the rest of the humanity.
He found solace in the works of Maurice Barrès and Friedrich Nietzsche,
whose ideas were then making a significant impact on Greece's intellectual
circles. Dragoumis did not hesitate to borrow from them whatever suited
him. The egoist in him demanded a critical re-examination of the self
in order to renew confidence in his abilities. Dragoumis agreed with the
Nietzschean idea that the exceptional individual, whom he considered
himself to be, was often submerged within the large and amorphous
mass of humanity much to his detriment.[7]

Barrès provided Dragoumis with just the complex of ideas that he
needed to satisfy his own psychological needs and his antipathetic feelings

toward that class of Greek society to which he belonged. In the intuitive and vitalistic world of Barresian thought each individual can find in the ego a source of strength and a focus from which to relate one's actions in the world at large. This posited a need for an analysis of the self (*le moi*) and a belief in the worth of the individual as the exception to the multitude. The ego was not envisaged as a passive element, however. Rather it was a dynamic entity capable of strength and aggressiveness. Pressing upon the need for individuality and even aloofness, Dragoumis spoke of his desire to become "better than myself."[8] He noted that man had basic motivating factors that went into the makeup of his personality. These factors or more precisely impulses were love (*eros*), friendship (*agape*), death, the will to survive, the homeland (*patrida*), and the need to succeed in life (*nike*).[9] It is obvious that these were all attributes based on emotion and subjective judgment. They belong to the Bergsonian world of irrationality and vitalism.

Dragoumis saw man as injecting himself into life rather than sitting passively on the sidelines. The choices that individuals had were presented by him in the form of antithetical and conflicting options. Man could be a winner (*nikites*), an outsider or one who withdrew from society (*monachos*), a part of the masses, or finally one who was unsuccessful in life.[10] Dragoumis had already decided that he could accept only the first or second alternatives for himself. Parallel to the "victor-outsider" archtype was another dualism. He believed that men could be either creative or destructive in two ways. They could make an impact on the world through physical work or "action" (*energia*) as Dragoumis called it, or through "thought" (*skepsis*), which was the way of the intellectual.[11] He preferred to combine the two in an "apollonian" synthesis that harmonized raw creative energy through mental discipline. His was an attempt to emulate what Nietzsche had divined about man. But in order to do it Dragoumis could not overcome his past.

Dragoumis rejected the safe, and to him mediocre values of his class, which he felt had achieved very little. But he could not withdraw completely from society. He acknowledged that he had ties to a particular place and time. Life had to have meaning and the "victor-outsider" felt that he could not find it except within the encompassing arms of the nation. Barrès, the Lorrainer, had at first denied his birthplace as a world of "barbarians" only to return to it as a convert to rootedness. Dragoumis, the Athenian, rejected his urban, middle class world for the roots and mission that he felt completed his life. The nation provided him with an outlet for his desire for "action" and with a mystical element that satisfied his neo-romantic impulse for self-fulfillment. He disagreed with Nietzsche on the German philosopher's dictum that men needed to remain free of national ties. As he stated:

But if you change yourself in such a manner so that you will be able to say 'I have no motherland,' . . . do you think you are better than other men, or placed higher or wiser or more free? Or is a man perhaps more free . . . who, *recognizing his obligations*, understanding them, accepts them? And is not a man better yet and more free who neither *doubts* nor has need of recognizing, or understanding in order to concede his bondage, and does not ever discuss the question, but rather living in his country (*patrida*), remaining a Greek or a Frenchman, thinks of other things or acts or simply lives? He seems to me a more *healthy type* without a doubt.[12]

Dragoumis feared the anonymity that he felt was attendant in the spread of European civilization. In his conception the nation provided the needed protective cover.

It was impossible as Dragoumis saw it to evade those ties that bound a person to his nation. There was even a hint of resignation in his acceptance of those binding forces.[13] Nevertheless, nations were ". . . only waking places for a few exceptional people."[14] Barrès had stated that nationalism was a form of energy. Obviously whoever possessed the ability to master and make use of that energy could have an impact on society.[15] While he was willing to submerge himself in the nation, Dragoumis at once sought to make this a highly personal relationship, one that would somehow increase his individuality in the process. By loosely interpreting Nietzsche's values he was able to assert that he was "leaning on his nation to become more of a 'man' (*anthropos*), that is, more than a man, an *übermensch (yperanthropos)*."[16] National consciousness was a deeply individual feeling for Dragoumis. It was *his* Hellenism that he was working for. He likened himself to the prophets of old; a man with a vision to guide his people to the goal of national greatness: "I worked for Hellenism. In working for Hellenism I work for myself."[17] The self took on a greatly enlarged perspective as it became part of the totality of a national tradition. Conversely this reduced nationalism to a single individual who embodied the essence of the whole.[18]

The two worlds that Dragoumis was bringing together, individualism and nationalism, were contradictory and ought logically to be incompatible. Whether viewed from a rationalist or a romantic point of view, the notion of individualism presupposes a confidence and a reliance in the powers, mental and emotional, that a person possesses in dealing with the world around him. Nationalism as it developed in the nineteenth century maintained that the natural unit in life was the group based on the possession of common characteristics. Its purpose was to establish an identity for the group as a whole and in the process for the individual. In combining these two currents of thought Dragoumis was not doing so on the same basis that had brought liberalism and nationalism together in the first half of nineteenth century. The goal then, as Herder had taught, was the expansion of human rights through those "natural" units that mankind belonged to, the nations. Now, in the thought of Dragoumis, that vision was narrowed and altered. The nation had taken on a life of its own independent of the people who made it up. This represented a radical departure from the idea that a nation was the collective expression of the wishes of the many. Mysticism had replaced rationality; the nation was now the possession of the few to be used on behalf of the many whether they liked it or not. Dragoumis found no contradictions in his views for they were based on intuition not reason.

Attack on a Disintegrating World

Dragoumis' call for rootedness reflected his fears and dislikes of Greek society. As individuals were judged in terms of vitality or feebleness, so it was with his view of nations. They were also organisms which were liable to laws of growth and decay.

As the exceptional individual Dragoumis considered that he was living within a society suffering from a national malaise. Nietzsche had written of the crisis of values in the West and had drawn a scathing picture of a civilization no longer dynamic. Dragoumis echoed these thoughts by trumpeting the failure of spirit in his society. He saw the Greeks as tired, weak and apathetic. Centuries of history had taken their toll and now they were reduced to listlessness. Hellenism was divided within itself and the chasm was both political and spiritual. Part of Greek society was content with a life of peace and prudence. The other, outside the frontiers of the Greek state, desired a bettering of its life and a union with the rest of the nation; yet, it too was divided. Dragoumis was convinced that the union of all the disparate elements of the nation was necessary if the Greeks were to have a vigorous civilization. But the state seemed to him incapable of bringing all the parts together, for it was ". . .lost in a sea of individual interest," which amounted to "opportunism" by the people.[19] This condition had not arisen overnight. Dragoumis emphatically placed the burden of guilt on the Greeks of the nineteenth century. Those who had created the small kingdom had somehow lost touch with the vital nerve of Hellenism. Dragoumis looked on the Greece of his day as a disoriented society and pointed an accusing finger in several directions.

Writing in the Athenian daily *Neon Asty* in 1906, Dragoumis characterized Greek society as "mixed-up." He revealed his prejudices when he noted that this confusion had resulted from the conflicting values of a world in flux. As he stated: "Of the old things [the Greek institutions and traditions of the Turkish period] many have fallen, others remain only half-standing, but these will be torn down also, others took on a Frankish appearance, others have been stolen from the ancients and from foreigners, and these have not been digested as yet."[20] This upheaval in values had been accompanied by a rupture in the physical unity of the Greeks. Those within the kingdom were as much or even more concerned with the Parisian scene as with events in Constantinople.

It was during this decade that the great outflow of emigration took place.[21] Most of those who left did so in search of better economic opportunities, and there was not a village in Greece that did not feel the impact of this exodus. This significant movement seemed to Dragoumis a national calamity. Emigration in his view upset the balance of society. Since most of these people were simple villagers, Dragoumis felt that it was proper and to their benefit if they remained at home, learned a trade as their fathers had done, and left the pursuit of riches to adventurers. If emigration was necessary then it ought to·be to areas in the Levant where Greek communities already existed. In this way Hellenism in Asia Minor would be strengthened. Emigration to America would be of little service to the nation. Greeks going there would forget their native land after two or three generations. Finally there was the question of foreign economic penetration. If the Greeks did not remain and invest in the economy, then outsiders from Europe would certainly step in and take their place. Dragoumis cited German interests in the Ottoman Empire as an example of this trend.[22] His reaction to these socio-economic developments was first and foremost a nationalist one. He was not interested in the financial benefits that the nation would gain from the Greek diaspora. The arguments for economic nationalism that were invoked in the inter-war period already had found expression.

Dragoumis saw the breakdown of unity in Greek society as having taken place long before the rise of emigration in the early twentieth century. Looking back to the days before the revolution, Dragoumis became almost nostalgic as he discussed that era. Life under Turkish rule had one aspect to commend it as far as he was concerned. It gave a certain uniformity to Greek society. The Greeks had an eastern way of life, *Romiosyne,* named after the traditions developed from the Byzantine or East Roman era. Socially this way of life meant the separation of men and women in society, with the women closed up in the homes. A large measure of influence was given to the Orthodox church in public affairs, religious, and otherwise. Education was sufficient to enable the Greek subject to carry on his work. He retained a rudimentary knowledge of the meaning of Greek civilization as it was during the days of the Byzantine Empire. From life around him he could easily understand his condition as a subject of the Ottoman state while retaining the dream of retaking the "City." Only a few Greeks, the merchants in the empire, gained the wealth and education to alter this pattern of life and even they found benefits to it. Dragoumis did not see the period of Ottoman rule, the *Turkokratia,* as anything good in itself. Yet life in the empire had forced the Greeks to accept a common outlook. The outbreak of the revolution of course disrupted this uniformity.

This disturbed Dragoumis, who believed that the struggle for national independence had brought social change as well. The Greeks in the new kingdom began now to look towards Europe for ideas and leadership. The world of *Romiosyne* had been upset.[23] Athens now rivalled Constantinople for the attention of the Greeks and they were transforming their society along Western lines. What was once looked upon among Greeks as a long sought and welcome change now filled Dragoumis with apprehension. Dragoumis' national consciousness now saw enemies were there had previously been liberating forces. This change in perspective had both a European as well as a Greek dimension.

We have already seen how the Greeks benefited from Europe's philhellenism in their drive for independence and how they eagerly accepted an image of themselves as the sons of Pericles. Dragoumis did not dispute the value of cherishing one's ancestry. The admiration of one's ancestors (*progonolatreia*) he defined as ". . . feeling one's origin, the continuity of one's national identity, the history which makes one aware . . . of the passing of one's nation through the centuries. . . ."[24] In lyrical terms he expressed his own admiration for ancient Greece:

> Ancient Hellenism, like a vast wave, broke and ended at the foot of the last century; the ripples of the wave still break quietly on the shore of some islands and Greek places still enslaved today. And the language, which was spoken by kings, like Theseus, is now looked down upon by street cleaners, because some pseudo-intellectuals were never able to free themselves from the honey of Attica. The mountains are many-hued behind the light colored marbles . . . . In such a land splashed with color and light should not true men reappear?[25]

It was fitting that the modern Greeks wished to emulate this rich legacy. He feared, however, that they had gone overboard in this matter. Admiration (*progonolatreia*) had become an obsession (*progonoplexia*). The emphasis on the ancients sacrificed the world of *Romiosyne* as something backward and unenlightened. The modern day *Romios* was seen by Greeks who thought themselves cultivated and urbane as the rustic whose sophistication only amounted to a peasant slyness. Dragoumis identified this outlook with that stratum of Greek society whose values he now rejected.

What stirred Dragoumis' wrath even more was his belief that the hand of the West was to be felt behind all of this. Indeed he believed that Europe's presence was there in a dual manner. He noted that Westerners had initially looked on the Greeks' efforts to identify themselves with the ancients with favor. But Europeans soon tired of their philhellenism and treated the modern Greeks as any other minor state.[26] This was damaging enough for Dragoumis without the burden of the Greeks' effort to imitate the West in every way possible. This *xenomania* was as irritating to him as it was to Giannopoulos. Greece, *la nouvelle arrivée,* in Dragoumis' estimation, was a nation of the *bourgeois gentilhomme* seeking to catch the latest fashion whether in wearing apparel or politics. The real threat to the nation was Europe

> with its Masonry, with its philanthropy, . . . its parliamentarianism, its leveling out, which makes all men equal with the lowest; all of this contemporary civilization which makes us mediocre, harmless and insignificant . . . .[27]

In pseudo-biological language Dragoumis asserted that the Greeks had been able in the past to absorb foreign elements, making them their own and in the end becoming stronger by each experience. But he feared that since the founding of the modern Greek state the inroads of the West had risen steadily as had the Greeks' willingness to accept them. If the process were not reversed the nation would lose its identity.[28]

To bolster his argument he enumerated several areas where this process had been at work. The educational system followed a European, in this case German, pattern with a curriculum whose content was heavily weighted with classical Greek material. In administration the Bavarian regime of Otho had replaced a centuries old system of self-sufficient communities with a centralized Western bureaucracy. Dragoumis pictured the monarchy as something alien, the domain of foreigners who could not possibly understand the Greeks and who desired only to turn the country into another Belgium or a Switzerland.[29]

In the end, however, it was the Greeks themselves who were held accountable for the "mixed-up" condition of the nation.[30] Whether they would simply overthrow these influences or whether they would have to become satiated before turning away, Dragoumis was not certain. Whatever means was used the Greeks needed to return to the real ". . . sources of modern Hellenic life, with its demotic tradition, which is the only genuine and far-reaching link with our older civilizations. Only then will we be saved from *xenolatria* and *archaiomania.*"[31]

Dragoumis attacked the middle class values of modern Greek society as misguided and uncreative. This world, which measured success in material terms, contradicted both his family background and personal preferences. He desired instead the world of the heroic. His critique of society around him was intended as a "realist" evaluation, but it served also to confirm his own prejudices.

Attack on Cosmopolitanism

While Dragoumis was concerned with the divisions that marked Greek society, there were other issues that he feared even more. National unity was desirable but not if the cost of achieving it was uniformity. A distinctive identity remained the sine qua non for the nationalists.

To most Europeans the thing they felt set them apart from the rest of humanity on earth was that they were "civilized." For Dragoumis European "civilization" meant having material goods, believing in progress and desiring peaceful relations among nations. Indeed, he wondered if being "civilized" was not simply another form of "degeneration."[32] He searched eagerly for indications that would bolster such an opinion. Dragoumis asserted that there were many Europeans who believed that philanthropy and compassion were desirable goals. To his way of thinking these were attitudes of a people who had ceased to see life as a struggle.[33] Likewise, he attacked those who believed that science could solve all of mankind's problems. Those who looked forward to an era free of superstition and prejudice were only deluding themselves.[34] Emotion, passion, and irrationality were an integral part of man's nature. His anti-rationalist vision considered these forces as crucial to the vigor and life of mankind.[35]

Modern Europe represented not only materialism to Dragoumis but the bogies of cosmopolitanism and socialism as well. He inveighed against individuals who supported international causes and believed that harmony among nations was possible. These people he regarded as immersed in their books and ideals with action taking up very little of their lives.[36] Such an outlook had made countries like Belgium and Switzerland into docile nations whose citizens no longer possessed the spirit needed to maintain a vital national life.[37] In this sense Dragoumis was hardly a "good" European.

Socialism, however, disturbed Dragoumis even more. As we have already noted it made its appearance in Greece at the end of the nineteenth century. The Greek socialists, following pretty much the strictures of German Marxism, criticized what they saw as a "bourgeois" society around them and called for the end to nationalist dreams that served to benefit only a few. Dragoumis, however, rejected socialism as a vision of a utopia for one particular class.[38] He refused to see it as an objective means of analyzing society and felt instead that it was a subjective ideology which sought to satisfy the "desire" of the working class for an easier life. It was to his elistist mind an unacceptable vision for it ". . . was born from the needs and the feelings of the workers, who desire to better their fate, that is, to work less, to win more . . . because they truly are exhausted people."[39]

The Greek socialists warned that conflict between classes was bound to occur and the country would one day face a crisis. The idea of struggle in society appealed to Dragoumis and he devoted considerable detail to his interpretation of this phenomenon. He considered the notion of conflict between groups as something hardly new. Competition was something that he felt existed in all societies. It was altogether natural and arose from economic as well as other causes. Struggle was necessary if society was to retain its vitality.[40] But class conflict vexed Dragoumis because he saw this as placing the people in the limelight at the expense of the individual. Socialism divided society up into classes instead of unifying it. Changes in society were not something pre-determined or inevitable due to broad economic developments. It was the individual who effected the changes of consequence. His distaste for humanity at large was evident in his statement: "I like individuals, I do not like the masses with their coarseness."[41]

But socialism was not meant to be appealing to persons. It claimed to be a theory of societal development and an alternative form of government. George Skliros, the Greek socialist, wrote that class conflict existed in Greece as it did in other states. The problem, however, was that the nation's political system was incapable of dealing with it. In effect the goals of the nation were misguided. Dragoumis responded with an argument that had concerned Europeans since the time of Machiavelli.

> I am, Mr. Skliros, a statesman (*politikos*). We statesmen follow the circumstances—that is, seeing and doing. The good statesman, with his strong psychological insight, foresees many things that will happen, and prepares himself to face them, to correct them as much as he can, to mend them temporarily, to uproot them entirely if he can and if it is necessary, to encourage them to grow . . . . if he judges that it must be this way. But what regulates all of his actions? How does he know how to diagnose *what is necessary* in every situation? If he is a statesman . . . he will have as an inviolable and firm principle the strict political interests of the state, and the victory of national life, even though it may be at the expense of other states. But pay attention Mr. Skliros, here is the difficulty. It is therefore necessary that the interests of each class be sacrificed? Must the proletariat become ill, remain without bread, naked, homeless, be destroyed and die? Yes, the workers must live like that, if the state has more important tasks to attend to, and if there is no serious danger to the state—let them still live this way. And if they wish to rise let them rise, and they will gain . . . another scrap in order to live. But if this uprising becomes massive, as with the French Revolution, the ruling class will change and another class will take power. But this does not concern me. Whatever class desires to, let it rule, if it can rule according to its interests and ideals. Suffice it that the state [continues to] live, stand on its feet and can hold its position among other states. Any class that rules a state must have among it ideals . . . the image of the state, the consciousness that all those who make up a state have something in common and that all classes of society . . . with all their differences share some common feelings, ideas, traditions, interests, needs and the great necessity of mutual help. The class that rules cannot ignore this, because otherwise it cannot rule.[42]

Dragoumis, who was not actively involved in politics at this time, reacted to Skliros' arguments as if they were a personal attack against his way of life. The writings of the socialists seemed to imply that his thinking and that of other nationalists was outmoded and irrelevant to the needs of the country.[43] He responded with the relish of a hero doing battle mocking his opponents and asserting his individuality by signing his articles in the name of "Ion the Hard" (*Skliros*).

Dragoumis did not meet the issues that the socialists raised head on. He sidestepped them with the argument that they were irrelevant to the problems then facing the nation. At the time the urban working class was of little consequence and while there was overpopulation on the land, there was an escape valve—emigration. Although socialists and nationalists found common ground over the language question, the views of the latter were attuned to visions of heroic actions against traditional enemies like the Turks or Slavs. Socialism offered nothing that would solve those problems.

Yet Dragoumis was flexible enough, or perhaps uncertain of himself, not to deny that conditions in the future might arise whereby socialism could offer an alternative way to organize society. Even so he envisioned it in the role of stimulating action in the people rather than as a solution to the economic and social ills of the nation. He saw this movement basically as a "phenomenon of an aged civilization" which worked at leveling society. It was not a doctrine that he desired to see gain support in Greece.[44]

For the period we are concerned with Dragoumis' attitude towards socialism remained as we have described it. Toward the end of his life, however, when he had lived through the momentous years of World War I, matters took on a little different perspective. Impressed by the Russian revolution and the importance of the socialist movements in Europe, Dragoumis expressed a willingness to consider socialism in a new light. He noted that his fundamental antipathy to socialist theories had led him to overlook the plight of the working people, but that he now looked with more sympathy on these issues. In articles that he published after his return to Athens from exile Dragoumis was willing to allow the idea that the workers would benefit greatly if they organized cooperatives. But this was hardly an admittance of any acceptance of socialism. Dragoumis still had no real liking for this doctrine.[45] We need not speculate here on what he would have done had he lived through the inter-war period. The fascist movement that developed so spectacularly after the war certainly drew in part upon nationalism for intellectual sustenance. But it must not be taken as simply an outgrowth or extension of the earlier doctrine. Fascism was a distinct ideology heavily indebted to the social and political conditions in Europe that were the legacy of WWI. Dragoumis needs to be evaluated in his own time and for what he was, an integrationist and irredentist nationalist who placed the nation before the state.

Let us return to the perspective of pre-world war Europe. Dragoumis was concerned with nationality and consciousness among the Greeks. His goal was to raise their level of self-awareness. European ideas and material goods would only hinder this.[46] To combat these products of "civilization" Dragoumis offered not revolutionary radicalism but tradition. His version of "tradition" was not concerned with preservation or conservation, but was a dynamic use of the past for the purpose of promoting the vitality of the nation in the future.

There is a link between the "civilizing" foes from the West and those from the East that Dragoumis felt threatened Hellenism. Socialism and cosmopolitanism would only serve to weaken the nation and thus make it easier for the eastern enemies, the Turks and the Slavs, to destroy Greece. Dragoumis, who felt that he was alone in life, applied the same view to his nation. His countrymen must depend on no one, Europe included, but rely only on themselves.[47] Personal antipathy towards egalitarian movements was transferred into the public sector by Dragoumis, who saw society in need of dynamism not of social justice.

The Nation Above the State

The rise of cohesive political units that we call nation states has been a process that, in the West at least, goes back several centuries. By the beginning of the nineteenth century when this development was well under way the concepts of the nation and the state seemed to be complementary, even natural, to one another. The former could broadly be defined as a group of people who, through the possession of common characteristics such as language, customs, religion and history, form a natural unit of mankind. The state is that governmental entity which gives political expression and territorial limits to a given group of people. The two can exist independently of one another but since the late eighteenth century historical circumstances led people to consider them as an inseparable combination. Practitioners and theorists alike of these doctrines labored to make them conscious expressions in the minds of their people. They were especially concerned that their doctrines be not mere abstractions of the configurations of mankind but rather ideologies that demanded action and commitment from the people. While the ideas of the state and the nation co-existed and were linked with one another, it was a matter of judgment whether or not they were coequal. Hegel, the social conservative, apotheosized the state as the embodiment of the collective will of its citizens, something far above the individual. Later another German, Bismarck, devoted his life to serving the state, in this case Prussia. The symbol of a world devoted to realism, he looked askance at nationalism disliking its overtones of popular rule. But what if the state failed to live up to what was expected of it? This was the feeling of many Frenchmen about their state after 1870 and Greeks about theirs after

1897. And most important of all in Eastern Europe the nation and the state were hardly ever conterminous. If the nation state presumed *a priori* a clear identity of frontiers and people these were precisely the factors which political and historical conditions could not guarantee.

Dragoumis, of all three individuals discussed here, was most concerned with these issues. His thinking on the nation state reflected his perception of the "reality" of conditions in the Balkans and his intellectual preferences. Reality in this case was a small, weak state, created through the intervention of the great powers of Europe with its continued existence heavily influenced by these states, a large number of Greeks still subjects of the Ottoman Empire and neighbors ready to compete with Greece for territorial prizes. These conditions were essentially as they had been for decades. Dragoumis, however, provided the most detailed theoretical analysis of the nation state relationship for his time.

While the modern Greek state was a reality, it was an unpleasant one for Dragoumis. It fulfilled neither his visions of national grandeur nor his own egoist strivings. His definition of the nation state then was appropriate to these feelings. In metaphorical terms he noted that the state ". . .is the shirt which a nation worthy of political self-existence (*afthyparxia*) can wear, and which at times does not cover it [the nation] entirely."[48] As with a shirt the state was something that could wear out in time and need replacement. The politics of greatness needed a larger stage than the modern Greek state could provide. This only the nation could provide. Witness his activities in Macedonia and Constantinople, both outside the frontiers of Greece.

History could even be brought in to support these views. It justified his desire to see the Greeks and thus himself at the center of great affairs. In succession, the ancient polis, Alexander the Great's empire, the Byzantine and Ottoman Empires and finally the modern Greek state were all vessels which had cradled the nation. The state, to continue the metaphor, would not always fit the nation. In the case of his own day Dragoumis pointed to the numbers of Greeks who remained outside the frontiers of the kingdom. Thus he felt that he was free to discard this particular "shirt" and look for one that would provide a better "fit."[49]

The function of the state then was clearly to serve as a means to an end. Dragoumis illustrated this conviction in his interpretation of the kingdom's history. The uprising in 1821 signified to him the force of nationalism at work among the Greeks. Thus the state that was created was a result of ". . .a burst of pan-hellenic force, when national consciousness spread somewhat among the people of the nation in the form of the *megale idea* . . . ."[50] Dragoumis implied that the Greeks were thinking of the long-deceased Byzantine state when they rose against the Turks. The result then was nothing but a partial realization of that "nostalgia" for past grandeur. The newly created kingdom was simply the kernel of the nation. By forming this small state the Greeks now had a "workshop" from which to continue their drive towards the attainment of the *Megale Idea*. Greece in Dragoumis' vision had the same function as did Sardinia-Piedmont in the unification of Italy. Until Venizelos, however, there was no one who might have been cast in the role of a Cavour. Dragoumis, to his credit, never had any illusions of filling this role himself.

As a nationalist Dragoumis found himself in much the same position as his German counterparts did even after the creation of the Reich. The satisfaction of having a state was not complete since all of the "nation" was still not within its borders. Frustrated by this and impelled by his nationalist outlook Dragoumis transferred his loyalty to a higher "reality." Only the nation expressed in terms of ". . .Hellenism, the Panhellenic, the *Genos,* the *Ethnos*," had meaning for him. A monarch, ministers, or members of parliament could come and go, this was not "reality" anyway. "What does the Greek government represent? Certainly not the nation."[51] Politics as such did not concern Dragoumis. The state had a nationalist mission to fullfill and this was the only reason for its existence.[52]

If the state meant little to Dragoumis it certainly was a most important institution to its citizens. It provided order and security. But he felt that in carrying out these functions it was in effect turning the people away from their real task. Reliance on the state diverted the people's attention from the needs of their fellow Greeks outside the frontiers of the kingdom. Dragoumis created for himself a personal mission with a double purpose as a response to these perceptions:

> I am not working for the state, because our state is not worthy of receiving help; it is simply a starting place. I am working for the nation. I must make men out of the Greeks, I must liberate them, be they free or enslaved, because they are all slaves and rayas.[53]

The goal to be attained was not that of simple irredentism, which had been part of the political vocabulary of countries like Greece for decades. To this traditional external mission Dragoumis added an internal one. The state as far as he was concerned was dominated by a growing class of bureaucrats. Its salvation had to come from within and without. Politics were now enmeshed in a world of nationalist mysticism.

In some part of the world, Dragoumis remarked, there is an area more fruitful, more beautiful, and more rich in memories for an individual than any other area. This was his national home.[54] These sentiments, expressive of one's love for his country, had altered significantly in their meaning since the time they were first expressed by Herder. While they still retained the cultural context in which Herder had formulated them, nationalists like Dragoumis now gave them an orientation that was far from the rationalism and individualism of the eighteenth century.

The nation was not just the totality of all the members that made it up. It was considered by Dragoumis as the repository of a people's social and cultural values and out of this entity they created whatever was of significance. Indeed it was the nation and only the nation which was capable of creating a civilization.[55] This was a significant function in Dragoumis' view since he presumed that a people's greatness in history depended on what sort of civilization they created. With a state to protect it, the nation was then free to see to ". . . the creation of civilizations and exceptional individuals."[56] It was the task of the state to see to the material needs of the people. Herder's humanist view of the natural institution within which a people found security and happiness was transformed into an aggressive and dynamic vision out of which extraordinary people and creations were expected.

Dragoumis was explicit in his writings that all nations were not the same. Echoing the contributions of social Darwinism to nationalist theory he believed in the idea of "natural" competition among nations with only a few excelling above the others. This was not a struggle in which only the fittest survived, however. Many nations were scattered over the earth. They could be strong or weak, civilized or barbaric. Each had its place in the scheme of things. In this scheme of course Dragoumis' approval went to those that stood out above the others. The weak and the barbaric provided a reference point by which strong and civilized nations could judge themselves.[57] Although all nations were needed to create a total picture, the uniqueness of each was ranked according to values instituted not by nature but by man.

In pseudo-biological terms Dragoumis saw nations as natural organisms. As such they were also subject to the law of growth and decay. In this instance those nations that developed tendencies towards a peaceful existence, and lacked the passion and opportunism which supposedly characterized a vigorous society were obviously in decline. Socialism, cosmopolitanism and Masonry, as we have already seen, were some of the "infections" that could bring on this condition.[58] Yet Dragoumis did not come to grips with what was obvious: national development governed by "natural" laws placed the destiny of such an institution in the hands of inexorable forces. This severely circumscribed the voluntarism available to nations and individuals and left them in the condition of responding rather than initiating action to a given set of circumstances.

In an article written in 1907 Dragoumis compared Greece and Russia as nations. He pictured the former as a country that had been shaped by history for centuries. While it was a civilized nation, it nevertheless bore the marks of such a long past. Russia, by the way of contrast, was an upstart, half-wild and as yet not really formed as a nation. These nations were as two women in Dragoumis' mind. Greece was a polite lady, careful of what she did, desirous of making a favorable impression and ever mindful of critics. The great Slavic state on the other hand was a woman of the provinces, as yet unrefined in the ways of civilization and unafraid of expressing her every thought. Her long period of existence had made of Greece a highly refined nation where form counted for everything. Dragoumis asserted that it was now time for this "more nobly civilized" nation to display not only its cherished traditions, but also to show new life and vitality in thought and action.[59] The question may be asked whether such a change was possible if nations were endowed with the collective natures of their peoples. Dragoumis seems here to have thought of the character of nations as a product of the culturally and politically creative elements in a society who in effect represent the nation. Since continuity through time was desired, then the nation as the vessel of a people's collective character seemed more appropriate than the state.

This approach to the problem of how nations developed led Dragoumis to assert that they all had some sort of "pattern" to complete. In effect their history was the record of their destiny as it unfolded. He cited England as an example of a nation that fulfilled its "pattern" by developing into the British Isles. In recent decades Germany and Italy were seen as having worked to complete their national configuration. The next and obvious step for Dragoumis was to argue that the Greek state must follow suit and gather in all the areas of the nation. This was a necessity since the Greeks in these territories would bring needed vitality to Hellenism.[60]

Since the days of Ottoman rule Greek intellectuals had used as we have seen expressions such as *genos* to designate the collectivity that was the Greek people. In the nineteenth century the term *ethnos* or nation provided temporal, geographic and even racial continuity. Through his writings Dragoumis sought to sanctify the idea of the nation elevating it to a position of primacy in the consciousness of its citizens. Emotion was more important than reason as a criterion of life to Dragoumis and the nation satisfied this need. It of course served the purpose of providing continuity which, as Dragoumis saw it, meant that change and growth took place in the process. The nation was a constant which assumed various forms as it developed through history. When Dragoumis demanded, however, that the state be devoted to a struggle for territorial enlargement in the name of a higher entity, he entered into a dangerous and unreal world. The consolidation of Germany, Italy and even England was the result of a process based on political power and not national will. Furthermore, whatever one may say of the merits of "natural" frontiers for nations, in the case of the Greek diaspora it made little sense. Dragoumis realized this and tried to find an "internal" essense common to all of the nation and combine it with a "realistic" appraisal of Greece's position in the Balkans. His conception of the nation as a consequence was a compound of cultural metaphysics and political irredentism.

The Organic Society: The Politics of Rootedness

How people have come together to form a society has concerned European intellectuals since the time of Rousseau. For their part nationalist writers quickly challenged the notion that people possessed inalienable rights as individuals and that they gathered together on the basis of some "social contract." Herder himself argued that they came into the world already belonging to some social unit be it family, clan, or tribe. This organic view of society formed as we have already noted an important part of Dragoumis' thought world. Applying this concept to the political and social conditions in his part of Europe Dragoumis saw the nation as representing Hellenism in its entirety while the local community (*koinoteta*) was a microcosm of this organic whole. "Hellenism is a family of Greek communities," he wrote. If the communities were vigorous and alive, then *a priori*, the nation must be in good condition, and vice versa. He saw these small social units as repositories of the nation's cultural character.[61]

The institution of the self contained local community in the Balkans and Asia Minor had existed for centuries. Under Ottoman rule with its organization of the subject peoples along religious lines, a great deal of self-rule could exist at the local level. Ottoman officials were in charge of administration, but at the village level it was to their advantage to allow the numerous subject peoples to regulate their own internal affairs, the central authority overseeing and intervening only when the state deemed it necessary. With the passing of time the importance of the community became firmly established and a well-defined pattern of social and political relationships evolved.[62] At the time when Dragoumis was writing Greek communities in the Ottoman Empire were still flourishing with their way of life little altered from that of preceding centuries.

In the early nineteen twenties, at the time of the Greek-Turkish imbroglio, Arnold Toynbee visited Asia Minor and became acquainted with many of the Greek communities. His account testifies to the longevity and importance of this institution in the ethnic life of the Levant.

The communal patriotism which one finds among the Anatolian Greeks to-day constantly reminds one of travellers' descriptions of Ydhra, Petses (sic), Ghalaxidhi, Ambelakia, and other European centers of Greek life a century ago. The mukhtar (head-man), the priest, the schoolmaster, the doctor, take a mutual interest in their respective duties and know how to work together. Voluntary subscriptions are forthcoming not only from merchants and land-owners but from shopkeepers and labourers for the building and upkeep of church, school, and hospital, and for the salaries of clergy and teachers.[63]

The community was a very self-sufficient institution by necessity if not by choice. What is relevant to our discussion is that it fostered attitudes and upheld values which Dragoumis saw as essential to the well-being of the nation: self-reliance, communal action, clearly defined relationships between individuals and a simple way of life in which customs and traditions were held in high esteem. If one remembers that Epiros, Macedonia, and Crete, areas presently for the most part in Greece, were part of the Ottoman Empire until 1913 Dragoumis' interest in the Greek communities becomes even more significant.

When the modern Greek state was created, the government of King Otho was faced with the problem of bringing about the recovery of the country from the depredations suffered during the struggle for independence. In order to do so the monarch's advisors felt that a centralized system with a state bureaucracy modeled along Western lines was necessary if order and security were to be maintained. The country was divided into ten provinces (*nomoi*). These were in turn subdivided into districts or *eparchies*. At the local level the state instituted the system of *demes*. These were made up of one or more villages depending on their size. A *demarch* or mayor was elected from each *deme* through ". . . an intricate process of limited suffrage, indirect election, and central appointment. He was a native of the *deme,* represented local interest, and served a three-year term. But the jurisdiction of the mayor and council was carefully circumscribed by the state, and all were subject to suspension or dismissal from office by the Crown without benefit of judicial decision."[64]

Dragoumis railed at what he saw as the uprooting of a long-functioning native institution at the hands of non-natives (the monarch and his Bavarian court) in favor of a system that really helped only them rather than the nation. The *demogerons* or elders elected by the communities during the period of Turkish rule represented in the eyes of Dragoumis the ". . . natural leadership of every Greek community, and not the *demarch,* the *paredros* (deputy mayor) and the *deme* council—self-rule has been from the time of Agamemnon the natural administration on Greek soil and not centralization."[65]

While locally-run communities could find a place and even flourish in an imperial world, they were at once at odds in the more tightly controlled bureaucratic system of the modern nation state. By 1900 the administrative arrangement of Greece had been considerably altered. During the premiership of George Theotokes local administration was reorganized for political reasons. The number of *nomoi* was enlarged to twenty-six and the *eparchies* were abolished. This left only the *demes* which numbered over four hundred at the beginning of the century.[66] The bureaucratic apparatus was well entrenched and it would have required a minor revolution to bring any real change. While Dragoumis certainly was a supporter of the communities he no doubt would have been much less harsh on the central government if it had placed nationalist visions ahead of everything else. "Ion the hard" preferred strength wherever he found it.

Dragoumis was shrewd enough to realize that localism was a double-edged sword. While it fostered in the individual an attachment to the soil and the place of his birth, it also could promote parochialism and disunity. The state of Greek society itself would provide Dragoumis with ample evidence of this. He supported localism,'however, as the more preferable alternative believing that centralization meant the uprooting and disorientation of a settled way of life. It seemed a valid solution to the trends that distrubed him most: emigration and the rush to the cities from the countryside.[67]

The localist schemes that Dragoumis supported did not approach anything like the all-encompassing commune of the Russian Slavophiles. The community, as he envisaged it, provided the social and political framework for villagers to regulate their affairs among themselves. The idea of common ownership of the land was repellent to Dragoumis, and the emphasis on religion that was present in the thinking of the Slavo-philes was also absent. The community did not imply any form of collective life as did the mir or commune. Dragoumis' interest was to allow the people as members of a nation to do as much for themselves as possible, thus becoming able to exercise individual initiative and at the same time to attain a greater consciousness of belonging to a larger but organic unit. The motivation behind these views of society was nationalist. Dragoumis desired a prosperous peasantry but their social welfare was not at the heart of his concern. He conceived of them as Greeks first. Keeping them settled on the land was his method of seeking to make them staunchly nationalist.[68] There was a romantic conservatism in Dragoumis' desire to see Greeks return to the "natural cycle" of life. This is readily apparent in his statement that "the farmer's son must remain a farmer, the shoemaker's a shoemaker, the baker's a baker. And in the same manner the son of a merchant a merchant, and that of a banker a banker. Only thus does the work of everyone get better."[69] Everyone thus had a station in life. The pluralism and mobility of modern society had no place in his stratified nationalist world.

Dragoumis went to some length in detailing what he felt the duties of the state and communities respectively ought to be. At the local level the communities would build churches and schools; provide priests and teachers; construct hospitals, maintain cemeteries, reservoirs and springs; administer local justice and watch over the forests and fields. For its part the state would be required to collect the state's taxes; build higher schools of learning (gymnasia, vocational schools and where necessary teacher's academies); provide a police; maintain higher courts of justice as needed; manage the large public works projects such as harbors, railroads, post offices, the telegraph and customs; and maintain the highest legislative body in the land made up of fifty men who would be chosen by indirect election. Every community would choose two representatives who in turn would elect the members of parliament.[70] As he elaborated it, the system seemed akin to local government in the Hungarian half of the Habsburg Monarchy with the estates dominating county affairs. Dragoumis obviously had little faith in democracy. His proposals were an attempt to balance off local interests against those of the central government rather than any radical reorientation of power.

Were these ideas to have been put into effect, Dragoumis envisioned several salutary results. More people would become interested in the problems at the "grass roots" level and they would be more active in the community's affairs instead of looking to the state to do everything. Political wire-pulling would decline, although Dragoumis realized that it would never cease entirely. Opportunist politicians would be curtailed and their influence could be localized. The state would remain above petty politics and would not have to intervene so often at the local level. Members of parliament would be known to all the nation and would thus be hindered from turning parliament into an institution dispensing patronage. Finally, the state's budget could be lightened of many expenses, with the local communities managing their own problems, and without a commensurate loss of revenue for the central government.[71] In presenting these ideas we can readily see Dragoumis' inherent distrust of the Greek political world. He embraced the *koinoteta* as a means of circumventing a political system that seemed incapable of being resolute and in the romantic idealist belief that organic politics were truly national politics.

His notions concerning the communities were of course largely shaped by his experiences in Macedonia and the Ottoman capital. His thoughts therefore cannot be divided into those that applied only to the Greek kingdom or only to the Greeks outside the country. While serving at the various diplomatic posts in the Ottoman Empire Dragoumis had ample opportunity to examine the relations between the communities, the Turkish authorities and the Orthodox officials.[72] He noted that often the communities found themselves caught in the dilemma of having conflicting advice offered by their Orthodox clergy on the one hand and the Greek consular officials on the other. He hoped that the communities would cooperate more closely among themselves especially in commercial affairs. Then they could exert a stronger influence in the political affairs of the empire.[73]

It is noteworthy that it was in Egypt that Dragoumis found communities operating as he envisioned. After a short visit there he felt that he had seen his ideas actually at work. There each party had his function clearly defined. Ecclesiastical affairs were the concern of the bishop, the communities managed their local problems through a council and political guidance was in the hands of the Greek consular official.[74] They accomplished the three goals that Dragoumis desired. They maintained their Hellenic traditions, ran their own affairs, and were conscious of being part of the nation as a whole. It is ironic, however, that Dragoumis chose the Greek diaspora communities in Egypt as exemplifying his notions of organic life. They had existed there of course for hundreds of years and pursued a life that had very little to do with the Greek world within the kingdom. They were a culture out of the past which survived into the twentieth century in an area where the power of the Ottoman Empire had already crumbled. Their circumstances were in certain ways unique and in a few decades this world would be destroyed as that of all the other communities of the Greek diaspora by the very kind of ideas that Dragoumis represented. Unity and diversity in the form of a nation state and small communities were now increasingly difficult to reconcile.

The Politics of the Volk: Language and Education

As we have previously shown Dragoumis conceived of the nation as an organic unit that represented the collectivity of a people. This raises the question of just exactly who constituted the nation. Did it include all of the people or just that part of society that lived on the land? In other words did Dragoumis have a conception of a distinct element in society that represented the Volk and maintained the customs and lore of the nation? He used terms such as *ethnos* (nation), *genos,* and *file* (race) indiscriminately so that we cannot count on them to help us make clear distinctions. His concern with promoting the unity of the nation while accepting the existence of divisions in society as long as they did not lead to class conflict indicates that national rather than social homogeneity was uppermost in his mind. By examining his thoughts on language and education we may come closer to understanding his idea of what and also who constituted the nation.

The language question, as Dragoumis saw it, affected everyone in the nation. Responding to a pamphlet by another writer, in which the question of what form of Greek ought to be taught in the schools was discussed, Dragoumis wrote:

> In regard to the argument that the national soul does not yearn for its native tongue, one cannot accept this as true regarding the Greeks, because the national soul is not constituted only by teachers and archaist intellectuals [who would use the *katharevousa*], but also by peasants, workers, women, intellectuals and writers who

feel, speak, sing, and write the common spoken tongue, regardless
if there is or is not an influence from the scholarly, written
language.[75]

It is clear then that language is a fundamental criterion in distinguishing
a nation, and it is this that brings together and binds a people. But in the
case of the Greeks language had served to divide and not unite the nation.
Who then embodied the consciousness of the nation? It was obvious to
Dragoumis that it could not be those who used the *katharevousa* and
identified with classical Greece. He accused these people of foisting a
false view of the nation on their countrymen. By focusing on the
classical legacy they had divided up Hellenism and had helped bring a
sterility to the life of the nation.[76]

The issue of language in Dragoumis' thought had both nationalist
and social ramifications. Thus the work of the demoticists had an
important "psychological" connotation for him: "The demoticists by
having been capable of dispelling a tradition, the classical, which had
become a superstition and a nightmare, are ready to study any other
superstition from close-up and to be rid of it."[77] In doing this the
demoticists freed the nation from the rigidity of relying on one set
tradition. Dragoumis conceived of a nation as a dynamic entity and its
culture, therefore, had to reflect this.

Language, like a people, was always developing. It took on new words,
even foreign ones, but it continued to retain its basic character. As
Dragoumis saw it every written language held something "artificial"
within it. By "artificiality" he meant ". . .the remembrance of the origin
of each word and the continuity of the language." This benefited the
nation by providing unity and a tradition. In this instance the Greek
language had sustained a continuity from Homer to the present. Each
civilization that arose, Archaic, Classical, Hellenistic, Byzantine and
modern Greek made its contribution to the language. These changes arose
from within a particular era with its own particular needs. It was wrong
then to consider any one period as having the correct form of the language
as the supporters of the puristic did by harking back to classical times.
But the extremists among the demoticists were equally in error when
they tried to base the nation's language on what was spoken at the time.
This meant a reliance on localisms that was just as disruptive to the continuity of the language.[78] Like the nation, a language belonged to a definite
historical era yet it needed to maintain its links with the past.

Dragoumis as a demoticist attributed to this tradition a proud lineage,
unlike Giannopoulos who saw it as an upstart movement of the modern
period whose aim was to bury all that came before it. Demoticism, in
Dragoumis' view, was not just the popular spoken language of his own
time. Each era of Greek history in fact had its own "popular demotic"

(*laike demotike*) which amounted to the "natural language" of the period. Thus Polybius, the Evangelists, the writings of Porphyrogenitos, the Byzantine epic *Digenis Akritas,* the Cretan writings of the sixteenth and seventeenth centuries, the writers of the Ionian islands and the demotic songs were all examples of the "natural language" of their time. Linguistically and historically this was a tenuous argument. Many of the works of the Byzantine era were a mixture of more than one form of Greek, as in the case of *Digenis Akritas.* But Dragoumis was concerned with illustrating a creative tradition rather than with philological accuracy.

We can better understand his intentions if we compare his version of the demotic tradition with what he labeled the "pedantic scholarly" tradition (*scholastike logiotate*). This and the popular tradition were both legacies of the Byzantine world to modern Greece. Dragoumis recognized that the "scholarly" tradition was the literary product of the Church and officialdom in the Byzantine Empire. He castigated it as a sterile effort to retain and preserve as much of the classical Greek as possible. What concerns us here is not a philological argument but Dragoumis' belief that whatever group dominated the social and political life of a society, in this case the aristocracy and clerics, determined the formal language of the period. He contended, therefore, that the creative efforts of the Greek nation had been thwarted for centuries by this scholarly activity which had monopolized formal culture. "The scholarly tradition is the last visible remnant of Byzantine civilization, like a dead leaf that has not yet fallen from the tree."[79]

From Dragoumis' vantage point these developments had had deleterious reprecussions in the modern era. When the Greek kingdom was created the educators and intellectuals who also were classically oriented set about to emulate that epoch. To wean the people away from the language they learned as children from their mothers they introduced the puristic or *katharevousa,* a mixture of modern and classical Greek. Dragoumis saw this as an attempt to transform the *Romios* or modern Greek into a Hellene of the classical period.[80] This destroyed continuity in language which also affected the unity of the nation.

While Dragoumis considered himself a demoticist, he refused to follow the lead of the most famous member of this group John Psicharis. Dragoumis rejected the efforts of Psicharis to devise a grammar for the demotic. It was a "natural" language and therefore it developed of its own accord through the creative efforts of the nation. Psicharis' heavy reliance on the spoken word in developing the written demotic must also have put off Dragoumis, who, as we have noted, believed in that "artificiality" that meant continuity with the past. He was in full accord, however, with the idea that the demoticists needed to convert as many of the "purists" as possible. But there seemed to him to be a dilemma here. Those who disliked the demotic were prejudiced against it from the beginning. Seeking to convert them by writing in the demotic was useless because they stumbled over the very fact of the language itself. Dragoumis preferred to see the demotic used in literature and all other areas where the language was used such as government and education in the belief that its spread would bring converts.[81]

From our examination it is obvious that Dragoumis considered all those who used the demotic to be part of the nation. Language was a means of identifying those who made it up. He included people from all social strata in this category and did not confine himself to any mystique of the peasant as the folk ideal. Yet the "language of the people" was used effectively by only a minority of the urban middle class. One can see in Dragoumis' ideas a distinction between those who employed the demotic, the creative elements of society, and those, generally associated with politicians, educators, the church and bureaucracy, who did not. Thus the nation could be identified with a particular elite. This was in keeping with Dragoumis' differentiation between the state and the nation. The demoticists could serve to help unify the nation while at the same time being its most conscious representatives. The nation was not identified with some version of popular sovereignty but with those who shared a particular cultural tradition whether consciously or not.

If a people is identified as a nation through the language that it uses, then institutions of learning are significant because of their influence in the maintenance and spread of literacy. Although the use of a language was a natural phenomenon, the formal teaching of it in schools raised immediate questions. In the case of the Greeks there was the problem of what form of the language should be taught. The choice that was made would have an impact on the character of the nation in Dragoumis' view and thus needed careful scrutiny.

The spirit and content of Greek education received the trenchant criticism of Dragoumis. "The schools of *Romiosyne* [that is, the schools in all the Hellenic communities], creations of a vacuous wisdom and abandoned to the complete discretion of the nation's learned [the educators], attempt to perpetuate the aridity of the scholarly tradition and every other dead . . . ." concept.[82] As he saw it there was much more to education that the content of what was taught. Dragoumis perceived it as a state of mind, where feeling and enthusiasm were all important. Students who were not motivated to work for their country were only half-educated. The fault in this case lay with many of the teachers. They had dulled the spirit of their students and produced citizens of little value to their nation.[83]

In this matter Dragoumis saw a nexus between the West and the Greeks. The Europeans had impressed upon his countrymen their love for the ancients. Then the Greeks themselves had indulged in the worship of the classical world (*archaiomania*) and drenched their educational system with it. Dragoumis rhetorically asked about the manner and content of instruction. What did educators teach their pupils?

> Enthusiasm for the Christian religion? Enthusiasm for the heritage of the Byzantine Empire? Enthusiasm for distant ancient Greece? Enthusiasm for the sciences? For the arts? For gymnastics and exercise? None of these things. They poison them slowly with. . . a false worship of the Ancient Greeks. . ."[84]

The implication was that if the nation possessed a living cultural tradition then the efforts of teachers to preserve the Greeks' ancient heritage were superfluous. Dragoumis' vitalistic outlook led him to see nothing but sterility in modern Greek paideia and to contrast it with the dynamism of the demotic culture based on the folk.[85]

Dragoumis attacked not only the spirit and content but the goals and structure of education. Using the teaching of language as an example, he argued that the child was introduced at an early age to a language form, the puristic, that was not natural to him. The *katharevousa* was then used as a stepping stone. As the student advanced he was confronted with ancient Greek. The further he progressed the deeper he became involved with the classical past. Dragoumis saw a narrowing effect in this whereby the student was forced to assume that ancient Greece was his only heritage. Thus he was drawn further away from *Romiosyne,* from the living present and the traditions of the modern nation.[86]

Overriding these particular criticisms was Dragoumis' sense of the general purpose of education. His attitude was similar to that of the teacher Bouteiller in Barrès' *Les Déracinés*. Dragoumis expressed his feelings when he wrote:

> Of what use are the sciences in the schools? Whatever the children learn, it amounts to the same thing. The question is not for them to become educated in order to live. The question is for them to become better human beings, if this is possible, that is more dissatisfied with their environment and with contemporary civilization, and to seek something better by overcoming contemporary civilization.[87]

An education which produced an individual alienated from his own immediate roots and possessing a distorted understanding of his heritage was not an education at all in Dragoumis' eyes. A student who was weaned on reason and lacked the emotion to identify with the nation was not an asset to the country. Dragoumis bemoaned the fact that his countrymen paid so much respect to letters for he saw this faith in booklearning as unwarranted.[88]

Given his conviction that those who made up the nation should be committed to work for it and that they should be aware of their place in it, Dragoumis' views on the methods of education went in two complementary directions.[89] First, he encouraged the tendency to simplify what the student needed to be taught. His idea was that the pupil be given only the amount of education necessary to make him a productive person: "Education must unburden the young Greeks from the weight of useless knowledge, which the teachers have encumbered them with up until now, and clear their minds of the archaic burden which the ignorance and stupidity of various teachers of the *Genos* and lawmakers of the State stuffed into the heads of their fathers . . . ."[90] A basic knowledge, without any frills, was adequate for a person to take his place in the community. Second, Dragoumis emphasized individual involvement in society. Education ought not to consist only of formal schooling. A tour of duty in the "Greek army or Macedonia" was quite enlightening for any young man. His curriculum should include not only the four "Rs", but lessons in the meaning of "danger" and "war".[91] "Most people do not need a great deal of schooling. It is enough for the children to learn a few beneficial things, whatever is useful for the work of the village or for their trade, nothing more."[92]

Such a view of education certainly placed a heavy emphasis on duty and service to the nation rather than on the development of the rational faculties. Even ethics were to be made simple and straightforward. A child in Dragoumis' view was not to be kept from seeing and hearing unpleasant things. Instead he should be made aware of the rough side of life. The books that he read ought to reflect this attitude and refrain from any moralizing or preaching. While recognizing the value of books in the education of children, Dragoumis was much less enthusiastic when it came to dealing with adults.[93] As far as he was concerned books for adults served often only as a pastime or else filled them with useless knowledge.

The basic thrust of Dragoumis' educational theories, at least in terms of methods and structure, was to keep people in their place with duty rather than opportunity coming first. The nation needed roots not upward mobility. It was a closed world to be guided by just as firm an elite as was already in charge of the educational establishment. The same contradictions existed here as in Dragoumis' theories about his egoism and his nationalism. If exceptional individuals were desired this was hardly possible in the educational structure that he envisioned. But then again Dragoumis probably intended that his system be applied to only a part of society, that which would follow the lead of those guiding the destiny of the nation.

If in methods and structure the educational system was intended to instill cohesiveness and loyalty to the nation, in content it was more likely to do so. Dragoumis, as we have pointed out, was a staunch supporter of tradition despite his talk of the need for change. He believed that it should be ever-present in the consciousness of the people. To promote this he advised that teachers provide their students with an understanding ". . .of the sources of modern Hellenic life, with the knowledge of contemporary demotic literature and the recent and more distant history of the nation."[94] By studying their past the people learned about their origins, could better understand who they were, and would learn who their enemies were.[95]

History was an instrument for the inculcation of a nationalist consciousness. It enabled a teacher to excite the student with enthusiasm for the nation. Dragoumis pictured a history lesson beginning with the war for independence in 1821:

> And from the great uprising of twenty-one he [Dragoumis] envisioned the teacher going backwards towards the time of the Turkish domination until the taking of the City with the death of Constantine Paleologos, to the point where he would make the children cry. And at this point he would give them to understand the plight of the nation, the reality about them, the geographical position of *Romiosyne* between the East and the West, the awakening of the neighboring nations, the influence of Western civilization with its good and bad points. . .and the inestimable strength that nations can rediscover by immersing themselves in some ideal.[96]

The emphasis on more "recent" history was deliberate. Dragoumis saw this as an opportunity for the people to feel their nation's successes as well as failures. He wanted to see comparisons made between these two polarities. Such a case would be the revolution of 1821 and the war of 1897. This sort of history would ". . .allow the mind of the child to feel the influence of the national humiliation."[97] In addition, all of the nation was encompassed in the Byzantine and Ottoman eras and it enabled the students to sense that they belonged to an entity greater than the kingdom. In an age of irredentist nationalism, Dragoumis was its most conscious and vivid exponent in Greece. He preferred the worlds of Byzantium and the Ottoman Empire to classical Greece because they were more relevant to his nationalist visions, which were based on immediacy, racialism, and collectiveness. Ancient Hellas had only recently begun to be seen as a dynamic civilization where forces of rationality and irrationalism mingled creatively. The traditional view which looked upon that culture as harmonious, serene and essentially timeless, still had a powerful following especially in Greece itself. Dragoumis disliked this as well as what he felt was Europe's appropriation of that culture for its own ideals. The nation not only had to find roots but it had to be unique as well. The version of history that suited Dragoumis' aims and needs was a compound of ethnicity and vitalism and it caught the spirit of his time.

Dragoumis was convinced that Greece possessed enough schools but of the wrong kind. The gymnasia seemed to him to be a little more than factories for producing civil servants. The kingdom did not need any more schools but the Greeks outside its frontiers did. He conjured up a romantic vision of a one room schoolhouse with a single teacher spreading nationalist ideas among the Greeks of Asia Minor and Macedonia.[98] To realize this dream Dragoumis actually attempted to found a teachers' academy along with several other demoticists. A few references to this scheme can be found in his work *Those Who Are Alive*. The mission of this school was to help bring about ". . . the union of the race into one state, the identification of the race with the state, which presumes the awakening of national consciousness, but with other qualities than what patriotic teachers, speech-makers and articles in newspapers are using now."[99] He did not state what happened to the enterprise, although presumably it never became a reality.

Through his theories on language and education Dragoumis put forth the strongest nationalist critique of the bourgeois dominated society in his time. It was, however, an attack made in defense of the past. Done in the name of the nation Dragoumis' vision conjured up a mythical dynamic folk that was both cohesive and creative. The society that he envisioned could hardly have been able to cope with the demands of the modern nation state, however. Dragoumis' theories implied the continuance of a stratified society in Greece but looked forward to its being more unified as an integral nationalist state.

Civilization: The Nation Writ Large

If the nation was the instrument through which Dragoumis fulfilled his ego, it was also the institution through which the highest level of culture, a civilization, was generated. It was Dragoumis' broadest vision of humanity yet it remained circumscribed by the nationalist framework that he imposed upon himself and everyone else.

As with the nation, time and place were critical factors in the rise of civilizations.[100] By engaging in this activity nations were able to exert an influence beyond their frontiers and even benefit humanity at large.[101] The process was, however, complex in Dragoumis' view and all nations did not produce their own original civilization.

A nation must not simply be civilized, but it must have a civilization of its own. Of course every civilization, however original it may seem, is in reality influenced either by foreign cultures (*politismous*) or by older ones born in the same nation, or by both of them. It is one thing to be influenced by foreign cultures, but quite another for a (foreign) civilization to be transplanted into a nation. There are nations which cannot create culture, but simply accept foreign ones and modify them according to their own nature. There are others that are not able to do even that . . . . But there are also such nations that can assimilate all the foreign and older civilizations, which then motivate them to advance . . . , and which become the seed in order for them to give birth to their own indigenous civilization. For these nations civilization has not been taken from another place, but is a native fruit . . . .[102]

Dragoumis made the distinction, which German intellectuals appreciated, between a civilized and a cultured society. In this manner he was able to compare his nation favorably with nations like France or England. It mattered not that Greece did not possess the latest in technical innovations. What really counted was that the Hellenes had produced significant cultures before. This interpretation handsomely accomodated the vicissitudes of Greek history as it allowed for the impact of foreign influences while asserting an overall constancy in that civilization. The factor that made this possible was of course the homeland, the geographic constant that insured a natural environment which both Dragoumis and Giannopoulos deemed basic in the shaping of any society.[103]

In the unfolding of a civilization Dragoumis posited the existence of two forces, one a conserving tendency tied to the past the other an impulse for change oriented to the future. Tradition or the remembrance of the past was, as we have seen, the conserving force that unified a nation. History was the process by which consciousness of the past was acquired. The attainment of consciousness was the sign that history was making itself felt in society.[104] The implication was that those individuals who acquired a consciousness of their past would be stimulated to either political or cultural creativity.[105]

The development of civilization as Dragoumis conceived of it was the product of a dynamic interplay between the individual, his environment, and his past. A civilization then was always in the process of becoming. It was creative because it was in a state of flux. Dragoumis liked to cite the Renaissance in Italy as a favorite example. Here was a society in upheaval. There was a dynamic interaction between the forces that Dragoumis had singled out, and it could be seen in the artistic and literary creations of the time. It was a society giving birth to a civilization. As this was an organic process, Italian civilization had then reached a peak from which it had gone into a decline. In Nietzschean terms Dragoumis argued that Europe in his time had reached a stage of being relatively well-off. It devoted itself to utopian dreams of material comfort, an indication to Dragoumis that the spiritual dynamism of that civilization had deteriorated.[106]

All civilizations then were faced with inexorable and cyclical change: "Nothing functions forever, all organisms die. How can . . . a body, an organization, or organism live and function forever if the one who gives life and fire to it tires or changes?"[107] The implication was that man himself was at the heart of these developments. New ideas, the incursion of a new people, a change in the nature of the people, all were indications of how man himself was the prime force in bringing change. A civilization was protected by its political system be it an empire, a nation-state or a city. If it received a damaging blow from either an external or internal upheaval there would be a corresponding impact on the civilization.[108] Yet the nation, embodied in the collectivity of the people or race, would remain. Thus man, who was subject to the organic laws of the universe, could overcome his transitory nature through the nation.

Dragoumis' thoughts on civilization were really manifestations of a concern with power. Since life meant change and strife then the way to challenge it was through adherence to the nation. Cultural creativity was another form of struggle. The creation of a civilization was proof that life's challenge had been met. It signified that a society, grouped as a nation, was able to dominate life. By doing so it had acquired power, which to Dragoumis was the real purpose for the existence of men and likewise nations.

We must now look to see how these ideas were applied to the Greeks. In an essay entitled *Hellenic Civilization* published in 1913, Dragoumis made his views known in some detail. What concerns us is how he interpreted the past in light of developments in his own day. The thrust of his argument was that the Greeks had too much of a good thing. While they could look back to a long and rich heritage, Dragoumis feared that it had become a burden. He implied that Greek society in his own day was not creative enough because it tied itself too much to the past. The idea was that there should be less dependence on what had gone before and more concern with the future.[109]

Dragoumis was enough of a traditionalist not to want a real break with the past, however. He asserted with pride that the ancient Greeks had created a civilization unsurpassed by anyone. The Phoenicians, Egyptians, Indians and early Greeks all had produced cultures of consequence, but nothing like that attained by Periclean Athens. Those civilizations that followed including the Roman, Byzantine and Italian Renaissance might have been as creative as that of classical Greece, but none had surpassed the perfection of that epoch.[110]

In the centuries that had passed since then the civilization of the Hellenes had continued to develop. Byzantium, however, as we have noted, generated two traditions, the scholarly and the demotic, which Dragoumis saw as a divisive legacy to the modern Greeks. He preferred to think that the Greeks had not created a new civilization since the fall of Constantinople. By this he meant that the scholarly and demotic cultures had survived but that neither had as yet emerged to create a single unified civilization.[111]

Dragoumis harbored no doubts that the Greeks could create a new civilization:[112] "If the new religion is the nation, again the Greeks will discover its expression and its form, and will present to the world the true love of the nation . . . ."[113] To do this two conditions had to be met. The people had to retain a collective consciousness of their continuity with the past. Dragoumis used the term "race" when referring to the Greeks here not with the implication of physical characteristics but of a metaphysical spirit.

He recognized that a people's physical characteristics could change. He therefore preferred to stress the importance of consciousness in a people as a criterion of identity much the same as it was for an individual.[114] Even if the "race" lost its independence it could not disappear as long as it retained a consciousness of its "nature" (*ypostasis*).[115] In this way Dragoumis raised history above the level of human actions to a metaphysical plane where emotion rather than reason was paramount.

This, however, was not enough to create a civilization. Dragoumis expected that an "aristocracy" of exceptional individuals would be needed if a new civilization were to be born. These people could be found in the military, in politics or in education. They might be rich or poor, possess a great deal of education or very little.[116] Nevertheless, it was obvious that the rebirth of the nation would take place from above. Dragoumis of course had in mind the Italian Renaissance in making these suggestions. In fact he fancied himself as a "link" between the past and the future of Greek civilization.[117] His egoism thus reached its highest peak!

Dragoumis never tried to present a detailed picture of what this new civilization would be like. It is obvious from the preceding discussion, however, that it would be unlike either that of classical Greece or Byzantium and certainly different from that of contemporary Europe. Its basis would be the demotic tradition and in geographic extent it would mean a much enlarged state in the Balkan peninsula. He expected that Hellenism in the future would exert a much greater influence in the area and was at least receptive to the idea that the Greeks could meditate between the civilizations of the East and West while maintaining their own unique culture.[118] In essence his views were an ambitious attempt to glorify the nation.

Dragoumis' appeal in Greece has taken many directions. Nationalist writers have eagerly sought to promote his ideas.[119] Demoticists have of course claimed him. A few have been intrigued by the "internal" aspect in Dragoumis' thought.[120] To properly understand his significance, however, we must place him in his own time. The established culture in Greece was being challenged by intellectuals who saw it as artificial and stagnant. Indeed after the defeat in 1897 there was criticism as we have seen of all aspects of society. Dragoumis' writings, grounded in certain European currents that we have discussed, caught the mood of the time. His books, which were as much demoticist tracts as nationalist appeals, seemed to be a fresh approach to what some preceived as the nation's ills.

He represented the nationalist ethos at its apogee. There was irony of course in the fact that his thoughts on Hellenism were in essence based on an intellectual framework derived from the West. Nevertheless, at a time when many Greeks felt frustrated with their society Dragoumis presented them with a vision of uniqueness. Rather than turning towards the West to fulfill themselves as had been the case before, he counseled them to look inwards and find the sources of strength within their native folk culture. He thus represented the last and most conscious effort of the traditional elements of society to hold off the westernization of Greece. This was the paradox of the nation that is seen as the "cradle of the West."

In their struggle for independence from the Ottoman Empire the Greeks defended their actions and appealed for European support in the name of justice and reason. They claimed that the war against the Turks was undertaken to regain natural rights that they had lost centuries before.[1] Once independence had been gained, the Greeks defended their need to continue their struggle against the Ottoman state on the premise that not all of the nation was free. What had begun as an eighteenth century justification for revolt based on the natural rights of man soon turned into a nineteenth century romantic vision of territorial expansion in the name of the "nation." As we have seen the Greeks became deeply committed to a vision conjured up from the past as a guidepost for the future. Enshrined as the "Great Idea" it remained a constant throughout all the political upheavals of the nineteenth century. It is, therefore, necessary for us to see how this nationalist dream fared after the defeat of 1897. To do so we need only turn and look at Dragoumis' life during the period under examination, since he embodied in thought and deed the pursuit of this goal.

Like those supporters of the Great Idea who preceded him, Dragoumis defined what were Greek lands and who was part of Hellenic society in broad terms.[2] Continuity with the past is evident in his thought.Yet, Dragoumis was disturbed by the obvious fact that after almost a century of effort the national dream had not been realized. This raises the question of how and in what way his views on the Great Idea varied from those of the preceding era.

Dragoumis liked to think that he assessed the situation from a realistic standpoint, separating what had been fantasy in the past from the objective conditions of the world: "Dreams and hyperbolic desires paralyze men and nations. If the nation becomes worthy once more, the City and the East and whatever it wishes will belong to it later."[3] The Great Idea, as far as Dragoumis was concerned, had to be evaluated in terms of what practical service it could perform for the country. In other words, the motivation remained the same but the means needed rethinking.

Dragoumis' view of the world, imbued with a strong sense of Bergsonian vitalism, asserted the need for creativity in man's actions. It was the same with nations. If life was in a state of continuous growth and change, then, like individuals, nations needed a purpose to give meaning to them. In the case of Greece this purpose or national ideal served a dual function. It would help to unite the people and keep them from quarreling among themselves and at the same time it would stimulate them to continue their struggle on behalf of the nation. The Greeks of course already had an ideal, one which had been nourished for decades. But in fact this was precisely what concerned Dragoumis. He considered whether or not it had perhaps become too natural a part of them. Referring to those Greeks who were within the frontiers of the kingdom, Dragoumis complained that they seemed to retain the form of the national ideal but had lost the essence of it. The Great Idea was an admirable vision, but were the Greeks actually acting on it?[4] Dragoumis betrayed his fears when he noted that the stimulative power of the national ideal had eroded significantly and that people were now being tempted by other visions such as socialism, or they simply did not care.[5] While this was hardly the case, such thoughts reflected the sort of anxieties that troubled the traditionalist elements in society. Dragoumis did not doubt the necessity of a national ideal. His main concern was the form that it should take. He knew that the Great Idea would appeal to the Greeks in the Ottoman Empire but he wanted them to be "realistic" in their understanding of it. They needed to recognize their national unity and assert their potential economic as well as political power. Turning to the mainland Greeks in the kingdom, who inhabited what Dragoumis referred to as the "Helladic" state, he questioned the appropriateness of the Great Idea. Dragoumis, the realist-hero asserted that the traditional hope of recapturing Constantinople was now an unrealizable dream, given the political and military circumstances of the day. It was his argument that the Greeks ought to concentrate on enlarging their country, i.e., creating a "great Greek state."[6] Though this was in effect the policy that governments in Greece had been following for decades, Dragoumis impatiently criticized them for their "timorous" policy of "chipping away" at the Ottoman Empire. What the country required, as "Ion the strong" saw it, was a more vigorous, bold and sustained foreign policy. He argued bitterly that past diplomacy had been confused and insufficiently aggressive, having left the initiative to Greeks outside the kingdom like the Cretans.

It was not Dragoumis' purpose to do away with what was by now a well-established tradition of nationalist expansion. What he did was to give primacy to action over thought, to offer alternative possibilities for this to occur. His own career in Macedonia and Constantinople suggests a willingness to make use of both concepts, the Great Idea and the great Greek state. Consistency in Dragoumis lies not so much in his thought but in his desire for action as a "realist-hero." The vision of the Great Idea was a personal challenge and an outlet for his energies. The two factors, nationalist commitment and individualist vitalism, were wedded together in his personality, in a symbiotic rather than a contradictory coexistence.[7]

We have already noted Dragoumis' fondness for remembering things long past. The Great Idea was of course the embodiment of this feeling, associated as it was with the civilization of East Rome that conquered the Near East. After the final destruction of this civilization in 1453, it was the *Romios,* the Greek subject of the Ottoman Empire, who retained a remembrance of what had gone before and dreamed of resurrecting the Byzantine Empire.[8] Dragoumis like Giannopoulos understood the great political and economic transformation that had taken place on the Continent by the time of the Greeks' revolt in 1821. He could not over-look the crucial role that the West had played even in such a remote area as the Balkans. Angry at the obviously slow progress the country had made, which in his mind meant political development foremost, Dragoumis turned against those who were supposedly of great benefit to the new nation—the European philhellenes.

Philhellenism then was a double-edged sword to Dragoumis. Abundantly useful for promoting an independent Greece, it offered, in his view, a disturbingly constricted idea of the nature of the modern Greeks. The Europeans' admiration of the ancient world had led, in Dragoumis' eyes, to their viewing modern Greece within a classical framework. It is worth noting here that Dragoumis exempted the Russians from this criticism. They it seems understood the Greeks' "vision" since they were not supposed to have labored under the misconceptions of the philhellenes. Dragoumis adduced this from the belief that the Russians did not possess the classical heritage of the western world! Needless to say, this did not endear them to Dragoumis, who felt that they were not about to allow the Greeks to fulfill their national "vision," which could only come at the expense of their own. It was, nevertheless, Europe with its rationalism and humanism that Dragoumis identified as the villain from the time that Greece was first created.[9]

Once the Greek state had been established, its political leaders were faced, according to Dragoumis, with the dilemma of dual loyalty. They had to deal with the needs of the country as well as with those of the Greeks outside the frontiers of the kingdom. There were indeed two alternatives to this dual political inheritance. The country could acquiesce and follow the lead of the great powers. In this case the argument was made that the needs of the kingdom came first and the policy of the government ought to be the strengthening of the state by slow territorial enlargement. This policy, which Dragoumis obviously rejected, he labeled "Helladic", one that was narrowly centered on the state. The more appealing alternative to Dragoumis was what he liked to think of as "Hellenic," a policy that had a broad scope and took into consideration the entire nation, which was both within and without the kingdom. Under the circumstances Dragoumis felt that there had been a misunderstanding of the scope of Hellenism. Influenced by Europe and lacking faith in the capabilities of the new state, Greece's political leaders had formulated a weak and poorly conceived national policy. They established Athens as the supposedly temporary center of the Hellenic world and then proceeded to forget about the real focal point of the nation, which Dragoumis asserted was Constantinople. Their strategy of expanding the frontiers of the state and retaking the City from the Turks was diluted by timid acts of diplomacy. They waited for the European powers to hand them "tidbits" of territory. The world of *Romiosyne* had been succeeded by a "Helladic" vision, which to him represented a failure of national policy.[10]

This line of reasoning led Dragoumis to certain conclusions. We have already noted his basic assumption that the Greek state encompassed only a part of the nation. In addition he felt that every nation had "natural" frontiers, i.e., those that were commensurate with the geographic extent of the "race."[11] He of course could see the political and territorial disintegration of the Ottoman Empire and the concurrent rise of aggressive nationalisms among all the peoples of the Balkans. Reacting to this he called for a policy that would insure that Greece's interests were protected. Specifically, he argued that neither the vision of a revived Byzantine Empire nor the retention of a small Greece with boundaries determined by what had existed in classical times was a correct policy. Dragoumis supported action that would have created a ". . . Greece which would have as boundaries those of the Greek race."[12] This he interpreted to mean the areas of Epiros, Macedonia, Thrace, Crete, and the Aegean islands. The Greeks in Anatolia were considered in a different context. He thought, as we have seen, that they would derive more benefit by cooperating more closely through their communities, working to enhance their position within the empire. Dragoumis supported both policies as complementary.[13] In other words, he sought to establish as the basis for a practical policy a distinction between a greater Greece and Hellenism in Asia Minor. Underlying all these ideas, however, was the attempt to stimulate action through heightened consciousness.

Dragoumis thought of his approach as a balance between the excessive visions of national glory and the cynicism of political life.[14] He was aware that southeast Europe was going through the process that is named after it—Balkanization. The splintering seemed to him to be going on inside of his country also. To forestall both the external and internal fragmenting Dragoumis offered cohesiveness through a nationalist vision of a people united by common action. It was the image of the *Volk* making its own destiny. Its outward looking orientation and aggressiveness, however, could only increase tensions in the area.

Macedonia and A Greater State

The twentieth century brought no respite to the political troubles that plagued Macedonia. If anything, the problems in the area worsened.

Bulgarians, Serbs and Greeks fought in varying degrees for this economically and politically important piece of Ottoman territory. A pattern of challenge and response developed among the various national groups creating a rising spiral of animosity not easily subdued. The problem was a major concern to all the Balkan nations involved. In the 1890's there were attempts at reaching an understanding over this area between certain of the concerned countries but nothing conclusive resulted.[15] How the region could be divided up amicably among the interested parties once the Ottomans were gone, remained an insoluble question for years.

All three nationalities had already organized groups to promote their cause in Macedonia. Probably the earliest and most effective was the Internal Macedonian Revolutionary Organization, IMRO. Originally founded to support the cause of "Macedonia for the Macedonians", it was soon confronted with another Macedonian organization which aimed at incorporating Macedonia into Bulgaria. IMRO had its hands full keeping clear of the Turkish authorities and at the same time resisting the efforts of those who desired union with Bulgaria. The matter came to a head in the ill-fated Ilinden uprising of July 20/August 2, 1903.

IMRO instigated a rebellion in the Macedonian vilayet of Monastir, hoping to liberate all of Macedonia from the Turks if possible. Though the uprising experienced some initial success, the mobilization of superior forces by the Turks doomed the movement. Much loss of life and property damage occurred in the villages, however, before the rebels were subdued. The Ilinden uprising brought the great powers into the affairs of the empire once more and they imposed a reform program for the area on the Ottoman government. Known as the Mürzsteg program and devised in October, 1903, the plan envisioned administrative and financial reforms as well as a reorganization of the police forces in the area. For the various Balkan states the Ilinden rebellion signaled a new stage in the development of the Macedonian problem.

In previous years Serbia had followed a moderate policy on Macedonia. She had been concerned by Bulgarian nationalist claims to the area and after 1870 with the rapid growth of the Bulgarian exarchate. To counter these forces Serbia had sought, and in 1903 obtained, recognition of the Serbs as a nationality in the empire by the Sultan. Her main hope was to keep the *status quo* if possible, and then to work out a solution, which would take Bulgarian interests into consideration, but keep the area from falling into their hands. The Mürzsteg program seemed to the Serbs a useful means of curbing both Bulgarian and Greek nationalist activities in Macedonia. Serbia was content after the Ilinden uprising to seek a solution that would allow Macedonian autonomy provided the Serbs would enjoy equality with the Bulgarians.[16]

The Macedonian question continued as a problem for Bulgaria, clouding efforts by the government to reach lasting agreements with the Serbs. IMRO split into two factions after the uprising. The Supremists, who believed in the use of terror and union with Bulgaria, gained control of the organization. They had no desire to work with the Serbs, and by 1904 there was a renewal of the conflict between the two nationalities in Macedonia. Serbian armed bands, known as Chetniks, increased their activity against the IMRO groups.[17] The most pronounced aspect of the problem in Macedonia remained, however, the conflict between the Bulgarians and the Greeks. Because an individual was still distinguished in the eyes of the Ottoman Empire by the faith he professed, religion entered inextricably into the matter. The Greeks were under the jurisdiction of the Patriarch in Constantinople. In 1870 the Bulgarians had obtained their own national church with the creation of the exarchate. For those who firmly considered themselves either Greeks or Bulgarians the issue was clear-cut; support of their respective national position was taken for granted. But there were thousands of villagers in Macedonia who had no wish to take sides, and if they did, they preferred to think of themselves simply as Macedonians. The conflict in Macedonia was not only between Greeks, Serbs or Bulgarians. Each party hoped to sway and eventually control those who did not consider that they belonged to any one of the three nationalities.

Macedonia continued to occupy a significant place in the nationalist aspirations of many influential Greeks, especially after the disaster of 1897. To these individuals the union of Crete with Greece was a dream that would come true eventually. Macedonia, on the other hand, was a present danger, and they demanded immediate action. Only in this manner, they argued, could Greece grow and maintain its political position in the Balkans. The Ottoman Empire was no longer the major threat, but mounting nationalist conflict in the Balkans was.[18] The Ilinden uprising only confirmed their fears for them.[19]

By the beginning of 1904 those individuals who actively supported a Greek effort in Macedonia had come together and formed a Macedonian Committee. Its membership included many who had belonged to the now disbanded National Society. The social background of these members was still largely that of the urban upper middle class: army officers, wealthy businessmen, professionals and political figures were all represented. A number of these individuals traced their origins to Macedonia, which made the cause even more important to them. Stefanos Dragoumis, father of Ion, was one of the founding members of the Committee. The organization carried on numerous activities, including circulating propaganda both in Greece and Macedonia, sending money and arms to the north and attempting to influence the government to undertake greater efforts in that region.[20]

The Greek government, burdened as it was at home by political instability, and desiring good relations with its Balkan neighbors and the European powers, responded cautiously to the issue. It made its presence in the area felt through the use of consular officials and the Greek church. Greek officers were allowed to travel to Macedonia under false names and on the pretext of doing business in the area. There they operated as leaders of secret organizations, and worked as agents carrying out assignments of organizing the Greek communities to compete with the rival nationalist groups.[21]

Macedonia in the next few years became the symbol to many Greeks of a crisis confronting Hellenism. They were convinced that the nation was being tested and they considered it their duty to respond. Often there was an intermixing of the public and private sector on this issue with regard to those who were involved. This is well illustrated in the activities of Pavlos Melas. Melas belonged to a family that was deeply committed to the Great Idea and its realization. His father, Michael Melas, had been associated with a nationalist organization called the National Defense (*Ethnike Amina*) in the late 1870's. Pavlos Melas himself had joined the National Society (*Ethnike Etairia*) while an officer in the army. The defeat of 1897 and the subsequent attacks on the National Society both left their marks on the young man. His nationalist zeal remained unabated, and was further bolstered by that of his wife, Natalia, sister of Ion Dragoumis.

In the spring of 1904 the Greek government, sensitive to the issue of Macedonia, began to plan some activity in the area. Army officers, among them Melas, were sent to the region to survey the situation and to begin organizing the Greek communities. Melas was convinced that it was necessary to send armed bands into the area if Greek interests were to be sustained. During the year he made several trips north into Macedonia. In August, 1904, the Macedonian Committee in Athens appointed him commander-in-chief of all the Greek bands in the areas of Kastoria and Monastir. Melas went to Macedonia for the last time on August 27/September 9, 1904. Several weeks later he was killed in the small village of Statista by Turkish troops, who mistakenly thought they were attacking a band of Bulgarian comitadjes.[22]

Melas as well as other Greek officers operated secretly in Macedonia. Most Greeks, therefore, were unaware of what was transpiring to the north of their country. When the news of Melas' death was made public, the surprise was all the greater. As the family was well known in Athens, the death of Melas caused a great stir of public emotion.[23] Later, his brother-in-law, Ion Dragoumis, characterized this event as significant in helping to crystalize Greek opinion on Macedonia. He felt that Melas' death amply illustrated what the nation's mission was, and showed that there were individuals who were ready to carry it out.[24] Greece was not at war with any neighboring state at the time. The death of an army officer in Macedonia vividly brought to the attention of many Greeks the fact that there were those of their countrymen who were deeply involved in an area most knew little about. In the past concern had been focused most often on the island of Crete. Those like Dragoumis now hoped that it would be re-directed to a region they believed should claim an equal share in the country's national interests.

Macedonia continued to absorb the attentions of many Greeks for several years following the Melas incident. This is graphically reflected in the life of Athanasios Souliotes-Nikolaides. The son of a civil servant and one of nine children, Souliotes characterized himself as belonging to a family far richer in ideals than in material goods.[25] For an individual from such a background, a career in the army was a natural route to take in life. The young man entered the Military Academy in 1895, graduating in 1900 as a second lieutenant. In the years following the defeat of 1897 we have seen how there was a constant and sometimes acrimonious debate over the military preparedness of the state. Many, including Crown Prince Constantine, strongly believed in the need for reorganizing the army. Yet for Souliotes, as undoubtedly for many other young officers, the question was not simply the need to strengthen the army. More important to them was the desire to make something of themselves. Service in the military was a natural and honorable outlet for their aspirations. The death of Melas only served to stimulate their nationalist sentiments.

Souliotes, who possessed the same sense of a national mission as Melas, welcomed the opportunity to work in Macedonia. He sought out Lambros Koromilas, the chief diplomatic agent for Macedonia and an ardent nationalist. Koromilas could not use any more officers in the consulate in Thessaloniki, but he proposed that Souliotes go to Macedonia and work there as a secret agent. Posing as the representative of a German sewing machine company, Souliotes arrived in Thessaloniki in March, 1904. There he set about creating a secret organization independent of the consulate called the Thessaloniki Organization. It remained a local unit working within the city. Some Greeks did go out into the country-side on their own to try and spread the system used by the Organization. This group performed several functions. It organized the Greeks of Thessaloniki into a more unified and politically conscious community. In furthering this aim the Organization encouraged the Greeks to buy and sell only to each other. The purpose of this scheme of course was to bring economic pressure on the Bulgarians who lived in the city. In addition the Organization opened schools and nurseries for children who spoke Macedonian or other Slavic languages but who sided with the Greeks. Souliotes himself wrote a pamphlet entitled the *Prophecies of Alexander the Great*, which was translated into Macedonian and distributed in the villages. In this pamphlet he presented the idea in pseudo-prophetic language that Macedonia could only be freed of Ottoman rule by the Greeks. Finally, the Organization had a section called the *Ektelestiko*, which carried out terrorist activities like the assassination of opponents and the enforcement of the society's orders.[26]

In a traditional society the place of a person's origin is important as it serves to give him an immediate identity and helps define him to others who do not know him. Association with a locality has been an enduring social custom for centuries among the peoples of southeast Europe. As we have noted, Macedonia retained a special significance for the Dragoumis family long after it had left the area. This interest in the area was the legacy that the young Ion inherited. He became more deeply involved with Macedonia when he entered the diplomatic service in 1899. By this time the nationalist struggle was already in full swing and centered on the religious loyalties of the population. During his service as a consular official in this area, Dragoumis soon came to meet and know many of the Greek nationalists as a part of his duties.[27] These individuals, including local clergy and bishops, teachers, doctors and village headmen, were known as Patriarchists, i.e., those who supported and looked for guidance to the Greek Orthodox Patriarchate. Their opponents, who looked to the Bulgarian Exarchate, were the Exarchists. From the conversations with both Patriarchists and Exarchists in his travels Dragoumis gained a knowledgeable understanding of the situation there. He became well aware of the value of Macedonia to the other Balkan states and with this in mind began to formulate schemes to promote Greek interests in the area.[28]

In keeping with his penchant for local initiative Dragoumis believed that the Greek nationalists or Patriarchists in Macedonia ought to rely on themselves rather than look to Athens for assistance. He endeavored to convince them of the benefits of promoting their own interests.[29] Using the past, Dragoumis argued that the Greeks had just as good a claim to the area as anyone else. To support his position he used historical arguments based on both culture and race. Dragoumis asserted that Alexander the Great was a Greek and then went on to state that there had been a Greek presence in the area ever since. He emphasized this with reference to Greek culture, language and religion, which he claimed had been the predominant influences in the area. The overall impression that he left was that the Greeks had a right to possess the area by virtue of longevity of presence as well as cultural supremacy.[30]

While he served in the various consulates to which he was assigned, Dragoumis carried on numerous nationalist activities. He saw to it that the Greek Orthodox church was supported, financially and politically. He made efforts at strengthening the Greek language schools in the region by obtaining more teachers and money from Greece and worked on organizing and coordinating the political activities of villages inhabited by Greeks. This included helping to organize several of the Greek communities into a society called the Defense (*Amyna*) for the purpose of opposing the Exarchists.[31] Recognizing the value of public opinion in the West Dragoumis urged friends to write in European newspapers and make propaganda on behalf of Greece's national interests. More generally he was a firm advocate of publicizing the Macedonian issue in Greece itself and raising money there to be sent north.[32]

Important as all these activities may have been for Dragoumis, the real significance of the Macedonian issue for us lies in his use of it for personal and nationalist purposes. In 1907 he published the *Blood of Martyrs and Heroes.* Dedicated to "the young" and written under a pseudonym, it was well received at the time. While the book focused on the Macedonian problem, it reflected at the same time Dragoumis' overriding concern with the nation and indirectly his relation to it. The work combined a criticism of what Dragoumis felt was an indifferent response to the issue with an overt appeal for greater involvement by Greeks in this matter. In setting down his thoughts on conditions in the area Dragoumis was guided by his own experiences and also by the death of his brother-in-law. Through a skillful description of the people and places he visited in his travels through Macedonia, he evoked a world where the fate of the nation was being determined.

Dragoumis castigated his countrymen in harsh terms. They were "worms" and had turned their culture and society into a "nest of worms" in their excess of "prudence." This was not a nation, he asserted, that he could respect. As if to shock his readers into reacting he announced that he would not hesitate to cause trouble for a government in which he had no confidence.[33] In a manner of speaking, he saw himself in the role of a nationalist gadfly.[34] He intended to use the Macedonian problem to "sting" and thus stir up the country in order that it might shake off the lassitude he felt had engulfed it after the debacle of 1897.[35]

The nation's ethos, Hellenism, seemed to Dragoumis to be locked in a struggle for survival. Although he referred to Macedonia, it is apparent that he had Greece in mind also. As he himself noted, Macedonia would save the nation, if only the nation wished to save Macedonia.[36] This had a personal significance for him as he sought to define his relationship to society about him. Macedonia was his instrument for personal salvation.[37] If it could be his then why not the nation's also?

The Ottoman East: The Greeks in Anatolia and Constantinople

On the littoral of Asia Minor from the Black Sea all the way around to the south there lived more than a million Greeks. We have already noted that their communities predated the coming of the Ottoman Turks. Having an established way of life most of these people could not conceive of living anywhere else. Some had even forgotten how to speak Greek.

By accomodating themselves to political realities they had been able to live side by side with the Turks in relative harmony. Through their corporate community life and active engagement in the commerce of the empire many Greeks had managed to create a thriving world for themselves.[38]

During the nineteenth century gradual but significant developments occurred with momentous consequences for the subject peoples of the empire. Ottoman statesmen of the Tanzimat era attempted to reorganize the millets so as to lessen the privileges that they derived because of religion and to bring them into line with a more secular concept of state citizenship.[39] Others who followed them and dreamed of reform, including the Young Turks, were more and more convinced that the millet, as a means of organizing the subjects of the empire, was outdated and an obstacle to a strong central state. In the meantime the sway that the Orthodox Patriarchate, dominated by Greeks, had over the Christian subjects of the sultan was diminished with the establishment first of a Bulgarian and then a Serbian millet. The Greeks, especially in Turkey-in-Europe, were by the beginning of this century only one of several competing Christian nationalities.[40] Finally, the existence of an independent Greek state with avowed irredentist aims could not help but stir up nationalist feelings among the Greek population especially in the European part of the empire. Instead of looking at the Ottoman Empire as a decrepit and disintegrating state, as Dragoumis did, it would be more appropriate to recognize that during the nineteenth century it was trying to revitalize itself. This presented both dangers and opportunities to its peoples.

The focal point of all these developments was of course the capital, Istanbul (Constantinople). Given the status of a separate province along with the surrounding countryside after 1877, it was still very much a polyglot city. When Dragoumis first came to know it the capital and neighboring areas had over 200,000 Greek inhabitants.[41] To them it was the only place to live and they called it simply the "City." All the different groups were there, merchants, professional people, artisans, and clergy, as they had been for centuries. Only now there was the additional factor of the Greek state which entered into the political calculations of the Ottoman Greeks.

Dragoumis became acquainted with the "City" in the spring of 1907, when he was assigned to the Greek embassy there. As he walked the narrow streets up and down the hills on which the city is built and explored the ancient sites, Dragoumis noted that he indulged in a reverie, associating himself with the grandeur of the Byzantine past.[42] As he recorded in his book *Those Who Are Alive,* Constantinople did not captivate him so much as it caused him to contemplate his relation to the past as well as the present. The "City" symbolized for him Greek accomplishments from the days of the Byzantine Empire. It served to remind Dragoumis of what the nation ought to be like in his own day. He linked the past to the present in presenting his view of contemporary Hellenism:

> The feeling is strong that we are losing the City completely, but Byzantine dreams do not disturb me as much as the knowledge that, whether we have the City or not, we are mediocre, worn out, asleep, hapless and mediocre, mediocre. The words 'To retake the City' are a symbol, which does not mean 'Let us remake the Byzantine Empire' but 'Let us be strong'. . . . [43]

Dragoumis was in effect claiming that he viewed the past in terms of historical realism not historical romanticism. Although he did attempt to break with the romantic Byzantinism that held a firm grip on the popular mind, there was, nevertheless, a neoromanticism in his ideas. By arguing that the Greeks in his own day were "mediocre" he was assigning values to them through a comparison with the past. In doing so he confirmed his own dependence on the uniqueness of the past, in this case Byzantium, in his estimation of the present.

His intermingling of the past with the present is apparent in his thoughts on what policies the Greeks in the empire ought to pursue. Hellenism in Asia Minor was a world from the past, that of the *Romios*. The community life and self sufficiency that these Greeks practiced and Dragoumis admired seemed to him proper as a means of handling local affairs. But this way of life was also parochial and as such Dragoumis was concerned that it could not meet the needs of Hellenism as a whole. Therefore he urged the Greeks to become more unified and better organized in order to be able to exert a greater influence in the empire as a nation. By taking a more active role in the affairs of the empire they could strengthen their position within it.[44] He envisioned himself in the role of promoting efforts for the greater benefit of the nation as a whole, that is, Hellenism in Anatolia.[45] The contradictory nature and incompatibility of these two worlds: empire and nation, Muslim and Christian, Ottoman and Greek failed to disturb Dragoumis as he pursued zealously his nationalist schemes.

As a consular official Dragoumis had regular contact with the Patriarchate and was well informed on its relations with the Greek communities in the empire.[46] The weight of tradition lay heavy on this institution and it worked as much to protect its own position as that of the faithful. Since it was an influential institution and religion had been a means for the Greeks to distinguish themselves from their rulers, Dragoumis was willing to support and make use of it. His attitude, however, was not that of a traditionalist. As a nationalist he expected that the church must change as new conditions arose in the empire. Its function was not the preservation of the past but leadership of the Greeks.[47] Dragoumis appreciated its value as a political instrument for maintaining group loyalty and mediating between the "nation," the Greeks in the empire, and the Ottoman state.

This, however, immediately raised the question of the nature of the relationship between the Patriachate and the Greek kingdom. Dragoumis resorted to a metaphor based on the Byzantine imperial symbol, the double-headed eagle. When it came to the leadership of the Greek subjects of the Ottoman Empire, the church, a remnant from Byzantine times, represented one head. In place of the other head, which had been the Byzantine state, there was now the Greek kingdom with influence through its consular officials. The symbolism ended, however, when Dragoumis insisted that one of the two institutions should take the lead. Although he stated that the choice of who should follow whose lead was not of critical importance, at the same time he made clear his belief that the secular institution could manage the task more effectively.[48]

It seemed then that the Greek state was a potentially powerful force, through its consulates and influence with the Patriarchate, on behalf of the Greeks in the Ottoman Empire. Yet Dragoumis saw a difficulty in this for he believed that the kingdom was not strong enough as a state to be able to carry out any long term nationalist program.[49] In the years just before the Balkan alliance was fashioned, Dragoumis was urging a policy of avoiding trouble with the empire for the time being. Greece ought to support her co-nationals in Turkey and see that they were treated justly, but to provoke a conflict did not seem practical to him at the moment.[50] At the same time he questioned whether one ideal could serve the national interests of both the kingdom and the Greeks in the empire. Even though he was an admirer and defender of the "nation", he appreciated the difference in power between a state and an ethnic group. The Greeks in Anatolia might desire independence and those in the kingdom an enlarged state. In either case Dragoumis understood that it would take a statesman of exceptional capabilities to accomplish both goals. Whether or not someone like this would appear Dragoumis' nationalism demanded a self-conscious effort from all parties concerned.[51] He toyed with two forms of nationalism in reality. On the one hand he believed that the Greeks in the empire must try and become co-rulers with the Turks by maximizing their economic and political strength. On the other hand if this did not work out and the "sick man of Europe" finally succumbed, then the Greek state ought to be prepared to step in and help bring about the unification of the nation.[52] For the state to do this Dragoumis was amenable to Greece's cooperation with other Balkan countries. But this was permissible, in his view, only if the kingdom had a military that would be respected by its counterpart in the other Balkan states. Within the empire itself Dragoumis saw the need for the Greeks to organize their communities better and to be able to manage without any aid from the kingdom if necessary. As we have noted previously Dragoumis advocated educational changes for both worlds, especially the use of the demotic in order to assure the vitality of the nation.[53] His political program envisioned both territorial expansion by the state and the assertion of collective autonomy by the *ethnos*. Greek nationalism was now not only expansionist or irredentist but integrationist as well as seen in Dragoumis' concern to maintain the nation's cultural identity.

In the spring of 1908 Dragoumis' friend Athanasios Souliotes arrived in Constantinople and together they worked to set up an organization similar to the one that had been established in Thessaloniki.[54] The reason for its formation was the same as for the earlier group: a Greek reaction to Bulgarian nationalist activities, in this case in the Ottoman capital and surrounding countryside. Although the Bulgarian population in the city itself was not anywhere near as large as the Greek, the surrounding area of the Istanbul province as well as the Edirne vilayet did contain numerous Bulgarian communities. This and the existence of the Bulgarian Exarchate prompted the Greek nationalist activities.[55]

Souliotes and Dragoumis promoted the Constantinople Organization (*Organosis Konstantinoupoleos*) as a means of employing direct action against competing nationalist groups and to provide more unity among the Greek populace of the empire.[56] Like all modern secret organizations it was to be small in size with a tight structure and demanding loyalty to the leadership.[57] Outside the capital the Organization used tactics already developed by its sister group in Thessaloniki to counteract the efforts of Bulgarian nationalists there. In Istanbul itself a list of Bulgarian merchants was drawn up and Greeks were urged to boycott them. In addition the Organization endeavored to intensify the nationalism of the Greeks resident in the capital. Many of them used a Western language in their business and sent their sons to Catholic schools in the city to learn a trade. Souliotes and Dragoumis feared and disliked this cosmopolitanism, which was called Levantinism in this part of the world, and saw it as antithetical to nationalism. To combat this the Organization helped establish a "Language and Business School." Also Greek merchants and restaurateurs were asked to use Greek lettering in their signs and advertisements. The importance of language was evident in the vigorous efforts of the Organization to promote its use among the community as much as possible. Perhaps the most important activity of the Organization was that of seeking to mediate the conflicts among the various factions within the Patriarchate. Individuals from the different factions were brought into the Organization as members in the hope that greater unity could be achieved.[58] Souliotes considered the Organization as independent from the Greek government. He sought to keep it localized deriving material and personal support from the Greeks in the Ottoman capital.[59] Its purpose, nevertheless, was to serve Greek nationalist interests.

The year that saw the creation of the Constantinople Organization also brought great changes to the empire. The Young Turk revolt forced a constitution on the absolutist regime of sultan Abdul Hamid. To the nationalities of the empire the revolution brought the possibility of new opportunities along with the anxiety of an uncertain future. The leaders of the Constantinople Organization including Souliotes saw this as an opportunity for a new form of activity. Up to this point the Organization had concentrated on counteracting the activities of other nationalities, dealing with the Patriarchate and stimulating the nationalism of the Greeks. Now a new avenue appeared: the possibility of political action directly through the Ottoman governmental system. The Young Turks demanded the restoration of the Constitution of 1876 and the sultan acquiesced in July, 1908. Equality before the law was to be granted to all the peoples of the empire. With the goal of strengthening the power of the state in mind the Young Turk leaders espoused a policy of Otto-manization, which would place all the peoples of the empire on an equal footing as citizens regardless of nationality. Their intention was to end privileges inherent because of religion not to turn the empire over to its subjects. Nevertheless, many among the nationalities believed that a new era of harmony and brotherhood was about to begin in the country. For its part the Constantinople Organization sought to take advantage of this "era of good feelings" and it broadened its political activities accordingly.[60] But hopes for a new era proved chimerical as the new rulers began to pursue a policy of Turkification within a few years after taking power.

During the first few weeks, however, there was a feeling of euphoria and the new regime received an enthusiastic response from many Greeks. There were visions of the Greeks in the empire cooperating more closely with the Greek Kingdom. Even the idea of linking the two centers of Hellenism, i.e., Athens and Constantinople, through the Patriarchate was brought up! When the liberal Ottoman prince Sabbahadin passed through Athens he was accorded a warm reception.[61] It seemed to some Greeks that a new era had begun, one that might lead eventually to full equality with the Turks and possibly even co-rule of the empire. In this spirit the Constantinople Organization decided on a policy of cooperating with the Young Turks in the new parliament and it persuaded some of the Greek deputies to go along with the idea. The policy did not meet with unqualified enthusiasm from either Greeks or Turks and the Organization found the going rough.[62] The Organization continued its activities until the creation of the Balkan alliances, and the outbreak of the Balkan wars in October, 1912, obviated the need for such efforts.

Dragoumis viewed the Young Turk revolution as a dilemma for Hellenism in the Ottoman Empire. It appeared to him that outwardly it had opened a new era of more rights and better conditions politically for the nationalities. Yet Dragoumis was far from optimistic about the future of the peoples of the empire. He felt that the nationalities had not gained anywhere near as much as many believed. That they had achieved equality before the law and the right to use their own language did not impress him as a substantive change. With a touch of cynicism he wondered how long the "era of good feelings" would last. Of his friend Souliotes, Dragoumis noted that he was very pleased with the change in the government. It brought to Souliotes' mind the "great eastern state" that he had often mused about. Rhigas' vision of a federated state made up of the Balkan peoples seemed to Souliotes that it might now come true.[63] Although both Dragoumis and Souliotes were filled with nationalist sentiment, the latter tended to lose himself in a reverie imagining that the multi-ethnic Hellenistic state of Alexander the Great could be re-created in the twentieth century. By personal inclination and in nationalist outlook Dragoumis was more practical. He believed in the idea that things do not come easily in life. "Liberty is won, it is not granted by others."[64] While the Turks might grant civil liberties, it was up to the Greeks to use them to better their own position. Only in this way did Dragoumis feel that they could achieve lasting gains.[65] In this period of political upheaval in the Ottoman Empire Souliotes' nationalism seemed open and optimistic. That of Dragoumis, by way of contrast, was more guarded and self-critical.

Spurred on by the dramatic developments in July the nationalities participated in elections which were held in late autumn. Political life blossomed in earnest when parliament was called into session in December by the sultan. Souliotes worked diligently through the Constantinople Organization seeking to coordinate the interests of the Orthodox Patriarchate and those of the Greek deputies in the Ottoman parliament. Dragoumis himself did not remain long in Istanbul. He returned to the Foreign Ministry in Athens at the end of February, 1909, but managed to visit the "City" again for a month in May. His nationalism sharpened by his experiences in the Ottoman capital, Dragoumis wrote *Those Who Are Alive,* which appeared in September, 1911. Discussing his experiences in Istanbul, he continued to stress his belief that the Greeks in Anatolia needed to be more concerned about their future and become better organized.[66]

Those Who Are Alive was the vehicle through which Dragoumis delineated his views regarding what the political goals of the Greeks in Anatolia ought to be. In it he debated the question of a great "eastern" state with Souliotes as we have already noted. We need to look more carefully at what was certainly the broadest possible vision for the encompassment of all co-nationals. As Dragoumis recorded them, Souliotes' views were that the pressure of the "Slavs and Germans" on the Ottoman Empire might serve to force the creation of an eastern empire and civilization:

> It will not have *one* language, but *one* spirit will breathe within it, the Ionian, the Hellenic. The Anatolian race, it will again create the new, and broader humanist ideal, more extensive than the Christian, this ideal that humanity needs now.[67]

The center of this new civilization would be the "City", . . . "eastern, wealthy and variegated . . . ." in character.[68] Souliotes' vision of this eastern state was not like that of the Great Idea with its strong implication of Greek nationalism and ethnicity. Rather it was conceived as a heterogeneous, cosmopolitan state, a mixture of peoples modeled on the empire that Alexander of Macedon had created. Souliotes believed that the Greeks would maintain their separate identity in such a state and once again attain the importance in cultural matters that they had held in empires of the past.

Dragoumis, however, was unwilling to expand his vision to that extent. Although the enthusiasm of Souliotes moved him, he remained bound to his nationalism. Souliotes' eastern empire seemed to him too closely akin to that "Levantine" spirit that he disliked. Such a state would lead to the blurring of national distinctions between people, something that Dragoumis was unwilling to see happen.[69] Since he wished to intensify the nationalism of the Greeks, the ideal of an eastern empire would militate against it. He believed that in any event such a state would be difficult to create. Dragoumis could not accept anything but the view that all peoples are separated by distinct characteristics. To create a state such as the one that Souliotes envisioned would require the development of a "common political ideal." Given what Dragoumis believed was the immutable nature of peoples, namely their national diversity, the idea of an eastern state was chimerical as far as he was concerned.[70]

By the beginning of the twentieth century the Balkan peninsula had gained a reputation in Europe as a politically unstable area where rival nationalisms clashed with disheartening frequency. Its strategic importance was undoubted, however, as the frontiers of three competing continental empires all bordered on that region. Still Europeans tended to consider the nations that had arisen there during the previous century as exasperating children with insatiable desires worthy only of a play by Shaw. But to see the Balkan states as nationalist carbon copies of one another was to overlook an important difference.

All the nationalities in the region developed aggressive irredentist movements including of course Greece. In practically all instances the co-nationals and the territory that the Balkan states wanted to incorporate were contiguous to those countries. The one exception was, however, Greece. While the country displayed irredentist intentions over areas such as Epiros and Macedonia, the Greeks in Anatolia were another matter. It is clear from our discussion above that Dragoumis was aware of the differences between these areas in terms of Greek nationalist aspirations. In the Balkans it was simply a matter of the territorial expansion of the state. Hellenism in Asia Minor was, however, geographically scattered. Dragoumis attempted to deal with this problem by accomodating his nationalist program. His complaints then were that others in Greece did not understand the differences between these areas when they formulated their nationalist goals.

Dragoumis certainly sensed that he was dealing with two different worlds as a nationalist. The one was made up of an ethnically homogeneous population inside the frontiers of a sovereign state, the Greek kingdom. The other, the Greeks in the Ottoman Empire, was a "nation" comprised of a series of communities geographically dispersed among the population of a multi-ethnic state whose cohesiveness was not a function of political boundaries but religion. His self-proclaimed task was to bring more unity and political strength to both worlds. Hence his work *for* the Greek kingdom and his work *with* the communities and the Patriarchate in the Ottoman Empire.

Of the areas in the Ottoman Empire that contained a sizeable Greek population Dragoumis was obviously most familiar with Macedonia. His understanding of Hellenism in Anatolia was gained through the refracting prism of the Ottoman capital. This was further influenced by his concern with reviving the nationalism of the Greeks in the kingdom. Consequently the policies and the advice that he offered to his co-nationals in the empire were filled with exhortations for political and cultural unity that would protect and promote the nation. They were also a compromise to meet the discrepancy between the territorial and the ethnic nation. To overcome this dilemma of Greek nationalism drastic measures were required: the destruction of the Ottoman Empire and the expansion of the Greek state across the Aegean. This, however, hinged on something that Dragoumis had already questioned: whether or not the state was powerful enough to execute and sustain such a radical nationalist solution. The answer came during the Great War.

Kostes Palamas

Perikles Giannopoulos

Ion Dragoumis

Certificate of membership in the "Hellenism Society." Note the symbols of Hellenism, the Acropolis and Aghia Sophia, and the map showing the domain of Hellenism.

Modern Athenians recapturing their past. A performance of an ancient drama at the Stadium in Athens.

Κωνσταντίνος ☀ Διάδοχος

1821   1912

ΠΑΝΤΟΤΕ   ΕΜΠΡΟΣ!

139

Postcard printed at the time of the Balkan wars, depicting the
Crown Prince Constantine, with the caption "Ever Forward!"

CHAPTER VII
EPILOGUE AND CONCLUSION

The Greeks' nationalist dream of revival and irredentism, the Great Idea, seemed to be coming true by the eve of WWI. A military revolt in 1909 helped bring to power an astute statesman and diplomat, Eleftherios Venizelos. He demonstrated his political ability by winning the elections that were held in the fall of 1910, and repeating this success with an overwhelming majority in March, 1912. Under the guidance of a number of capable ministers who served in the government, the economic, judicial and military affairs of the country were put in order. At the same time Venizelos himself skillfully set out to promote closer relations with Greece's Balkan neighbors. By 1912 alliances between Serbia, Bulgaria, Montenegro and Greece had been consolidated. They were the basis of the successful wars that were waged against the Ottoman Empire in 1912 and 1913. Greece significantly increased both her territory and population. Nationalist sentiment at the time saw these gains as only the first step in the eventual ouster of the Turks from Europe and the taking of Constantinople.[1]

The acquisitions in territory and population that resulted from the Balkan wars may have been looked upon as the product of nationalist efforts by the Greeks but they introduced something far more significant into the country. Greece's area and population increased by more than sixty per cent. Before the wars the population of the country was estimated at 2,666,000. It now rose to 4,363,000.[2] But these enormous gains did not include only co-nationals. Some 400,000 of these people were Muslims including Turks and Albanians.[3] Where Greece had been ethnically homogeneous with but a handful of non-Christians before 1913, it was now becoming a multi-national state. The Great Idea, a nationalist vision from an imperial past, was being realized in a manner that was bound to produce significant consequences in the character of Greece as an integrated nation state.

Before the process of assimilating the new territory and population could really get started, war broke out again in southeast Europe. Its expansion in the fall of 1914 with the entrance of the Ottoman Empire on the side of the Central powers placed Greece in a difficult position. Her strategic location in the Balkans was abundantly evident to both her leaders and to the belligerent states which were now seeking to bolster their respective camps with as many allies as possible. To align the country with one side or the other was fraught with the possibility of serious political and military consequences. The effort to decide upon a politically proper position foundered on the rocks of two conflicting views. Premier Venizelos, motivated by both political sympathy and calculation, quickly came to the conclusion that the country's best interests would be served by coming out on the side of the Entente. Before the entry of the Ottoman Empire (October, 1914) and Bulgaria (September, 1915) into the war on the side of the Central powers the opposing view of King Constantine had just as much merit. In his opinion, Greece was susceptible to pressures from both sides: by sea from the Entente and on land by the Central powers. He felt that the nation should remain neutral and not involve herself at all. National unity in the country was soon compromised by political conflicts that reflected disagreements between personalities as well as over policies.

In January, 1915, a new element was introduced that only served to complicate matters. Sir Edward Grey, Foreign Secretary of England, acting with the approval of France and Russia, offered "most important territorial compensations for Greece on the coast of Asia Minor."[4] What followed in the wake of this offer was literally the division of the country into two implacable political camps. Whether or not to enter the war depended on each group's estimation of the benefits versus the costs of territorial expansion into western Asia Minor. Colonel Ioannis Metaxas, a member of the army's General Staff who had studied the problems involved in acquiring territory in Anatolia, argued forcefully that such a scheme would have little chance of success given the military, geographic and economic realities of the area involved. Only under very favorable circumstances, i.e., the full military support of Greece by the Entente powers and the severe reduction of Turkish political sovereignty in Asia Minor, did he feel that the country ought to participate.[5] The king, diplomatically conservative and personally sympathetic to the Central powers, accepted Metaxas' strictures about involvement in Asia Minor. He set himself against an alliance even with the military support of the Entente. Venizelos, on the other hand, mindful of the dangers inherent in any territorial claims by Greece in western Asia Minor, nevertheless felt that intervention on the side of the Allied states would place his country in an advantageous position with regard to territorial aspirations at the end of the war. His was a diplomat's gamble on the future through a shrewd perception of the realities of the time. Both individuals were firm nationalist supporters of the country's expansion, having worked to that end in the Balkan wars. They now disagreed violently, however, not on the goal, which was dear to both, but on the means of attaining it.

The political crisis that began in the early spring of 1915 deepened steadily until September, 1916, when Venizelos, feeling that he could no longer accept such a situation and seeing no possibility of a compromise, left Athens to set up a rival government in Thessaloniki. It was not until June of the following year that the impasse between the king and Venizelos was resolved. The Entente powers, angry at the king for what they regarded as a pro-German attitude on his part and declaring that his government was a threat to their forces stationed in Macedonia, intervened. Constantine was forced to step down and was sent into exile. With him went other political opponents of Venizelos, including Metaxas and Dragoumis. Venizelos returned to Athens, becoming premier once more. The government, armed forces and the civil service were purged of royalists and replaced by supporters of the premier.

When the war finally ended and a peace settlement was being arranged in Paris, Venizelos, representing his country at the conference, now asked for that "territorial compensation on the coast of Asia Minor" that the Allies had offered more than four years before. By the treaty of Sèvres, signed in August, 1920, the Greeks received most of what they had dreamed for a century of acquiring. The Ottoman capital, however, was still beyond their reach as it was to be internationalized. Venizelos' supporters hailed him as the creator of the "Great Greece" of "two continents and five seas." Yet even at this moment of undoubted success the country remained bitterly divided politically. This was ominous in view of the burden that it was about to take on. The treaty of Sèvres increased Greece's territory by approximately 49,000 square kilometers and lengthened its land frontiers by some 950 kilometers spread over two continents. This new territory contributed 1,665,000 people to the country. Included in this population were some 699,000 Muslims and 159,000 others such as Bulgarians, Armenians and Jews.[6] Greece was now well on the way to becoming a state with sizeable ethnic minorities, creating a problem that would plague most states in eastern Europe between the wars.

In a general election in November, 1920, Venizelos' party suffered a resounding defeat. The victorious royalists quickly brought back Constantine from exile and assumed the burden of power. Despite the change in government the country still faced the dilemma of what to do about Anatolia. The Allies had allowed the Greeks to occupy Smyrna and the surrounding countryside in May, 1919, and the Sèvres treaty gave them the right to administer the Smyrna enclave for five years at which time a plebiscite would enable the population to decide whether or not it wanted to formally become a part of Greece. Despite an electoral campaign that criticized the Venizelists for unduly burdening the country with so many years of fighting, the new government headed by Demetrios Gounaris, with the concurrence of the king, proceeded to continue with the imbroglio in Asia Minor. A century of nationalist aspirations and a by now expectant Greek population in Anatolia were too much to resist.

In early January, 1921, the Greeks launched a third offensive in an effort to destroy the growing Turkish Nationalist forces under the leadership of Mustafa Kemal. Two more followed that same year, but the end for the Greeks was already evident. The size and power of the Nationalist forces grew as more and more of the Turkish peasantry rallied to the cause. At the same time Kemal exploited the divisions among the Allied powers bolstering his position diplomatically and leaving the Greeks with only minimal support from England.

The critical Greek offensive of 1921 began in August but after a month of fighting the Turks had not been dislodged much less destroyed. Hostilities dragged on for another year with the Greeks now in retreat. In August, 1922, the Turks launched their final offensive that forced the Greeks out of Asia Minor completely. The Kemalist forces reoccupied the city of Smyrna in early September and burned what they felt symbolized the presence of Hellenism in Anatolia. By the treaty signed at Lausanne between the two belligerents on July 24, 1923, Turkey asserted her independence and Greece was forced to accept a mandatory exchange of populations.

Thus ended Greece's "Anatolian adventure" and with it the idea that the modern Greek nation was destined somehow to inherit the imperial world of the Byzantines and the Ottomans. George Theotokas, born in Constantinople in 1905, caught the significance of this moment in history in his novel *Argo,* which he published in Greece, in 1933, the years after he arrived there. Damianos Phrantzes, a character in the novel who is forced to leave Constantinople as the author himself had done, muses about the past:

> Just as the refugee ship began to move from Galata . . . Damianos felt that something in his heart was being cut finally and irrevocably . . . It was a deep longing . . . the sensation of a forcible uprooting, the rude and decisive separation from the land of one's ancestors, . . the negation of all of the past and all the traditions of the *genos,* the destruction of the Great Idea . . . Rumpled up in a corner of the deck, the young Damianos Phrantzes . . . was traveling alone and uncared for to the West, without the ideals of his ancestors, . , . bringing with him to free Greece, the great and incurable grief of the refugee.[7]

The ethnic, expansionist, and revivalist nationalist movement of the Greeks had not been able to surmount the political discord in the country. Weakened by this and without the united support of the Western powers it faltered before the rival ethnic, and integrationist nationalist Turkish movement. While the Greeks had looked to the historical past in formulating their nationalist ideal, the Turks broke with the past and based their movement on the present in terms of ethnicity and territorial unity.

Although both movements were aggressive, that of the Greeks was expansionist and tended to lead unwittingly to the growth of a multi-ethnic state, while that of the Turks was exactly the opposite, contractive and ethnically unified. From the point of cohesiveness the latter movement could not help but be stronger. An era in the history of Southeastern Europe had come to an end.

We must now assess the significance of the individuals discussed here to their own era and more broadly to modern Greek history itself. We have noted that by the late eighteenth century intellectuals like Koraes strongly felt the contrast between the traditional society into which they were born and the rational and dynamic "West." In attempting to reconcile these two conflicting worlds they sought to use the rational methods of the West to achieve the national regeneration of their people. In Koraes' case he believed that in imitating the West the Greeks would rediscover their own heritage, which was really the basis of western civilization.[8] By reestablishing contact with the culture of classical Greece, the intellectual renascence of the modern Greeks would take place.

The desire for intellectual liberation from the eastern world of theocracy and superstition inherently meant political liberation. When the Greeks finally achieved their freedom from Ottoman rule and created an independent state they had overcome, in their own eyes as well as those of Europe's, the first barrier to national regeneration. As we have observed they then concerned themselves with making their state politically, culturally and economically viable. In order to do so they focused their attention on two things. By emulating the civilization of the ancient Greeks they could assert their unique identity vis-a-vis the rest of the world and advance culturally. By expanding the state to include more territory inhabited by their co-nationals they expected to thrive economically and politically.

By the 1880's these optimistic expectations had failed to materialize. The prevailing assumptions of enlightenment and material progress through the emulation of the West now began to be questioned. The controversy over language was evidence in part of the rising feeling among a number of intellectuals that the nation needed to assert its identity anew. The political and diplomatic difficulties at the end of the century only served to reinforce the awareness of the need for change.

In dealing with the problem of Greece's identity and destiny Palamas was able, as we have seen, to move easily through the entire Greek cultural spectrum, classical and Christian. He better than any other writer at the time was able to wed the varied heritage of the Greeks to the demotic and create images that were appealing to a society bound to the past. In doing this he helped legitimize a movement that was still considered suspect and unworthy of the nation by many intellectuals. Palamas sensed the potential of a native, folk-based culture. It was a rough and unpolished gem which, when properly exploited by the artist, yielded both a rich cultural treasure and creative energy for the nation. In this emphasis on the folk-demotic there was also the implicit assumption that the race would always survive no matter what adversity might confront the nation.

There was a second contribution that Palamas made to the country's collective identity. We saw how the historian Paparrigopoulos fashioned a continuity for all of Greek history, past and present. Palamas took this into the realm of literature and emphasized the *dynamism* inherent in the continuity itself. As he conceived it, Greek culture had been continuously innovative because it constantly assimilated new and vigorous ideas.

When it came to dealing with the relationship between his nation's culture and that of the "West" Palamas sought to obviate the issue. He did not deny his native world but on the other hand he felt no compelling need to defend and protect it from other cultures. The difference between him and Giannopoulos and Dragoumis was that he did not envelop his writing and his life, indeed his complete existence, in the nation as a solution to the conflict between contradictory worlds. Palamas sought to transcend this vexing dilemma by concentrating not on the content of the two opposing thought worlds, but on the creative force in both realms, the artist himself. From Orpheus to Nietzsche, the essence of every culture was the creative spirit of the artist as individual.

Turning to Giannopoulos we are struck by the contrast in outlook. Here we are confronted with an intellectual who could only cope with the contradictions within his culture, and those between his native world and the "West," by finding a single essential standard in the remote past on which to base his life. Though he agreed with the other figures on the need to invigorate the nation's culture he rejected the idea that this could be accomplished through the demotic tradition, which as we saw, he felt was inferior to what had come before. Giannopoulos "resolved" this problem and also the differences between his culture and that of the "West" by denigrating the latter and seeking out an era in his people's past that he felt was the essence of their civilization. It was classical Greece, whose culture was unsurpassed in his view, which possessed the true spirit of the nation. It and the physical surroundings of the country were all that the modern Greeks needed. Giannopoulos' ideas represented a major departure from the presuppositions of the preceding century. He asserted that it was no longer necessary for the Greeks to look outward to Europe and seek guidance in order to better their society. They had only to look inward upon themselves and to their physical world to rediscover their creative powers. Giannopoulos made an even more striking departure by insisting on separating Europe from classical antiquity even though its civilization was based on the ancient world. This was a distinction that Greek intellectuals of a century before would have rejected.

Dragoumis represented a third form of nationalist reaction combining elements present in the thought of the other two figures. Because of his upbringing and personality he could not accept the premises upon which Europe's power rested. His solution to Greece's predicament in the modern world was not to look to any *one* era in the nation's past. Instead, he sought out a native tradition that he thought would be able to meet the dynamism that Europe exuded. He chose demoticism and identified it with the nation as the manifestation of its collective energy. In making this choice, however, he was seeking to counter a world based on materialism, secularism and a disregard for tradition, with one founded on exactly the opposite principles. It was an uneven match. Both Dragoumis' nationalism as well as that of Giannopoulos were essentially defensive in that they were attempts to protect and preserve the ethnic identity of the nation.

Despite the variations in their thought all three individuals manifested common views. That this should be so is not surprising. They grew up in a relatively homogeneous society sharing its common traditions and outlook. Each was convinced that his nation must display its uniqueness and that it could not be imitative of any other culture or era. Hellenism needed to be based on its own sources. What disturbed them was the feeling that the established culture of their day was nothing more than an imitation of an imitation, that is, Greece imitating Europe, which in turn imitated classical civilization. In asserting their nation's uniqueness they all looked upon Greece as neither western nor eastern but something in-between. The Byzantine and Alexandrine empires intrigued them as societies that managed to establish a separate identity despite contacts with other peoples. Through such beliefs, which they all shared, they sought to demonstrate their nation's distinctiveness.

Consciously or not all three figures came under the shadow of European civilization. We have noted their borrowings already. What is important, however, is not what they took from the West but the reasons for their doing so. It was first of all a reaction to their *own* world that led to their expressions of nationalist sentiment. They perceived around them a country frustrated by ignominious defeat in 1897, a stifling cultural establishment, political mediocrity, growing external threats to the nation, and a populace more willing to leave the country than to stay and deal with the problems confronting it. A century of enlightenment and emulation of Europe had brought no success. Action was needed but of what kind? The answer seemed apparent from the past. A society that was not dynamic was doomed to decline. They then correlated that dynamism with the cultural creativity which had given past Greek civilizations their grandeur. Europe itself obligingly provided all the justification that was needed for this view through the writings of Nietzsche and Bergson.

There is another dimension to this issue, however. Dragoumis and Giannopoulos certainly recognized that significant developments were taking place in their society. Greece was entering the European world slowly but steadily. Sensing these changes yet disliking them, these two individuals searched for some form of stability and defense against what was happening. They found it in nationalism, which also served to quench their thirst for identity. Palamas, who was more confident and optimistic about these developments, had less need of collective reassurance.

Just as the various forms of nationalism are bound by historical conditions and time so it is with these figures. They belong to an era that ended with the defeat in Asia Minor. Their impact on later generations has varied through the years in intensity and substance. After 1922 in' the geographically narrowed world of Hellenism the ideas of Dragoumis and Giannopoulos continued to retain a relevancy. In the case of both men this interest has developed along parallel lines. When the notions of race and nation were given a heightened significance in Europe during the 1920's and 1930's, nationalist writers inevitably turned to Dragoumis' writings for inspiration.[9] This aspect of his thought has continued to have an appeal down to recent times.[10] The same is true to a lesser extent of Giannopoulos.[11] Other writers, however, have been attracted to another and different facet of their work. It was their commitment to as well as their conflict with the society around them that appealed to those who had to come to terms with post-1922 Greece.[12]

A century now lay between the first stirrings of Greek nationalism in figures like Koraes and Rhigas and the era of Palamas, Dragoumis, and Giannopoulos. Even after a century of development as a nation-state the Greeks were still seeking answers to questions that they had asked when they launched their struggle for independence: "Who are we?" and "What do we wish to accomplish?" Koraes regarded the modern Greeks as the "natural" and legitimate descendants of the ancient Hellenes who had fallen on hard times. Through enlightenment they could prepare for independence as a nation and take their rightful place among the nations of the world.

Once independence was attained, however, the Greeks entered into another phase of nationalism; the acquisition of territory and people considered to be part of the nation but as yet not liberated. The humanist confidence of Koraes was replaced by a romantic aggressiveness. As the decades passed changing political conditions in the Balkan peninsula and the failure to achieve the romantic-irredentist dream of the Great Idea led those like Dragoumis and Giannopoulos to question both their society and the bases on which it rested. The end of the century produced a period of criticism and self-doubt. Out of it came the assertion by those figures examined here that the nation was not to be identified "subjectively" merely with a linguistic group but "objectively" as the intuitive as well as reasoned understanding of the past. History was not to be studied merely as a means of understanding the present. Rather it represented the essence without which a people could not exist. Nationalism of this sort must always seek to prove itself in history.

NOTES
INTRODUCTION

1. Hans Kohn, *The Idea of Nationalism: A Study in Its Origin and Background,* 1944, pp. 329-334, 572-576. Elie Kedourie, *Nationalism,* 1960, rev. ed. 1961, p. 9. Carlton J. Hayes, *The Historical Evolution of Nationalism,* 1931. Louis Snyder, *The New Nationalism,* 1968, p. 48.

2. K.R. Minogue, *Nationalism,* 1970, pp. 26-29. Hugh Seton-Watson, *Nationalism Old and New,* 1965, p. 15.

3. Anthony D. Smith, *Theories of Nationalism,* 1971, Chapter 10.

CHAPTER I

1. Arnold J. Toynbee, *The Western Question in Greece and Turkey,* 1922, p. 20.

2. For the purposes of this study I have used the last years of the eighteenth century as a starting point in the discussion of Greek nationalism. Several authors, however, have traced the roots of modern Greek nationalism much further back in time to the end of the Byzantine Empire. See for example Stephen G. Xydis, "Mediaeval Origins of Modern Greek Nationalism," *Balkan Studies,* v. 9 (1968), pp. 1-20 and Ap. Vacalopoulos, "Byzantinism and Hellenism. Remarks on the Racial Origin and the Intellectual Continuity of the Greek Nation," *Balkan Studies,* v. 9 (1968), pp. 101-126. For an opposing view see Cyril Mango, "Byzantinism and Romantic Hellenism," *Journal of the Warburg and Courtald Institutes,* v. 28 (1965), pp. 29-43.

3. Hans Kohn, *The Idea of Nationalism,* 1961, pp. 534-537.

4. An interesting discussion of the reaction of the Greeks to the West from the medieval period to the nineteenth century is found in Philip Sherrard, *The Greek East and the Latin West,* 1959, *passim.*

5. Biographical material for both men is contained in the *Megale Ellenike Enkyklopaidia* (The Great Greek Encyclopedia), 1932, on Rhigas, v. 21, pp. 125-27, on Koraes, v. 14, pp. 859-66. See also K. Th. Dimaras, *Istoria tes Neoellenikes Logotechnias* (History of Modern Greek Literature), 4th ed., 1968, chapters 11, 13, hereafter cited as Dimaras, *Modern Greek Literature.* L.I. Vranousis, *Rhigas Feraios,* 1957 and K. Th. Dimaras, *O Koraes kai e Epoche tou* (Koraes and His Epoch), 1958 provide good introductions to these men along with the texts of their most important works. In addition see Nicholas Pantazopoulos, *Rhigas Velestinlis,* 1964.

6. Dimaras, *Modern Greek Literature,* p. 175.

7. Vranousis, *op. cit.,* pp. 7-112. See also the comments of Cyril Mango, "The Phanariots and the Byzantine Tradition," in *The Struggle for Greek Independence,* ed. Richard Clogg, 1973, p. 57. A print of the map can be found in both Vranousis and Pantazopoulos.

8. *Ibid.,* pp. 197-201.

9. Kohn, *op. cit.,* p. 535. George Finlay, *A History of Greece,* 1877, v. 6, p. 7.

10. John Petropulos, *Politics and Statecraft in the Kingdom of Greece, 1833-43,* 1968, pp. 20, 37.

11. Ap. Vacalopoulos, *Istoria tou Neou Ellenismou (History of Modern Hellenism)*, 1961, v. 1, pp. 66-77. Mango, *op. cit.,* pp. 32-35 gives an opposing view of the reasons for the use of the word "Hellene".

12. The period of Turkish rule of the Greeks from the 15th to the 19th century.

13. D. Zakynthinos, *E Politike Istoria tes Neoteras Ellados* (The Political History of Modern Greece), 1965, pp. 44-45. Pantazopoulos, *op. cit.,* pp. 27-28.

14. Pantazopoulos, *op. cit.,* pp. 28-29. S. Zambelios, *Byzantinai Meletai Peri Pegon Neoellenikes Ethnotetos* (Byzantine Studies on the Sources of Modern Greek Nationality), 1857, pp. 47-58, was one of the first attempts in the nineteenth century to link the modern Greeks with their Byzantine past. It dealt with the transformation of the *genos* into the *ethnos.* Zambelios pictured the Greeks as moving forward in history preserving their traditions while transforming their society.

15. Stephen G. Xydis, "Modern Greek Nationalism," in Peter F. Sugar and Ivo Lederer, *Nationalism in Eastern Europe,* 1969, p. 209, fn. 6.

16. Nicholas Svoronos, *Histoire de la Grèce moderne,* 1953, pp. 49-53.

17. Petropulos, *op. cit.,* pp. 4-16. There was a Russian party led by Metaxas, an English headed by Mavrokordatos and a French party guided by Kolettis.

18. A vivid example of newspaper polemics is given in three articles on the *"Megale Idea"* which appeared in the pro-Russian paper *Aion,* September 10, 13, 17, 1847 (o.s.) attacking the policies of the Francophile Kolettis.

19. Petropulos, *op. cit.,* p. 507. Petropulos makes the following observation: "One might say that the basis for this kind of unanimity . . . was nationalist sentiment with its ultimate goal (Great Idea) and the requirements imposed by its institutional expression in the nation-state (national unity)."

20. Arnold Toynbee, *op. cit.,* p. 128, states that political romanticism" . . . is essentially unhistorical, being an attempt to telescope past and present into one another. . . ." The irony of course lies in the fact that the stress in ideas of this kind is on history and they are used as a national weapon.

21. Some authors have argued that the origins of the Great Idea are to be found in the last years of the Byzantine Empire. J. Voyatzidis, "La Grande Idée", *L'Hellénisme Contemporain,* 1953, pp. 279-287, discusses the basic features of Byzantine civilization with particular reference to the Hellenic elements within it, and then goes on to trace the Great Idea in outline form from its inception, as he sees it, at the time of the Lascarid Empire in Nicaea in the 13th century to the 19th century. See also Stephen G. Xydis, "Mediaeval Origins of Modern Greek Nationalism," *Balkan Studies,* v. 9, (1968), pp. 1-20 and Anthony Bryer, "The Great Idea," *History Today,* March, 1965, pp. 159-68. Edouard Driault, *La Grande Idée, La Renaissance de L'Hellénisme,* 1920, is composed of a series of lectures that were given by a philhellene historian in Athens in 1920. It traces in part the course of the Ottoman Empire vis-a-vis the European powers. Most of the book is devoted to a consideration of the French and Germans in the Near East during the last century. The nineteenth century development of the Great Idea, which is the approach taken in this study, is covered in the following accounts. Petropulos, *op. cit.,* pp. 23, 345-48. K. Th. Dimaras, " 'Tes Megales taftes Ideas' " ('Concerning this Great Idea'), offprint of *Iatrologotechnike Stege,* Spring, 1970, pp. 35-41 presents the philological argument for the rise of the term *"megale idea"* in the early 1840's as seen in the parliamentary speeches of John Kolettis. See also D. Zakynthinos, *op. cit.,* pp. 47-53, Cyril Mango, "Byzantinism and Romantic Hellenism," *Journal of the Warburg and*

the Courtald Institutes, v. 28 (1965), pp. 29-43, Edouard Driault and Michel Lhéritier, *Histoire Diplomatique de la Grèce de 1821 a nos jours,* 1925, 4 vol.

22. *The Greeks of Today,* 1878, 2nd ed., p. 120. See examples of this in Kolettis' speech in the 1844 parliament as cited in E. Kyriakides, *Istoria tou Sychronou Ellenismou 1832-1892* (History of Contemporary Hellenism 1832-1892), 1892, v. 1, p. 494, and Konstantine Paparrigopoulos, *IstorikaiPragmateiai* (Historical Essays), 1858, p. 1.

23. Svoronos, *op. cit.,* p. 63.

24. *Ibid.,* pp. 63-64.

25. The entire issue is discussed in Kyriakides, *op. cit.,* v. 1, pp. 487-505. See the rather unfavorable description of Kolettis and his methods in John Campbell and Philip Sherrard, *Modern Greece,* 1968, pp. 87, 89.

26. Kyriakides, *op. cit.,* p. 501.

27. *Ibid.,* p. 494.

28. Both views are well summarized in Petropulos, *op. cit.,* pp. 507-08. Svoronos, *op. cit.,* p. 58, sees this difference as that between bourgeois liberals of the Mazzini type and the official position of conservatives about the king.

29. For a recent discussion and revival of this question see Romilly Jenkins, "Byzantinism," in *Lectures in Memory of Louise Taft Semple,* 1967, pp. 137-178, which basically agrees with the views put forth by Fallmerayer. Opposing views are given in Ap. Vacalopoulos, "Byzantinism and Hellenism. Remarks on the Racial Origin and the Intellectual Continuity of the Greek Nation," *Balkan Studies,* v. 9 (1968), pp. 101-26, and G.G. Arnakis, "Byzantium and Greece," *Balkan Studies,* v. 4 (1963), pp. 379-400. The Greek reaction to Fallmerayer at the time is well treated in Dimaras, *Modern Greek Literature,* pp. 263-66.

30. Jenkins, *op. cit.,* p. 175. Tuckerman, *op. cit.,* p. 330.

31. The Greek prelude to romanticism is examined in K. Dimaras, "E Ellenike Skepsi kai to Thema tou Romantismou sta Chronia 1829-39" (Greek Thought and the Theme of Romanticism in the Years 1829-39), *Grammata,* VIII (1945), pp. 77-88.

32. Biographical details in S.V. Kouyeas, "Konstantine Paparrigopoulos," *Megale Ellenike Enkyklopaidia* (Great Greek Encyclopedia), v. 19, pp. 573-4. See also K. Dimaras, "Oi Protes Ekdoseis tes Istorias tou K. Paparrigopoulou" (The First Editions of the *History* of K. Paparrigopoulos), *Eranistes,* 1967, no. 29, p. 146. Hereafter cited as: Dimaras, "First Editions," *Eranistes.*

33. I have used the edition published in his *Istorikai Pragmatiai* (Historical Essays), 1858.

34. Kouyeas, *op. cit.,* p. 574.

35. K. Paparrigopoulos, *op. cit.,* p. 1. This was originally a lecture delivered at the university in 1854.

36. Dimaras, "First Editions," *Eranistes,* pp. 145-46. Kouyeas, *op. cit.,* p. 574.

37. K. Paparrigopoulos, *Istorikai Pragmatiai* (Historical Essays), 1889, pp. 240-53. This is an essay entitled: "Ancient, Medieval and Modern Hellenism."

38. A concise account of this issue is given in Robert Browning, *Medieval and Modern Greek,* 1969, pp. 103-118. A biography of Solomos by Romilly Jenkins, *Dionysius Solomos,* 1940, sees him as the hero and the romantic classicists such as

Alexander Soutsos, who wanted a revived classical Greek, as the villains. This gives a misleading view of the problem and the issues of the period.

39. Tuckerman, *op. cit.,* p. 126.

40. The various positions are discussed briefly in Petropulos, *op. cit.,* pp. 504-5. See also Campbell and Sherrard, *op. cit.,* pp. 89-91.

41. A French version appeared in 1855 with the title *Solution de la question d'Orient,* and a Greek edition in 1853.

42. Melas, *Hints,* pp. 6-7.

43. *Ibid.,* p. 30.

44. *Loc. cit.*

45. *Ibid.,* pp. 66-69. Campbell and Sherrard, *op. cit.,* 92-95. George Aspreas, *Politike Istoria tes Neoteras Ellados* (The Political History of Modern Greece), 1922-30, v. 1, pp. 257-66. Hariton Korisis, *Die Politischen Parteien Griechenlands 1821-1910,* 1966, pp. 63-4.

46. Svoronos, *op. cit.,* pp. 61-2, 73-5.

47. Leften Stavrianos, *Balkan Federation,* 1964, pp. 131-33. H.N. Brailsford, *Macedonia,* 1906, pp. 76-108.

48. Leften Stavrianos, *The Balkans Since 1453,* 1958, pp. 371-75.

49. John Notares, ed., *Anekdota Eggrafa gia ten Epanastasi tou 1878 ste Makedonia* (Unpublished Documents on the Uprising of 1878 in Macedonia), 1966, pp. 21-54.

50. Neokles Kazazis, "Political and Intellectual Life in Greece," *Contemporary Review,* September, 1879, p. 165.

51. Demetrios Bikelas, *Le Rôle et les aspirations de la Grèce dans la question d'Orient,* 1885, pp. 41-2. Bikelas, a moderate on the nationalist issues of the day, commented that: "Greece does not have any excessive claims. The Great Idea of the resurrection of the Greek Empire can still inflame some generous souls, . . . who find pleasure in nourishing themselves with the dreams of the past; but it has ceased for a long time to guide the thoughts of those who govern the destinies of Greece . . . . Our efforts and our aspirations are directed toward the formation of a Greek State whose northern frontier would begin from the point in the Adriatic which is above Corfu and would extend as far as the Aegean beyond the Chalcidice, including the Greek part of Macedonia; the island of Crete would form the southern limit of this state." Bikelas was sketching the idea of a greater Greek state as opposed to a Great (Byzantine) Idea; a statist rather than an ethnic concept.

52. George Ventiris, *E Ellas tou 1910-1920* (The Greece of 1910-1920), 1931, v. 1, p. 26.

53. Giannes Psicharis, *To Taxidi Mou* (My Journey), 1971, p. 37. This edition in the series "Hermes" is edited by Alkes Aggelou. The passage is from the Prologue.

54. An article by Kostes Palamas in *Nouma,* 1903, no. 1, p. 2, reproduced in Giannes Psicharis, *Apanta* (Collected Works), n.d., v. 1.

55. Psicharis, *My Journey,* p. 37.

56. Svoronos, *op. cit.,* pp. 76-9.

57. Aspreas, *op. cit.,* v. 2, pp. 216-40. The author goes into great detail on the activities of the National Society with complete certainty that it was to blame for much of the demand to go to war. See also the article on the Society in the *Great*

Greek Encyclopedia, v. 9, p. 724. Also William Miller, *Travels and Politics in the* \
Near East, 1898, pp. 282-88.

58. William Miller, *History of the Greek People,* n.d., pp. 105-08. William Langer,
The Diplomacy of Imperialism, 1950, 2nd ed., pp. 361-63.

CHAPTER II

1. Editorial, "Oi Ypefthenoi" (Those Responsible), *Akropolis,* May 5, 1897,
p. 1. The government of premier Deligiannes received a stern rebuke from the paper.
He and other politicians were depicted as men who simply were looking out for their
own welfare. "It [the war] was a struggle for the saving of privileges and parliamentary
seats. It sufficed for the fragments [of the nation] to survive the national catastrophe. This was the only worry of our rulers. Now they are busy collecting the pieces
that were saved. But we do not believe that this time they will be able to settle
their accounts with the Nation as cheaply as they did before, always getting the
upper hand." See also the article entitled "Ti kakon mas ekame e Ethnike Etairia"
(What Harm the National Society Did to Us), *Akropolis,* May 6, 1897, p. 2. As the
most vociferous nationalist organization the National Society received the brunt
of the blame.

2. "Tes Amynes!" (On Defense!), *Akropolis,* May 7, 1897, p. 1.

3. Editorial, "O Ethnikos!" (The Nationalist), *Akropolis,* May 23, 1897, p. 1.

4. "To Ethnikon Programa" (The National Program), *Ellenismos,* v. I (1899),
no. 1, pp. 3-9.

5. *Ibid.,* pp. 7-8.

6. To Periodikon Mas, "Ta Ellenika Ideode kai e Megale Idea: Gnomai ton
Synchronon" (The Greek Ideals and the Great Idea: Opinions of Contemporaries),
To Periodikon Mas, May 1, 1901, pp. 105-106.

7. *Ibid.,* p. 106.

8. *Loc. cit.*

9. All quotations from *ibid.,* p. 107.

10. *Loc. cit.*

11. In another response the highly regarded German trained folklorist, Nicholas
Polites, was unable to express an opinion concerning Greek ideals. He excused himself on the ground that he was still conducting research on Greek folklore and therefore felt unqualified to give, as he put it, "a categorical opinion on that question"!
Ibid., p. 139. As in the case of Karolides, erudition was no guarantee of insight into
the problems of one's country.

12. *Ibid.,* p. 110. This idea was expressed by Andreas Karkavitsas, a well known
short story writer. In the same issue of the periodical there was an announcement
that Karkavitsas would soon publish a novel entitled *The Great Idea.* This never
appeared, but it is indicative of the outlook of the author.

13. *Ibid.,* pp. 108, 110-11, 141-42. Alexander Pallis, who spent many years outside
of Greece but remained a firm believer in the Great Idea, voiced what must have
been the feeling of individuals like those discussed in this study. The translator of
the Gospels into demotic argued that the nation needed many "dreams" as he called

the ideals. Good schools, justice and the bringing of the "unredeemed" Greeks into
the kingdom were mentioned. His wrath was directed at foreign influences in the
country. It was necessary, in his view, for the Greeks not to imitate foreign practices.
Such imitation would lead to "levantinism", i.e., the taking on of European customs
and manners by the Greeks. An attitude of hostility towards Western influences was
already evident in Greece at this time.

14. *Ibid.,* pp. 140-41.

15. Hariton Korisis, *Die Politischen Parteien Griechenlands,* 1966, p. 156.

16. George Aspreas, *Politike Istoria tes Neoteras Ellados* (Political History of
Modern Greece), 1922-30, v. 3, p. 37.

17. William Miller, *Greek Life in Town and Country,* 1905, p. 27.

18. *Ibid.,* p. 158.

19. *Ibid.,* p. 140.

20. *Ibid.,* p. 143.

21. George Drosines, "Epi to Ergon" (On With the Work), *Ethnike Agoge,* no. 1
(March 1, 1898) p. 2.

22. *Ibid.,* p. 127-28.

23. Giannes Psicharis, *The Language Question in Greece,* 1902, p. 40.

24. There are varied accounts concerning whether or not the translation was passed
by the theological review board. George Aspreas, *The Political History of Modern
Greece,* v. 3, p. 23, states that the translation was rejected and the queen quietly
withdrew it. Elias Boutierides, *Syntome Istoria tes Neoellenikes Logotechnias*
(Short History of Modern Greek Literature) 2nd ed., 1966, p. 275, notes that the
translation was approved. A report by the British embassy in Athens, PRO: FO
32/729, November 19, 1901, supports the account of Aspreas insofar as rejection
of the Queen's translation was concerned.

25. Boutierides, *op. cit.,* v. 3, p. 19, accepts this reasoning uncritically. The queen
had nothing like this in mind when she commissioned the translation.

26. A description of the events is given in Aspreas, *op. cit.,* v. 3, pp. 24-26, and
Psicharis, *op. cit.,* pp. 52-53. See also an account by the British embassy in Athens,
PRO:FO 32/729, November 19, 22, 24, 28, 1901, and PRO:FO 32/736, Jan. 2, 1902.

27. A few months after the Gospel riots another incident, known as the "Boards"
affair or *Sanidika,* brought turmoil to Greek political life. As a result of the fall of
the government after the Gospel riots new elections were scheduled for March,
1902. At this time supporters of one political party set out to make an impression
on their opponents by tearing boards off the fence around a new building being
constructed in Athens and beating them over the head. See Aspreas, *op. cit.,* v. 3,
pp. 29-30. The following year in the winter of 1903 another incident, similar to the
Gospel riots, shook Athens. A performance of Aeschylos' drama the *Orestia* in a
version that was not suitable to the linguistic tastes of the purists brought the
university students into action once more. Another riot ensued and yet another
government fell. See Miller, *op. cit.,* p. 158.

28. Boutierides, *op. cit.,* p. 243.

29. Schlumberger published the following: *Un Empereur Byzantin au dixième
siècle: Nicéphore Phocas,* Paris, 1890; *L'épopée byzantine à la fin du dixième siècle,*
Paris, 1896-1905, 3 vols; *Konstantinos Palaiologos kai e poliorkia kai alosis tes
Konstantinoupoleos ypo ton Tourkon to 1453* (Constantine Paleologos and the
Seige and Capture of Constantinople by the Turks in 1453), Athens, 1914.

Penelope Delta, whose patriotic children's book *Gia ten Patrida* (For the Mother-land), 1st ed., 1909, had as its setting the epoch of Basil Bulgaroctonos, was inspired to write this work partly from reading the works of Schlumberger, with whom she corresponded. See *Correspondance P. Delta-G. Schlumberger,* Athens, 1962.

30. Giannes Psicharis, "The Gospel riots in Greece," in *The Language Question in Greece,* p. 60.

31. Alexander Delmouzos, who had studied in Germany, returned to Greece to become a leading demoticist exponent of reform in the educational system. In 1908 he wrote that the language question affected all of society from the "shoe-shine boy" trying to learn a few phrases to a soldier wearied of listening to lectures in the puristic Greek. See Alexander Delmouzos, *Meletes Kai Parerga* (Studies and Exercises), 1958, v. 1, pp. 27-8.

32. Psicharis began to publish his multi-volume linguistic work *Roda kai Mela* (Roses and Apples), dealing with the demotic Greek in 1902. For the reaction to Psicharis see Boutierides, *op. cit.,* p. 274.

33. See Kostes Palamas, *Apanta* (Collected Works), v. 6, pp. 255-56.

34. The latest edition was in 1969. All references are to this edition.

35. Elisaios Giannides, *Glossa kai Zoe* (Language and Life), pp. 34-37, 109.

36. *Ibid.,* pp. 27, 44.

37. *Ibid.,* pp. 43-44.

38. Elias Tsirimokos, *Istoria tou Ekpaideutikou Omilou* (History of the Educational Society), pp. 4-5. Giannes Kordatos, *Istoria tou Glossikou mas Zetematos* (History of Our Language Question), p. 135.

39. Tsirimokos, *op. cit.,* p. 4.

40. Kordatos, *op. cit.,* p. 149.

41. Tsirimokos, *op. cit.,* p. 4. The military revolt of Goudi had taken place and many felt that this would begin a new era for the country.

42. Ekpaideutikos Omilos (Educational Society), *Katastatiko* (Statutes), 1915, p. 14. Hereafter cited as *Statutes.*

43. *Statutes,* p. 15.

44. *Ibid.,* pp. 15-16.

45. Boutierides, *op. cit.,* p. 277.

46. *O Noumas,* January 2, 1903, p. 2. Demetrios Tangopoulos, the editor of *Nouma,* described his first meeting with Ion Dragoumis. The latter had brought a piece for publication, which later became a chapter in his book *Those Who Are Alive.* Tangopoulos notes that he was rather condescending to the young author because the periodical did not care to publish traditional nationalistic material. But Dragoumis' type of nationalism impressed the editor, and the journal went on to publish numerous articles by him. See D.P. Tangopoulos, *Idas,* p. 5.
Romios was the term used to describe the type of Greek who represented the eastern way of life, with its stress on folk-culture, demotic Greek, distrust of cities and government, that was the legacy of the Ottoman period. The counterpart to the *Romios* was the Hellene, representing those Greeks who looked to the West, emphasized the classical culture of the ancient Greeks, accepted the need for change and rejected the legacy of the Ottoman era.

47. One of the important debates occurred in 1907-08 between socialists and nationalists. Ion Dragoumis was one of the protagonists for a nationalist outlook,

and George Skliros supported the socialist view. See Panos Tangopoulos, "To koinonikon mas zetema apo tis steles tou *Nouma"* (Our Social Question from the Columns of *Nouma*), *Ellenika Grammata,* March 1, 1929, pp. 296-300.

48. Ion Dragoumis, *O Ellenismos mou kai oi Ellenes* (My Hellenism and the Greeks), 1927, p. 125.

49. Kostes Palamas, *Apanta* (Collected Works), v. 6, p. 442. Palamas discussed Macedonia and the problem of the "Bulgarophone Greek-Macedonian" as he called it. He argued that if this person were not taught a "living" Greek language he would not acquire a Hellenic national consciousness. Palamas then branded all those who taught in the katharevousa in Macedonia as "allies of the Bulgarians."

50. Leandros Palamas, "Ion Dragoumis", *Deltio tou Ekpaideutikou Omilou,* v. 9 (1921), p. 107.

51. Penelope Delta, "Stohasmoi peri tes anatrofes ton paidion mas" (Thoughts on the Education of Our Children), *Deltio tou Ekpaideutikou Omilou,* v. 1 (1911), pp. 80, 92.

52. *Ibid.,* p. 92.

53. *Ibid.,* pp. 90, 93. Delta wrote that we ". . . *all* belong to the motherland before we may belong to the family, that there is no sacrifice, either material or ethical, that we would not be *required* to perform for the motherland." Italics in the original.

54. George Skliros, *To Koinonikon mas Zetema* (Our Social Question), pp. 54-55. Giannes Kordatos, *Istoria tou Ellenikou Ergatikou Kinematos* (History of the Greek Labor Movement), 1956, 2nd ed., p. 127. Hereafter cited as *The Labor Movement.*

55. Skliros, *op. cit.,* pp. 53-55. Kordatos, *The Labor Movement,* p. 127, fn. 1, points out that Skliros himself did not actively take part in the working class movement. He preferred instead to write and engage other intellectuals over the issue.

56. Kordatos, *The Labor Movement,* p. 123. Kordatos quotes a letter from Kostas Hatzopoulos, a socialist, to a friend. Hatzopoulos, discussing the editor of *Nouma,* Tangopoulos, stated that the latter was mistaken if he thought that socialists and nationalists would be able to work together in harmony within the demotic movement.

57. Photograph of the inscription in K. Dimaras, *Istoria tes Neoellenikes Logotechnias* (History of Modern Greek Literature), photo no. 134.

58. Ion Dragoumis, "Gia to Vivlio tou Giannopoulou" (Concerning the Book of Giannopoulos). *O Noumas,* October 15, 1906.

59. Kostes Palamas, "Liga Logia gia ton K. Perikle Giannopoulo" (A Few Words about Mr. Perikles Giannopoulos), *Apanta* v. 6, pp. 439-446.

CHAPTER III

1. Kostes Palamas, *Ta Chronia mou kai ta Chartia mou* (My Years and My Papers), pp. 3-5, 17-19, 37, 61, 74-75.

2. K. Th Dimaras, *Istoria tes Neoellenikes Logotechnias* (History of Modern Greek Literature), 4th ed., 1968, pp. 386-394.

3. Kostes Palamas, "E Idea tes Patridos" (The Idea of the Homeland), *Estia,* November 1, 1896, p. 1.

4. Kostes Palamas, "O Enthousiasmos kai o Logos" (Enthusiasm and the Word), *Akropolis,* February 28, 1897, p. 1.

5. Vardas Fokas [Kostes Palamas], "Ethnike Anagennesis" (National Renaissance), *Estia,* February 8, 1897, p. 1.

6. *Loc. cit.*

7. [Kostes] Palamas, "To Ellenikon Pneuma: (The Greek Spirit), *Akropolis,* March 22, 1897, p. 1. In this piece Palamas compared his own era with that of ancient Greece just before the Persian wars. The implication was that the Greeks were facing a threat from the east once more, this time the Turks, and that they would be victorious as the ancient Greeks had been.

8. Kostes Palamas, "Pro Ekaton Eton 1797-1897" (One Hundred Years Ago 1797-1897), *Akropolis,* March 25, 1897, p. 1. Published on Greek independence day the article compared the two dates and argued that just one hundred years before Greek national consciousness was stirred and the Greeks sought aid from Europe. Continuing the parallel Palamas noted that like his own era many of the great powers and, of course, the Turks, were against the Greeks.

9. Kostes Palamas, "Synapantemata me ten dystychian" (Encounters with Misery), *Akropolis Esperine,* July 31, 1897, p. 1.

10. Kostes Palamas, "Tourkoi eis tas Athenas" (The Turks in Athens), *Akropolis,* June 25, 1897.

11. Kostes Palamas, "Thanatos tes Patridos" (Death of the Homeland) *Akropolis Esperine* September 10, 1897.

12. Kostes Palamas, Threskia tou Sovinismou" (The Cult of Chauvinism), *Akropolis Esperine,* September 16, 1897. The comparison of Moltke epitomizes the professional thoroughness of a modern military strategist and organizer. Onesandrus was a Greek philosopher of the 1st century A.D. who composed a treatise dealing with the duties of a general but treating the subject without any practical knowledge and in philosophical commonplaces.

13. *Loc. cit.*

14. Diagoras [Kostes Palamas], "Peitharchia" (Discipline), *Akropolis Esperine,* October 1, 1897. p. 1. See also: *Idem.,* "Duo apo tous Pollous" (Two Among the Many), *Akropolis Esperine,* September 5, 1897 and K[ostes] Pal[amas], "Oi Evelpides" (The Cadets), *Akropolis Esperine,* August 7, 1897, p. 1, for Palamas' criticism of the army. He, like many others at the time, felt that the military had failed in its one main objective; the retaking of Constantinople and the fulfillment of its national mission. There seemed little hope of the army's doing much of anything in the future given the economic controls that the European powers imposed on the country as far as Palamas was concerned.

15. Diagoras [Palamas], Discipline, *Akropolis Esperine,* October 1, 1897, p. 1.

16. Kostes Palamas, *E Poietike Mou* (My Poetics), in *Apanta* (Collected Works), v. 10, p. 505. *Idem., Apanta,* v. 6, p. 285.

17. Palamas, *My Poetics, Apanta,* v. 10, p. 507.

18. *Ibid.,* p. 506.

19. Palamas, *Apanta,* v. 14, p. 183.

20. Kostes Palamas, "E Fantasia kai e Patris" (Imagination and the Homeland), *To Asty,* August 9, 1899, p. 1.

21. Kostes Palamas, "Protochroniatike Efchi Gia to 1899" (A New Year's Wish for 1899), *Apanta,* v. 14, p. 40. The article cited originally appeared in the Athenian daily *To Asty,* January 1, 1899.

22. Palamas, *Apanta,* v. 3, pp. 43-44.

23. Kostes Palamas, *My Poetics, Apanta,* v. 10, p. 421. Palamas penned this in

1906, referring to the era when the language controversy was at its height. At the same time, however, the argument is of a general nature.

24. *Ibid.,* pp. 416, 421-22.

25. *Ibid.,* p. 417.

26. Palamas, "Imagination and the Homeland," *To Asty,* August 9, 1899, p. 1. *Idem., My Poetics, Apanta,* v. 10, p. 422.

27. Palamas, *My Poetics, Apanta,* v. 10, p. 453. *Idem.,* "Enthusiasm and the Word," *Akropolis,* February 28, 1897, p. 1.

28. Kostes Palamas, "Anefthynoi kai Ypefthenoi" (The Irresponsible and the Responsible), *Estia,* November 12, 1896, p. 1.

29. Kostes Palamas, *Apanta,* v. 6, pp. 163-171. See also in Palamas' *Apanta,* v. 6, pp. 172-178, pp. 245-283, 307-316, which contains articles on the language question and his involvement in it. The article by Rigas Golfes, "O Demotikistes" (The Demoticist), *Grammata,* 1943, pp. 283-290, is a concise sketch of Palamas' involvement in the demotic question.

30. Palamas, *Apanta,* v. 6, pp. 164-167.

31. *Ibid.,* pp. 307-316. See also *Apanta,* v. 16, pp. 501-02.

32. *Apanta,* v. 15, pp. 282-298, 318-321.

33. Kostes Palamas, *E Flogera tou Vasilia* (The King's Flute), 1910 pp. 137-38. All translations, unless otherwise noted, are by the author from the first edition of this work. Hereafter cited as Palamas: *The King's Flute.*

34. See Golfes, *op. cit.,* p. 288. Kostes Palamas, "Gia na to Diavasoun ta Paidia" (For the Children to Read), *O Noumas,* February 20, 1911.

35. *Apanta,* v. 16, pp. 435-440.

36. *Loc. cit.*

37. See *O Noumas,* April 17, 1911, p. 251.

38. I.K. Kordatos, *Demotikismos kai Logiotatismos* (Demoticism and Erudition), p. 186.

39. A. Hourmouzios, *O Palamas kai e Epoche tou* (Palamas and His Era), 1959, v. 2, p. 20.

40. *Ibid.,* v. 2, p. 19, fn. 1.

41. The best translation into English of Palamas' poem and the most recent is that by Theodore Ph. Stephanides and George C. Katsimbalis, *The Twelve Words of the Gipsy,* London, n.p., 1974. All quotations from the poem, except as otherwise indicated, are from this translation. From here on the work will be cited as Palamas, *Dodecalogue.* For the above quote see p. 14.

42. Palamas, *Dodecalogue,* pp. 32-38.

43. *Ibid.,* pp. 39-41.

44. *Ibid.,* pp. 47-49.

45. *Ibid.,* pp. 73-79.

46. *Ibid.,* p. 79.

47. *Ibid.,* p. 82.

48. *Loc. cit.*

49. *Ibid.,* pp. 87-89.

50. *Ibid.,* p. 90.

51. *Ibid.,* p. 92.

> A day will come when you shall both clasp hands,
> Pagans and Galileans, with clear sighted eyes,
> Strong with the herb of life's reviving fare;
> Then phantoms you will recognize as phantoms,
> And you will both stretch out your arms to grasp
> Of all that lives your share!

52. *Ibid.,* pp. 93-94.

53. *Ibid.,* pp. 117-123.

54. *Ibid.,* p. 119.

55. *Ibid.,* pp. 119-120.

56. *Ibid.,* pp. 126-127.

57. *Ibid.,* pp. 130, 132, 133, 134.

58. *Ibid.,* pp. 134-135.

59. *Ibid.,* pp. 141-142.

60. *Ibid.,* pp. 142-144.

61. *Ibid.,* pp. 151-152.

62. *Ibid.,* pp. 152-156.

63. See Hourmouzios, *op. cit.,* v. 2, p. 206.

64. This overview is based on the synopsis of each canto given by the poet himself in the second edition of the poem and reprinted in his *Apanta,* v. 5, pp. 519-524.

65. A. A. Vasiliev, *History of the Byzantine Empire, 324-1453,* 1952, v. 1, p. 300. See also George Ostrogorsky, *History of the Byzantine State,* 1957, pp. 264-279.

66. Vasiliev, *op. cit.,* v. 1, p. 320.

67. See M. Angold, "Byzantine 'Nationalism' and the Nicaean Empire," *Byzantine and Modern Greek Studies,* v. I (1975), pp. 49-70 for a recent discussion of the problem.

68. Kostes Palamas, *The King's Flute,* p. 61 has this to say about the Cretans:

> They come also from Crete, from the island that
> never grows old, never bends,
>
>   . . . .
>
> and enslaved, yet not enslaved, forever it exists to
> give
> freedom's lessons and to bathe with its blood
> the motherland's parched tree, making it grow.

69. *Ibid.,* p. 50.

70. *Ibid.,* pp. 50, 63.

71. *Ibid.,* pp. 73-86.

72. *Ibid.,* p. 73.

73. *Ibid.,* p. 80

74. *Ibid.,* p. 81.

75. *Ibid.,* p. 84.

76. See Palamas' own characterization of this theme in *Apanta,* v. 5, pp. 521-23.

77. Palamas, *The King's Flute,* p. 55.

78. *Ibid.,* pp. 94-107.

79. *Ibid.,* pp. 53-54, 127.

80. *Ibid.,* pp. 121-22.

81. *Ibid.,* p. 145.

82. *Ibid.,* p. 144.

83. *Ibid.,* p. 146-49.

84. *Ibid.,* p. 149.

85. *Ibid.,* p. 7.

86. *Ibid.,* pp. 66-67. The poet was referring to the role of the Arites. In the *Dodecalogue of the Gypsy* he described them at a low point in their history. Now in *The King's Flute* the tone has changed and it is their accomplishments and valor that are eulogized.

87. *Ibid.,* pp. 125-26, 130, 136, 140. On page 130 Basil recalls the words of a former teacher. The man's advice was that life is a constant struggle. In this struggle most took part, but only a few elect were allowed to sit by and merely observe. The emperor's reply was that among the many there were only a few that were exceptional. Above the many and even higher than the exceptional individuals were those who stood out as the strongest; those who were always in the forefront. Following Nietzsche Palamas argued that while nature endowed some more hand-somely than others, only those who made use of these gifts were truly the select.

88. *Ibid.,* p. 158.

89. Palamas said of the nation in *The King's Flute:* "A gathering becomes a race, a race becomes a people and there you have the Nations!" (p. 150). Concerning Europe the poet noted:

> And above all the fair races
> . . . .
> there are the scales of Justice,
> and the source of Wisdom, there
> is the joy and the power
> . . . and above everything else
> the autocrat that hears herself
> praised
> by the world's instruments: Europe,
> Europe, Europe! *(p. 151).*

90. Palamas, *The King's Flute,* p. 152.

91. *Ibid.,* pp. 153, 157.

92. Friedrich Nietzsche, *The Will to Power,* trans. Walter Kaufman, 1967, p. 77.

93. Palamas, *The King's Flute,* pp. 152-54.

94. *Ibid.,* p. 153. See also the comments by E.P. Papanoutsos, *Palamas, Kavafes, Sikelianos* (in Greek) 1955, pp. 113-14.

95. Palamas, *The King's Flute,* pp. 155-57.

96. *Loc. cit.*

97. *Ibid.,* pp. 151, 156. In another example the poet speaks of Michael Paleologos' return to Constantinople. He comes not to take the City, says the poet, for this is

no longer possible. Constantinople is now a "mere shadow" a "cold image" of that splendid capital that had once been the heart of Byzantium. See p. 161. The poet's historical mindedness saw the Greek past in terms of dynamic development and continuous evolution.

98. *Ibid.,* p. 156.

99. E.P. Papanoutsos, *op. cit.,* p. 94., in an essay on *The King's Flute* points out a contrast between the view that the poet Solomos had of Greece and that of Palamas. In Solomos' view, Papanoutsos notes, Greece ". . .exists above history . . .immovable through eternity above historical time." Palamas, the critic argues, conceived of Greece ". . .not as static but dynamic, like an historical phenomenon, like something which undergoes changes and inevitable alterations with the passage of time, but remains and will remain a struggling force. . . ." See Palamas' own statement in *Apanta,* v. 14, pp. 131-32, on the development of nations. In an article which originally appeared in *Eleftheros Logos* on January 17, 1924, the poet asserted that nations ". . .do not advance by rhetorical schemes or idyllic dream. . . . We will go forward first of all through competition, by fighting, by struggling. . . ."

100. A. Hourmouzios, *op. cit.,* v. 2, p. 213. See also Papanoutsos, *op. cit.,* p. 115, and Andrea Karantone, *Gyro Ston Palama* (About Palamas), pp. 178-181.

101. Diagoras [Kostes Palamas], *"Syntoma Logia apo ten Istorian"* (A Few Words From History), *Akropolis Esperine,* September 21, 1897, p. 1.

102. This is the title of Hourmouzios' three volume study of Palamas.

103. Georgios Theotokas, *Pneumatike Poreia* (Spiritual Development), 1961, p. 207.

104. Palamas, *Dodecalogue of the Gypsy,* p. 14.

CHAPTER IV

1. Perikles Giannopoulos, *To Neon Pneuma* (The New Spirit), 1906, p. 5.

2. There is little biographical material on Giannopoulos' life. For his early years I have relied on the article in the *Great Greek Encyclopedia* V. 8, p. 351. In addition there is the biographical note in the Jan.-March, 1938 issue of *Ta Nea Grammata,* which was devoted to Giannopoulos, pp. 295-96.

3. Perikles Giannopoulos, *To Neon Pneuma* (The New Spirit), 1906, p. 36.

4. Perikles Giannopoulos, "To Kathekon Mas" (Our Duty), *O Noumas,* January 12, 1903, p. 4.

5. Perikles Giannopoulos, *Ekklesis pros to Panellenion Koinon* (Appeal to the Panhellenic Public), 1907, pp. 54-55. *Idem., The New Spirit,* p. 9.

6. Perikles Giannopoulos, "Ta Dyo Idanika: Dyo Medenika" (The Two Ideals: Two Naughts), *Akropolis,* February 19, 1903.

7. *Loc. cit.*

8. Giannopoulos, *The New Spirit,* p. 51.

9. *Ibid.,* pp. 15-16.

10. *Ibid.,* pp. 22-23. The term Helladic (*Elladikos*) in Greek refers to those Greeks who come from the mainland of Greece as opposed to the islands or Asia Minor. Giannopoulos and Dragoumis used the term to mean those Greeks who did not believe in the Great Idea.

11. Perikles Giannopoulos, "Apo ta Nea Ereipia Pros ten Anagennesin: Salpisma"

(From the Modern Ruins Towards Rebirth: A Trumpet Call), *To Asty,* September, 30, 1904, p. 1.

12. Perikles Giannopoulos, *E Ellenike Gramme* (The Greek Line).

13. Giannopoulos, "The Two Ideals: Two Naughts", *Akropolis,* February 9, 1903.

14. *Loc. cit.* Giannopoulos did not coin the term "archaism." It was used, especially by demoticists, to distinguish those writers who used as pure a form of Greek as could approximate the classical.

15. Giannopoulos, *The New Spirit,* pp. 30-31.

16. Giannopoulos, "The Two Ideals: Two Naughts," *Akropolis,* February 19, 1903.

17. *Loc. cit.*

18. *Loc. cit.*

19. Giannopoulos, *Appeal to the Panhellenic Public,* p. 11.

20. *Ibid.,* p. 13.

21. *Ibid.,* p. 14.

22. *Loc. cit.*

23. *Ibid.,* p. 18.

24. *Ibid.,* p. 27.

25. *Loc. cit.*

26. *Ibid.,* p. 13.

27. *Ibid.,* pp. 29, 34.

28. *Ibid.,* pp. 34-37.

29. *Ibid.,* pp. 26-27.

30. *Ibid.,* pp. 11, 43.

31. *Ibid.,* pp. 38, 45.

32. Giannopoulos implied the Slavs though he most often preferred to name the Bulgarians as enemies of Greece.

33. The term "Frank" (*Frangos*) stems from the days of the Latins in the Levant. It is the Greek expression for any Westerner in general. Giannopoulos used it as a term of derision that served as his means of disapproval of everything Western.

34. Giannopoulos, *Appeal to the Panhellenic Public,* p. 39.

35. *Ibid.,* pp. 46-47.

36. *Ibid.,* p. 46.

37. *Ibid.,* pp. 30-31.

38. *Ibid.,* pp. 47-48.

39. *Ibid.,* pp. 49-50.

40. *Ibid.,* p. 16.

41. *Ibid.,* pp. 38, 42, 44.

42. Perikles Giannopoulos, *E Ellenike Gramme* (The Greek Line), 1961, pp. 85-87. This first appeared in an article entitled "E Ellenike Gramme" in the periodical *Anatole,* March, 1903.

43. Giannopoulos, *Appeal to the Panhellenic Public,* p. 52. This work appeared after the Russo-Japanese war of 1905. The Japanese victory made a great impression and even led to the organization of a Japan party.

44. *Ibid.,* p. 52.

45. *Ibid.,* pp. 52-53.

46. Giannopoulos, "The Two Ideals: Two Naughts," *Akropolis*, February 13, 1903.

47. Giannopoulos, *Appeal to the Panhellenic Public*, p. 10. *Idem.*, "Philologia kai Patriotismos" (Literature and Patriotism), *Estia*, August 16, 1899, p. 3. At this time men such as the amateur archaeologist Heinrich Schliemann were excavating the Greek antiquities. It was not until the first years of the twentieth century that the works of Byzantinists such as Karl Krumbacher and Gustave Schlumberger were translated into Greek.

48. Perikles Giannopoulos, "Syndrome tou Typou" (The Contribution of the Press), *To Asty*, April 22, 1903, p. 2. *Idem.*, "The Two Ideals: Two Naughts", *Akropolis*, February 12, 1903. *Idem.*, *The New Spirit*, p. 7.

49. Giannopoulos, "The Two Ideals: Two Naughts," *Akropolis*, February 9, 1903.

50. Giannopoulos, "Literature and Patriotism," *Estia*, August 13, 1899, p. 1.

51. *Ibid.*, p. 3. See also Perikles Giannopoulos, "Xenomania", *O Noumas*, January 11, 1903, p. 4. *Idem.*, "The Contribution of the Press", *To Asty*, April 22, 1903, p. 2. *Idem.*, *The New Spirit*, pp. 28-30.

52. Giannopoulos, *The New Spirit*, p. 33.

53. *Ibid.*, pp. 41-43.

54. *Ibid.*, p. 10.

55. Giannopoulos, "From the Modern Ruins Towards Rebirth: A Trumpet Call", *To Asty*, September 29, 1904, p. 1.

56. Giannopoulos, "From the Modern Ruins Towards Rebirth: A Trumpet Call", *To Asty*, October 13, 1904, p. 1.

57. Giannopoulos, *Appeal to the Panhellenic Public*, p. 59. *Idem.*, "Poietai kai Patris" (Poets and the Motherland), *Akropolis*, August 15, 1899.

58. Giannopoulos, *The Greek Line*, p. 73.

59. Giannopoulos, "The Contribution of the Press", *To Asty*, April 22, 1903, p. 2. *Idem.*, "From the Modern Ruins Towards Rebirth: A Trumpet Call", *To Asty*, October 15, 1904.

60. Giannopoulos, "The Contribution of the Press", *To Asty*, April 22, 1903, p. 2. Perikles Giannopoulos, "To Kathikon Mas" (Our Duty), *O Noumas*, January 12, 1903, p. 4.

61. Giannopoulos, "Literature and Patriotism", *Estia*, August 16, 1899, p. 3.

62. Giannopoulos, "Literature and Patriotism", *Estia*, August 15, 1899, p. 1. *Idem.*, "Xenomania", *O Noumas*, January 16, 1903, p. 4. *Idem.*, "O Dynatos Pothos" (The Strong Desire), *To Asty*, April 18, 1903, p. 2.

63. Giannopoulos, "Our Duty", *O Noumas*, January 12, 1903, p. 4.

64. *Loc. cit.* Perikles Giannopoulos, "Ohi Xena" (Not Foreign Things), *O Noumas*, January 30, 1903, p. 2. *Idem.*, "From the Modern Ruins Towards Rebirth: A Trumpet Call", *To Asty*, October 1, 1904, p. 1.

65. Giannopoulos, *Appeal to the Panhellenic Public*, pp. 29-30.

66. Giannopoulos, *The New Spirit*, p. 45. Dragoumis wrote the following in his copy of this pamphlet next to this statement: "What is character?—Freedom. What does 'a man with character' mean? It means a *free* man' and not one enslaved."

67. Giannopoulos, *Appeal to the Panhellenic Public*, p. 67.

68. *Loc. cit.* Giannopoulos, "Two Ideals: Two Naughts", *Akropolis*, February 10, 1903

69. Claude Levi-Strauss, *Race and History*, 1958, pp. 19-23.

160   NOTES

70. Giannopoulos, *Appeal to the Panhellenic Public,* pp. 7, 27. *Idem., The Greek Line,* p. 12.

71. Giannopoulos, *Appeal to the Panhellenic Public,* pp. 12, 14, 15, 17. *Idem., The New Spirit,* pp. 13-14.

72. Kostes Palamas, *Apanta* (Collected Works), v. 6, pp. 438-446.

CHAPTER V

1. For biographical material see the article on the Dragoumis family, including Ion, in the *Great Greek Encyclopedia,* v. 9, pp. 530-531. See also the biographical sketch in Kleon Paraschos, *Ion Dragoumis,* 1936, pp. 11-19.

2. Ion Dragoumis, *Osoi Zontanoi* (Those Who Are Alive), 2nd ed., 1926, p. 4.

3. Ion Dragoumis, *Ellenikos Politismos* (Hellenic Civilization), 1913, p. 10.

4. *Ibid.,* pp. 10-11.

5. Published by his brother, Philip, in 1925. Dragoumis made a reference to it in an article he wrote on May 11, 1908, entitled: "Koinonismos kai Koinoniologia" (Socialism and Sociology), *O Noumas,* republished in *Deka Arthra sto Nouma* (Ten Articles in Nouma), 1920, p. 99. He called it ". . . a psychological analysis of myself through the stages I have passed from the time as a child when I began to recognize my passions."

6. In his copy of Nietzsche's *Will to Power* (Dragoumis possessed a French translation: *La Volonté de Puissance,* trans. by Henri Albert, 1903., 2 vols.) he wrote in the margin of v. 1, p. 114: "ce n'est pas la vie qui est la cause de tous mes maux; c'est ma faiblesse."

7. See Friedrich Nietzsche, *The Will to Power,* trans. by Walter Kaufman, 1967, p. 19, paragraph 27. In his copy Dragoumis wrote in the margin: "mais les hommes d'exception doivent surmonter cette tyrannie".

8. Dragoumis, *The Footpath,* p. 71. The phrase is repeated constantly after almost every paragraph from pages 171-178.

9. Ion Dragoumis, *O Ellenismos mou kai oi Ellenes* (My Hellenism and the Greeks) 1927, pp. 148-49.

10. Ion Dragoumis, *Osoi Zontanoi* (Those Who Are Alive), 2nd ed., 1926, pp. 67, 174.

11. *Ibid.,* pp. 66, 68. *Idem.,* "Socialism and Sociology" in *Ten Articles in Nouma,* p. 100.

12. Dragoumis, *My Hellenism and the Greeks,* p. 60. In "Socialism and Sociology" in *Ten Articles in Nouma,* p. 99, Dragoumis wrote: ". . .I was born a Greek and a Greek I will remain, like it or not, until I die. I recognize my bondage and do not believe that *free will* exists, because if it existed I would be able to become a citizen of the world."

13. Dragoumis, *Those Who Are Alive,* p. 88. *Idem., My Hellenism and the Greeks,* p. 83.

14. Dragoumis, *My Hellenism and the Greeks,* p. 74. This was a favorite saying of Dragoumis and can be found scattered in several of his works.

15. *Ibid.,* p. 49. Barrès had entitled a trilogy *Le roman de l' énergie nationale.*

16. Dragoumis, *My Hellenism and the Greeks,* p. 83. *Idem., Those Who Are Alive,* p. 88. *Idem, The Footpath,* pp. 16, 217-18.

17. Dragoumis, *My Hellenism and the Greeks*, p. 4. Also pp. 1, 7, 156.

18. Ion Dragoumis, *Martyron kai Eroon Aima* (The Blood of Martyrs and Heroes), 2nd ed., 1914, p. 31. Hereafter cited as: Dragoumis, *Martyrs and Heroes. Idem.,* "O Dromos tes Makedonias" (The Macedonian Road), *Neon Asty,* Oct. 16, 1906, p. 1.

19. Dragoumis, *Those Who Are Alive,* p. 150. *Idem., My Hellenism and the Greeks,* p. 87. *Idem.,* "Socialism and Sociology", *Ten Articles in Nouma,* p. 104. *Idem.,* "Gia to Vivlio tou Giannopoulou" (Concerning the Book by Giannopoulos), *O Noumas,* October 15, 1906, p. 3.

20. Ion Dragoumis, "The Macedonian Road", *Neon Asty,* October 16, 1906, p. 1.

21. Theodore Saloutos, *The Greeks in the United States,* 1964, pp. 21-45.

22. Dragoumis, *Those Who Are Alive,* p. 2. *Idem.,* "E Mikre Patrida" (The Small Homeland), *Ten Articles in Nouma,* p. 61. *Idem.,* "A' Prokeryxe pros tous Sklavomenous kai tous Eleftheromenous Ellenes" (First Proclamation to the Enslaved and Liberated Greeks) in *Ten Articles in Nouma,* pp. 54-55. This was first published in 1908. Hereafter cited as "First Proclamation."

23. Dragoumis, *My Hellenism and the Greeks,* pp. 22-23. *Idem., Those Who Are Alive,* pp. 150-152.

24. Dragoumis, *Hellenic Civilization,* p. 29.

25. Dragoumis, *The Footpath,* p. 169.

26. Dragoumis, *Those Who Are Alive,* p. 151.

27. Dragoumis, *My Hellenism and the Greeks,* pp. 72-73.

28. Dragoumis, *Hellenic Civilization,* p. 22. *Idem., My Hellenism and the Greeks,* pp. 2, 75, 79. Philip Dragoumis, "Selides apo to Anekdoto Emerologio tou Dragoume" (Pages from the Unpublished Diary of [Ion] Dragoumis), *Nea Estia,* March 15, 1941, v. 29, p. 232.

29. Dragoumis, *My Hellenism and the Greeks,* p. 93. *Idem., Those Who Are Alive,* p. 3.

30. Ion Dragoumis, "O Nomos Plakonei Enan *Ellenikotato* Antho" (The Law Crushes a Most Hellenic Flower), *O Noumas,* April 2, 1906, pp. 1-2. Hereafter cited as: Dragoumis, "The Law Crushes."

31. Dragoumis, *Hellenic Civilization,* pp. 24-25. *Idem., My Hellenism and the Greeks,* p. 68.

32. Dragoumis, *Martyrs and Heroes,* p. 47.

33. Dragoumis, "To Ethnos, oi Taxes Kai o Enas" (The Nation, the Classes and the Individual), *Ten Articles in Nouma,* pp. 27-28. Hereafter cited as: Dragoumis, "Nation, Classes, Individual", *Ten Articles in Nouma.* The article was published originally in *O Noumas,* November 25, 1907. Dragoumis referred to a Greek socialist when mentioning these attitudes, but he indicated that they would be taken as signs of the times.

34. *Ibid.,* p. 26. *Idem., Ellenikos Politismos* (Hellenic Civilization), 1914, p. 29.

35. Dragoumis, *My Hellenism and the Greeks,* pp. 95-96.

36. See Dragoumis' attitude toward an uncle of his, Jacob Novikov, who was a Russian-Greek sociologist, as found in *My Hellenism and the Greeks,* p. 50. His remarks on pages 95-98 of the same work are also pertinent.

37. Dragoumis, *Hellenic Civilization,* p. 44. He labeled these two countries, "dairy fed Switzerland" and "bourgeois Belgium".

38. For a discussion of the controversy see the article by Panos Tangopoulos,

"To Koinonikon mas Zetema apo tis Steles tou *Nouma"* (Our Social Question from the Columns of *Nouma),* Ellenika Grammata, March 1, 1929, pp. 296-300.

39. Dragoumis, "Socialism and Sociology", *Ten Articles in Nouma,* p. 97.

40. Dragoumis, "Nation, Classes, Individual", *Ten Articles in Nouma,* pp. 23-24. *Idem., Those Who Are Alive,* p. 102.

41. The quote is from Dragoumis, "Nation, Classes, Individual", *Ten Articles in Nouma,* p. 29. *Idem., Those Who Are Alive,* p. 106.

42. Dragoumis, "Nation, Classes, Individual", *Ten Articles in Nouma,* pp. 26-28.

43. *Ibid.,* pp. 31-32.

44. Dragoumis, "Socialism and Sociology", *Ten Articles in Nouma,* pp. 101, 103-104. *Idem., Those Who Are Alive,* pp. 98-99. *Idem., My Hellenism and the Greeks,* p. 158.

45. See excerpts from his diary as printed in *Koinotes, Ethnos, kai Kratos* (Society, the Nation and the State) ed. by Philip Dragoumis, 2nd. ed., 1967, pp. 125-126. Ion Dragoumis, "Ti Einai o Socialismos?" (What is Socialism), *Athenaike,* Nov. 26, 1919. *Idem.,* "E Socialistike Protomaya" (The Socialist First of May), *Athenaike,* April 19 and 20, 1920, reprinted in *Society, the Nation and the State,* pp. 165-169.

46. Dragoumis, *Martyrs and Heroes,* pp. 46-47. *Idem.,* "O Evgenikotera Politismenos Laos" (The More Civilized People), *Ten Articles in Nouma,* p. 45. This article originally appeared in *O Noumas,* December 23, 1907.

47. From a letter by Dragoumis quoted in Natalia Mela, *Pavlos Melas,* 2nd ed., 1963, p. 184.

48. Dragoumis, *Hellenic Civilization,* p. 14.

49. *Loc. cit.*

50. *Ibid.,* p. 5.

51. Dragoumis, *Martyrs and Heroes,* pp. 30-31. *Idem., My Hellenism and the Greeks,* pp. 34-35. *Idem,* "The Macedonian Road", *Neon Asty,* October 16, 1906, p. 1.

52. Toxotes [Ion Dragoumis], "Ex Ellados" (From Greece), *Politike Epitheoresis,* May 23, 1910, p. 1.

53. Dragoumis, *Those Who Are Alive,* p. 89.

54. Dragoumis, *My Hellenism and the Greeks,* p. 62.

55. Dragoumis, *Hellenic Civilization,* p. 14. *Idem., Those Who Are Alive,* p. 157.

56. Dragoumis, *Those Who Are Alive,* p. 157.

57. Dragoumis, *Hellenic Civilization,* pp. 15-16.

58. Dragoumis, *Those Who Are Alive,* pp. 72-73.

59. Dragoumis, "The More Civilized People", *Ten Articles in Nouma,* p. 44.

60. Dragoumis, *Hellenic Civilization,* pp. 15-16, 178-180.

61. Dragoumis, "The Small Homeland", *Ten Articles in Nouma,* p. 65. Dragoumis wrote the article under the pseudonym, "Ion the Hard" (Skliros). This was intended as a jibe at the Greek socialist, George Skliros, who used the name "Skliros" as a pseudonym. Dragoumis' article, The Law Crushes", *O Noumas,* April 2, 1906, was an attempt to present his case for the communities.

62. Nicholas Kaltchas, *Introduction to the Constitutional History of Modern Greece,* 1940, p. 29.

63. Arnold Toynbee, *The Western Question in Greece and Turkey,* 1922, p. 124.

64. John Petropulos, *Politics and Statecraft in the Kingdom of Greece, 1833-1843*, 1968, p. 173.

65. Dragoumis, "The Law Crushes", *O Noumas*, April 2, 1906, p. 2. *Idem., My Hellenism and the Greeks*, p. 11.

66. William Miller, *Greek Life in Town and Country*, 1905, pp. 173-175.

67. Dragoumis, *My Hellenism and the Greeks*, pp. 13-14.

68. *Ibid.*, pp. 11-12. *Idem.*, "The Small Homeland", *Ten Articles in Nouma*, p. 60.

69. Dragoumis, "The Small Homeland", *Ten Articles in Nouma*, p. 60.

70. Ion Dragoumis, "Stratos kai Alla" (The Army and Other Things), *Ten Articles in Nouma*, pp. 79-81. This is the "Third Proclamation" of Dragoumis. It originally appeared in *O Noumas*, October 11, 1909. In the reprinting of it in the *Ten Articles in Nouma* the headings have been reversed by mistake. The duties of the state appear under the heading of the community and vice versa.

71. *Ibid.*, pp. 81-82.

72. A.Y.E., Consular Reports 1908, Constantinople to the Foreign Ministry, no. 209, March 15, 1908; no. 6927, November 11, 1908; and no. 947, December 2, 1908.

73. Dragoumis, *My Hellenism and the Greeks*, pp. 45-46. *Idem.*, "The Army and Other Things", *Ten Articles in Nouma*, p. 85.

74. Dragoumis, *My Hellenism and the Greeks*, pp. 45-46.

75. Idas [Ion Dragoumis], "Ena Fylladio" (A Pamphlet), *Deltio tou Ekpaideutikou Omilou*, v. 1, 1911, p. 123.

76. Dragoumis, *My Hellenism and the Greeks*, p. 123.

77. Dragoumis, *Those Who Are Alive*, pp. 24-25. *Idem., My Hellenism and the Greeks*, pp. 122-123.

78. Dragoumis, *My Hellenism and the Greeks*, p. 63. *Idem., The Footpath*, pp. 11-14.

79. Dragoumis, *Hellenic Civilization*, pp. 19-21. *Idem., The Footpath*, pp. 25-26. *Idem.*, "The Army and Other Things", *Ten Articles in Nouma*, p. 88.

80. Dragoumis, "The Army and Other Things", *Ten Articles in Nouma*, p. 90.

81. Dragoumis, *My Hellenism and the Greeks*, p. 38. *Idem.*, "The Law Crushes", *O Noumas*, April 2, 1906, p. 1. *Idem., Those Who Are Alive*, pp. 96-97.

82. Dragoumis, *Those Who Are Alive*, p. 147.

83. *Ibid.*, p. 154. Dragoumis in a vexed mood commented: "Teachers who do not have [the ability] to convey enthusiasm should be shot."

84. *Ibid.*, pp. 152-153.

85. *Ibid.*, p. 153. *Idem., My Hellenism and the Greeks*, pp. 115, 124.

86. Dragoumis, "The Army and Other Things", *Ten Articles in Nouma*, pp. 89-90. *Idem., Those Who Are Alive*, p. 154.

87. Dragoumis, *My Hellenism and the Greeks*, pp. 36-37.

88. Dragoumis, "The Army and Other Things", *Ten Articles in Nouma*, pp. 93-94.

89. Dragoumis, *My Hellenism and the Greeks*, p. 71.

90. Dragoumis, "The More Civilized People", *Ten Articles in Nouma*, p. 46.

91. *Loc. cit. Idem.*, "The Army and Other Things", *Ten Articles in Nouma*, p. 90.

92. Dragoumis, "The Small Homeland", *Ten Articles in Nouma*, p. 62.

93. Dragoumis, *My Hellenism and the Greeks*, pp. 75, 107.

94. Dragoumis, *Those Who Are Alive*, pp. 155-56.

95. Dragoumis, "The Small Homeland", *Ten Articles in Nouma*, p. 62.

96. Dragoumis, *Those Who Are Alive*, p. 156.

97. *Loc. cit.*

98. Dragoumis, "First Proclamation", *Ten Articles in Nouma*, pp. 53-54.

99. Dragoumis, *Those Who Are Alive*, pp. 155, 157.

100. Dragoumis, *Hellenic Civilization*, p. 45.

101. *Ibid.*, p. 14.

102. *Loc. cit.*

103. Dragoumis, *My Hellenism and the Greeks*, pp. 2-3.

104. Dragoumis, *Hellenic Civilization*, pp. 26-27. *Idem., Those Who Are Alive*, p. 25.

105. Dragoumis, *Hellenic Civilization*, p. 45.

106. Dragoumis, *My Hellenism and the Greeks*, pp. 153-155.

107. *Ibid.*, p. 66.

108. *Ibid.*, pp. 1-2.

109. Dragoumis, *Hellenic Civilization*, p. 18. *Idem.*, "The More Civilized People", *Ten Articles in Nouma*, pp. 44-45.

110. Dragoumis, *My Hellenism and the Greeks*, pp. 149-150.

111. *Ibid.*, pp. 21, 47. *Idem., Hellenic Civilization*, pp. 18-19, 22.

112. Dragoumis, *Hellenic Civilization*, p. 17. *Idem., Those Who Are Alive*, pp. 157-58.

113. Dragoumis, *Hellenic Civilization*, p. 45.

114. Dragoumis, *Those Who Are Alive*, p. 160.

115. Dragoumis, "The More Civilized People", *Ten Articles in Nouma*, p. 46. In his *My Hellenism and the Greeks*, p. 3, Dragoumis asserted: "If I were the only Greek remaining and all the rest died, and if the Swedes, the Irish and the Egyptians came to inhabit Greece . . . they would become Greeks. The one live Greek would teach them the language and his Hellenism would be shared among them. . . ."

116. Dragoumis, *My Hellenism and the Greeks*, pp. 31-32. *Idem., Those Who Are Alive*, p. 157.

117. Dragoumis, *My Hellenism and the Greeks*, pp. 5-6.

118. Dragoumis, *Hellenic Civilization*, p. 44.

119. For Example see Petros Orologas, *Ion Dragoumis*, 1938. Constantine Hatzipateras, *O Ion Dragoumis Kai e Syneidese tes Ethnotetos* (Ion Dragoumis and National Consciousness), 1948. D.S. Soutsou, *O Ion Dragoumis, Profetes tou Ellenikou Ethnikismou* (Ion Dragoumis, Prophet of Hellenic Nationalism), 1949.

120. George Theotokas, "Enas Neos Dragoumis" (A New Dragoumis) *Anagennese*, May-June, 1928, pp. 394-399 and July-August, 1928, pp. 473-481. Demetrios Tsakonas, "O Ion Dragoumis os Exairesis" (Ion Dragoumis as an Exception), *Ellenike Demiourgia*, October 1, 1952, no. 112, pp. 391-92.

CHAPTER VI

1. John Comstock, *History of the Greek Revolution*, 1829, pp. 499-500 as cited in Jonathan F. Scott and Alexander Baltzly, *Readings in European History Since 1814*, 1930, pp. 353-55.

2. Ion Dragoumis, "Koinonismos kai Koinoniologia" (Socialism and Sociology), in *Ten Articles in Nouma*, p. 100. *Idem.*, "A' Prokeryxe pros tous Sklavomenous kai tous Eleftheromenous Ellenes", (First Proclamation to the Enslaved and Liberated Greeks), in *Ten Articles in Nouma*, p. 48. Dragoumis stated that: "Greek lands are those which for thousands of years now are settled and worked by Greeks, those in which are buried the bones of thousands of Greek generations." Hereafter cited as "First Proclamation," *Ten Articles.*

3. Ion Dragoumis, "Stratos kai Alla", (The Army and Other Things) in *Ten Articles in Nouma*, p. 74. In the same articlep. 73, Dragoumis notes that the Greeks no longer held a leading position among the Balkan peoples. All these nations now were equal before the leadership of the great powers of Europe. The only powerful force that remained for Greece from past centuries was the Greeks' own aptitude for business.

4. Ion Dragoumis, *Osoi Zontani* (Those Who Are Alive), pp. 78, 82, 146. *Idem.*, *Ellenikos Politismos* (Hellenic Civilization), pp. 16-17.

5. Ion Dragoumis, *Those Who Are Alive*, p. 78. Significantly, Dragoumis notes that it is not the masses but rather the intellectuals that need to be challenged by an ideal. See *idem.*, *"Socialism and Sociology"*, *Ten Articles*, pp. 101-102. *Idem.*, "To Ethnos kai oi Taxes" (The Nation and the Classes), in *Ten Articles*, p. 32.

6. Ion Dragoumis, *Those Who Are Alive*, p. 80. *Idem.*, "First Proclamation," *Ten Articles*, p. 51. *Idem.*, "The Army and Other Things:, *Ten Articles*, pp. 74-75.

7. Ion Dragoumis, *Those Who Are Alive*, p. 81. *Idem.*, "The Army and Other Things", *Ten Articles*, pp. 75-76. See also George Theotokas, "Enas Neos Dragoumis" (A New Dragoumis), *Anagennese*, July-August, 1928, p. 474.

8. Ion Dragoumis, *Hellenic Civilization*, p. 8. *Idem.*, "The Army and Other Things", *Ten Articles*, pp. 71-72.

9. Ion Dragoumis, *Hellenic Civilization*, pp. 6, 23. *Idem.*, "O Dromos tes Makedonias" (The Path of Macedonia), *Neon Asty*, October 16, 1906.

10. Ion Dragoumis, *O Ellenismos mou kai oi Ellenes* (My Hellenism and the Greeks), p. 108. *Idem.*, *Hellenic Civilization*, pp. 6-9. *Idem.*, "The Army and Other Things", *Ten Articles*, p. 72.

11. Ion Dragoumis, *My Hellenism*, pp. 109-110. Dragoumis cited England as an example of a nation living within its "natural" frontiers. Italy was another example. The principle that interested him most was not national self-determination but the use of nationalism as a stimulant for a people to enlarge their nation.

12. *Ibid.*, p. 118.

13. Ion Dragoumis, *Those Who Are Alive*, p. 138. Dragoumis, refering to himself stated: "Perhaps he [Dragoumis] has a greater liking for the union of the race into one great and powerful, purely Greek state, while his friend [Souliotes] has a greater weakness for the other, the Eastern state, and the two of them can work together for both [objectives]. . . .Whichever of the two succeeds will be beneficial to the nation."

14. Ion Dragoumis, "The Army and Other Things", *Ten Articles*, pp. 68-69. Dragoumis presented an economic argument for national expansion. In his view, the cost of supporting schools, churches and consulates by the Greek government in lands where Greeks were found meant that the internal needs of Greece were not taken care of. If these areas became part of the Greek state, they would bring in the wealth and abilities of the diaspora Greeks. The argument is analagous to that proposed by Kolettis in the nineteenth century; salvation by expansion.

15. Wayne Vucinich, *Serbia Between East and West,* 1954, p. 133. L.S. Stavrianos, *The Balkans Since 1453,* 1958, p. 522.

16. Vucinich, *op. cit.,* pp. 123-30.

17. *Ibid.,* pp. 124, 131.

18. See the comments by Athanasios Souliotes in his book: *O Makedonikos Agon, E 'Organosis Thessalonikes' 1906-1908* (The Macedonian Struggle, the 'Organosis Thessalonikes'), 1959, p. 16. Hereafter cited as *Macedonian Struggle.*

19. Ion Dragoumis, *Martyron kai Eroon Aima* (The Blood of Martyrs and Heroes), pp. 85-88. Hereafter cited as *Martyrs and Heroes.*

20. Athanasios Souliotes, *Macedonian Struggle,* p. 12. K. Mayer, *Istoria tou Ellenikou Typou* (History of the Greek Press), I, pp. 254-255. Mayer quotes the Committee's declaration of purpose as published in the Athenian daily *Empros,* May 29, 1904. The publisher of the paper, Demetrios Kalapothakes, was a founding member of the organization. The declaration reads in part: "The Macedonian Committee through this proclamation gives notice to all Hellenism of its formation; it declares that it will not resort to anarchic measures, it will not blow up railroad tracks, nor will it destroy public institutions, but it will use measures unremittingly for the vigorous defense of its brothers from Macedonia, and it announces that *not one crime against Greeks will go unpunished"* (italics in the original). See also the editorial entitled "O Makedonikos Kindinos" (The Macedonian Danger) in *Akropolis,* January 26, 1904, p. 1 as an example of Greek journalistic efforts on behalf of the Greek cause in Macedonia.

21. AthanasiosSouliotes, *op. cit.,* p. 12.

22. For an account of Melas' life see Natalia Mela, *Pavlos Melas, passim.* I.S. Notaris, *Pavlos Melas, passim.*

23. The Athenian daily *Akropolis* in an editorial entitled "Where?" on October 20, 1904, p. 1, noted: "The blood of Pavlos Melas must serve as a pause in our national thoughts: Where are we going? How are we conducting ourselves?" As part of the funeral service children from all the schools in Athens were brought to the square in front of the parliament building. From there the funeral procession went to the Metropolitan Cathedral for services. See *Akropolis,* October 22, 1904, p. 2.

24. Anonymous [Ion Dragoumis], "Metaxy Ellenon kai Boulgaron" (Between Greeks and Bulgarians), *Neon Asty,* October 13, 1905, p. 1. Ion Dragoumis, "The Path of Macedonia", *Neon Asty,* October 16, 1906. *Idem., My Hellenism, p. 26.* Dragoumis saw the event in even broader terms: "His death is life to those tired of the mediocrity of life. His death resurrects the sleeping, shakes the numb, strengthens the weak, refreshes the thirsty. . . ." *Martyrs and Heroes,* p. 136.

25. AthanasiosSouliotes, *Macedonian Struggle,* p. 7.

26. *Ibid., passim.* See Douglas Dakin, *The Greek Struggle in Macedonia,* 1966, for an account in English.

27. Souliotes met Dragoumis in July, 1906, while in Macedonia. The two became good friends and later in Constantinople, co-workers in the Constantinople Organization.

28. Ion Dragoumis, *Martyrs and Heroes,* pp. 52, 118-120.

29. *Ibid.,* p. 52. Ion Dragoumis, "Socialism and Sociology," *Ten Articles in Nouma,* pp. 100-101.

30. Ion Dragoumis, *Martyrs and Heroes,* pp. 98-100. On page 101 Dragoumis argued: "We do not separate villages and cities in a location; the area is Greek, villages and cities. No area has been created as yet without villages and cities living together, undivided. In a Greek area it is impossible that Bulgarian villages could

exist. And if it were true that the majority of villages speak a special language—and I maintain it is not Bulgarian—Macedonia is a Greek land; the villages remain faithful not to the Patriarchate, but to their nation; the villagers wish to be Greeks, and they desire this so much, that you [the Bulgarians] call them with disdain 'Grecomaniacs'. In their minds the words 'Hellenism' and 'Civilization' mean the same thing." Dragoumis' ideas illustrate the continued simplistic outlook of Greek nationalists concerning Macedonia. The area was still considered Greek though they acknowledged there was another serious rival for control of the area, the Bulgarians. Greek nationalism is evident in Dragoumis' attempts to characterize Macedonia's inhabitants as loyal to the Greek 'nation' rather than the Greek church. Notice Dragoumis' equation of 'Hellenism' with 'civilization' as if to show the superiority of the Greek position on the basis of culture rather than race or religion.

31. Philip Dragoumis makes note of this organization in his editing of Ion Dragoumis' work, *My Hellenism*, p. 7. See also Natalia Mela, *op. cit.*, p. 187.

32. Ion Dragoumis, *Martyrs and Heroes*, p. 27. Natalia Mela, *op. cit.*, p. 181-82. Dragoumis mentions having written to Maurice Barrès personally in an appeal for European support.

33. Ion Dragoumis, *Martyrs and Heroes*, pp. 29-30, 103. *Idem.*, "The Path of Macedonia", *Neon Asty*, October 16, 1906, p. 1. *Idem.*, *Those Who Are Alive*, p. 82.

34. Ion Dragoumis, *Martyrs and Heroes*, p. 30.

35. *Ibid.*, Prologue, p. 3.

36. Ion Dragoumis, *My Hellenism*, pp. 15-16, 104-06. *Idem.*, *Martyrs and Heroes*, pp. 5, 89-90. Anonymous (Ion Dragoumis), "Between Greeks and Bulgars", *Neon Asty*, October 13, 1905, p. 1. Compare these ideas with those expressed by Giannopoulos in: *Ekklesis pros to Panellenion Koinon* (Appeal to the Panhellenic Public), p. 16. "The sword is the only justice" he argued chiding the Greeks for hesitating to assert their rights in Macedonia. They should take what is theirs and not look to the West for help.

37. Ion Dragoumis, *Martyrs and Heroes*, pp. 8, 10, 11, 12, 109, *Idem.*, *My Hellenism*, p. 84. Natalia Mela, *op. cit.*, p. 183.

38. Arnold Toynbee, *The Western Question in Greece and Turkey*, pp. 131-32.

39. Roderic Davison, *Reform in the Ottoman Empire 1856-1876*, 1963, pp. 114-135.

40. George Eliot, *Turkey in Europe*, p. 291.

41. Dimitri Pentzopoulos, *The Balkan Exchange of Minorities and Its Impact Upon Greece*, pp. 31-32 cites figures of over 200,000 Greeks living in the Constantinople sandjak in 1910. For Smyrna figures cited on pp. 29-30, show that in 1910 this province had a Greek population of over 600,000.

42. Ion Dragoumis, *Those Who Are Alive*, pp. 48-49.

43. *Ibid.*, p. 7.

44. *Ibid.*, pp. 122-23. *Idem.*, *My Hellenism*, p. 42. Dragoumis compared the Greeks of a "subject" Hellenism, those in Turkey, with those of a "free" Hellenism, who lived in Egypt. Without elaborating on this comparison he argued that in Egypt the Greeks were prospering, while in Turkey Hellenism was losing ground. His knowledge of the Greeks in Egypt apparently stemmed from a short period of service with the Greek consulate in Alexandria in 1905. The idea that Greeks were thriving in a society free from Turkish rule certainly appealed to him. See *Idem.*, *Hellenic Civilization*, p. 10.

45. Ion Dragoumis, *Those Who Are Alive*, pp. 70-71. Dragoumis worked as an

official of the Greek embassy, secretly through the political organization set up by some of the Constantinople Greeks, and with members of the Patriarchate. An organization espousing the demoticist cause called the "Brotherhood" (*Aderfato*) also interested Dragoumis. His ideological flexibility is apparent from his ability to work with both demoticists and officials of the Patriarchate.

46. AYE, Consular Reports Constantinople, 1908, doc. no. 209, March 15, 1908; doc. no. 728, July 26, 1908; doc. no. 1230, November 30, 1908. All dates are Old Style.

47. Ion Dragoumis, *Those Who Are Alive*, p. 71. *Idem., My Hellenism*, p. 85.

48. Ion Dragoumis, *My Hellenism*, pp. 77-78.

49. *Ibid.*, p. 137.

50. Toxotes [Ion Dragoumis], "Ex Ellados" (From Greece), *Politike Epitheoresis*, May 23, 1910, p. 1.

51. Ion Dragoumis, *Those Who Are Alive*, pp. 144-45.

52. *Ibid.*, p. 137.

53. Ion Dragoumis, "The Army and Other Things", *Ten Articles*, p. 75.

54. Unpublished manuscript by Athanasios Souliotes dealing with the Constantinople Organization written in Athens, Greece, p. 1. Hereafter cited as O.K. Text.

55. O.K. Text, p. 54.

56. *Ibid.*, p. 38. Ion Dragoumis, *Martyrs and Heroes*, p. 52. Dragoumis, musing about Macedonia, stated that he could envision ". . . an immense, secret organization within all of Turkey, a second Greek state, formed from all the Greek communities and districts with a Greek discipline among them, and with such a hierarchy binding them together that the communities would be able to work, to aid one another, and to struggle together at the same time against every enemy." Souliotes noted in his work that ". . . he always believed that there had to be an internal organization of Hellenism in Turkey."

57. O.K. Text, pp. 13-14.

58. *Ibid.*, pp. 38-39, 51-52. "Organosis Konstantinoupoleos" (The Constantinople Organization), *Megale Ellenike Enkyklopaedia*, v. 21, p. 32.

59. O.K. Text, p. 77.

60. *Ibid.*, p. 51.

61. *Ibid.*, pp. 73-75.

62. *Ibid.*, pp. 162-63.

63. Ion Dragoumis, *Those Who Are Alive*, pp. 115-116.

64. *Ibid.*, p. 120.

65. *Ibid.*, pp. 117-120. On page 117 Dragoumis wrote: "Then I cannot share the happiness of the rayahs, the *Romios*, because we ourselves did not struggle to breathe freely, we are not worthy of the liberty that they supposedly give us." *Idem.*, "The Army and Other Things", *Ten Articles*, pp. 72-73.

66. The book was dedicated to Perikles Giannopoulos, who had committed suicide the year before.

67. Ion Dragoumis, *Those Who Are Alive*, p. 128.

68. *Ibid.*, p. 80.

69. *Ibid.*, chapter 5, *passim*.

70. *Ibid.*, p. 119.

CHAPTER VII

1. Jerry Augustinos, "The Dynamics of Modern Greek Nationalism: The Great Idea and the Macedonian Problem," *East European Quarterly,* VI, 4 (1973), 444-453.

2. *Report of the International Commission to Inquire into the Causes and Conduct of the Balkan Wars,* New York, 1914, p. 418.

3. A.A. Pallis, *Greece's Anatolian Adventure—And After,* London, 1937, p. 224.

4. Christos Theodoulou, *Greece and the Entente August 1, 1914-September 25, 1916,* Thessaloniki, 1971, p. 92.

5. Pallis, *op. cit.,* pp. 22-25.

6. *Ibid.,* pp. 222, 224.

7. Georgos Theotokas, *Argo,* Athens, 1936, pp. 162-63.

8. Adamantios Koraes, "Report on the Present State of Civilization in Greece," in *Nationalism in Africa and Asia,* ed. Elie Kedourie, 1970, pp. 153-188.

9. See for example Petros Orologas, *Ion Dragoumis,* 1938.

10. A new edition of Dragoumis' writings began to appear in the 1920's published by his brother Philip. In 1949 there appeared an article by a member of the "National Union", Demetrios Soutsos, concerning Dragoumis as a "prophet of Greek nationalism." A selection of Dragoumis' works for high school children was published in 1953, and in 1963 the "Society for the Dissemination of Useful Books" brought out yet another selection of his works. New editions of some of his works continue to be published.

11. See the selection published in 1963 by Dem. Lazogeorgos, *Perikles Giannopoulos-Apanta* (Perikles Giannopoulos-Collected Works).

12. See Georgos Theotokas, *Elefthero Pneuma* (Free Spirit), ed. K. Th. Dimaras, 1973, *passim.* Also the issue of *Ta Nea Grammata* Jan-March 1938, which is dedicated to Giannopoulos.

Bibliographies

American School of Classical Studies. *Catalogue of the Gennadius Library.* 7 vols. Boston: G.K. Hall & Co., 1968.

Dragoumis, Ion. *Koinotes, Ethnos kai Kratos* (Community, Nation and State), sel. & ed. by Philip Dragoumis. Thessalonike: Etairia Makedonikon Spoudon, 1967.

Fousara, G.I. *Vivliografia ton Ellenikon Vivliografion 1791-1947* (Bibliography of Greek Bibliographies 1791-1947). Athens: Estia, 1961

Katsimbalis, George. *Vivliografia Koste Palama* (Bibliography of Kostes Palamas). Athens: Ellenike Ekdotike Etairia, 1943.

_____. *Vivliografia Koste Palama 1954-1958* (Bibliography of Kostes Palamas 1954-1958). Athens: n.p., 1959.

_____. *Vivliografia Koste Palama 1959-1963* (Bibliography of Kostes Palamas 1959-1963). Athens: n.p., 1964.

–_____. *Vivliografia P. Giannopoulou* (Bibliography of P. Giannopoulos). 2nd ed. Athens: n.p., 1960.

Politou, N.T. *Ellenike Vivliografia* (Greek Bibliography). v. 2 Athens: Sakellariou, 1911.

Unpublished Material

Souliotes, Athanasios. *Organosis Konstantinoupoleos* (The Constantinople Organization). Athens.

Newspapers & Periodicals

Ellenismos (Hellenism), 1898-1904.
O Noumas, 1903-1912.
Politike Epitheoresis (Political Review). Constantinople, 1910; Athens, 1916-1920.

Selected Works by Kostes Palamas

Books

Palamas, Kostes. *O Dodekalogos tou Gyftou* (The Twelve Words of the Gypsy) Athens: Estia, 1907.

_____. *The Twelve Words of the Gipsy.* Trans. By Theodore Ph. Stephanides and George C. Katsimbalis. London, n.p., 1974.

_____. *E Flogera tou Vasilia* (The King's Flute). Athens: Estia, 1910.

_____. *Eroika Prosopa kai Keimena* (Heroic Persons and Texts). Athens: Ekdoseis Foitetikes Syntrofias, 1911.

_____. *E Politeia kai e Monaxia* (Society and Solitude). Athens: Estia, 1912.

_____. *Pezoi Dromoi* (Footpaths). 3 vols. Athens: Demetrakos, 1928-1934.

_____. *Ta Chronia mou kai ta Chartia mou: E Poietike mou* I. (My Years and My Papers: My Poetics I.) Athens: Estia, 1933.

_____. *Apanta Koste Palama* (Collected Works of Kostes Palamas). 16 vols. Athens: Govostes, n.d.

Articles

Palamas, Kostes. "E semerine Ellas" (Present-day Greece), *Estia* 2nd sem. (1892): 91-93.

_____. "E ethnike glossa: O k. Palles" (The National Language: Mr. Pallis). *Estia* 1st. sem. (1892): 397-399.

_____. "Byzantine kai neotera Ellas" (Byzantine and Modern Greece). *Efemeris*, June 29, 1893.

_____ (Vardas Fokas). "E idea tes patridos" (The Idea of the Motherland). *Estia*, November 1, 1896.

_____ (Vardas Fokas). "E dynamis ton ideon" (The Power of Ideas). *Estia*, November 9, 1896.

_____ (Vardas Fokas). "Anefthyn kai ypefthynoi" (The Irresponsibile and Thoie Responsible). *Estia*, November 12, 1896.

_____ (Vardas Fokas). "Epameinondas Delegiorges." *Estia*, December 6, 1896, p. 1, and December 7, 1896, p. 1.

_____ (Vardas Fokas). "Ethnike anagennesis" (National Renaissance). *Estia*, February 8, 1897, p. 1.

_____. "O enthousiasmos kai o logos" (Enthusiasm and Intellect). *Akropolis*, February 28, 1897, p. 1.

_____ (K.P.). "Ear" (Spring). *Akropolis*, March 14, 1897, p. 1.

_____. "To Ellenikon pneuma" (The Greek Spirit). *Akropolis*, March 22, 1897.

_____. "Pro ekaton eton 1797-1897" (One Hundred Years Ago 1797-1897). *Akropolis*, March 25, 1897.

_____. "To mega oneiro" (The Great Dream). *Estia*, March 25, 1897.

_____ (K. Pal.). "Ai skiai ton progonon" (The Shadows of our Ancestors). *Akropolis Esperine*, June 4, 1897.

_____. "Tourkoi eis tas Athenas, En poiema profetikon" (Turks in Athens; A Prophetic Poem). *Akropolis*, June 25, 1897.

_____ (K. Pal.). "Apo ten Kreten to fos" (Light from Crete). *Akropolis Esperine*, July 16, 1897, p. 1.

_____ (K. Pal.). "Synapantemata me ten dystychian" (Encounters with Misfortune). *Akropolis Esperine*, July 31, 1897, p. 1.

_____ (K. Pal.). "Vouleftai, georgoi, stratiotai" (Deputies, Peasants, Soldiers). *Akropolis Esperine*, August 4, 1897, p. 1.

_____ (K. Pal.). "Oi evelpides" (The Cadets). *Akropolis Esperine*, August 7, 1897, p. 1.

_____ (K. Pal.). "O thanatos tou Parthenonos" (The Death of the Parthenon). *Akropolis Esperine*, August 12, 1897, p. 1.

_____ (Diagoras). "Dyo apo tous pollous" (Two Out of the Many). *Akropolis Esperine*, Sept. 5, 1897.

—————————— (Diagoras). "Ethnika mise" (National Hatreds). *Akropolis Esperine*, Sept. 7, 1897.

—————————— (Diagoras). "O thanatos tes patridos" (The Death of the Motherland). *Akropolis Esperine*, Sept. 10, 1897.

—————————— (Diagoras). "E threskia tou sovinismou" (The Religion of Chauvinism). *Akropolis Esperine*, Sept. 16, 1897.

—————————— (Diagoras). "Syntoma logia apo ten istorian" (Brief Words from History). *Akropolis Esperine*, Sept. 21, 1897, p. 1.

—————————— (Diagoras). "Peitharchia" (Discipline). *Akropolis Esperine*, October 1, 1897, p. 1.

—————————— (Vardas Fokas). "E prosefche" (The Prayer). *Estia*, October 30, 1897.

—————————— (Vardas Fokas). "O didaskalos" (The Teacher). *Estia*, November 13, 1897, p. 1.

—————————— (Vardas Fokas). "O prodotes" (The Traitor). *Estia*, November 23, 1897, pp. 1-2.

—————————— (Diagoras). "Filosofia tes ellenikes efthymias" (The Philosophy of Greek Humor). *To Asty*, February 28, 1899, p. 1.

——————————. "E fantasia kai e patris" (Imagination and the Motherland). *To Asty*, August 9, 1899, p. 1.

——————————. "Poiesis kai paidagogike" (Poetry and Pedagogy). *Estia*, June 6, 1900, p. 1.

——————————. "E techne kai e koinonia. Oi katafronitai tou koinou" (Art and Society. Those Who Scorn the Public). *To Periodikon Mas* 1 (1900): 65-70.

——————————. "Romios kai Romiosyne". *To Asty*, Oct. 12, 1901.

——————————. "E Megale Idea" (The Great Idea). *To Periodikon Mas* 3 (1901): 140-41.

——————————. "Filologika anathemata" (Literary Anathemas). *O Noumas*, no. 6 January 19, 1903, p. 4.

——————————. "Liga logia gia ton k. Perikle Giannopoulo" (A Few Words About Mr. Perikles Giannopoulos). *O Noumas*, no. 213, September 17, 1905, pp. 1-3.

——————————. "E 25 Martiou tou 1821 kai tou 1908" (The 25th of March 1821 and 1908). *Akropolis*, March 25, 1908, p. 1.

——————————. "Anamneseis kai entyposeis" (Reminiscences and Impressions). *Nea Estia*, 66 (1959): 1214-18.

Works by Perikles Giannopoulos

Books

Giannopoulos, Perikles. *To Neon Pneuma* (The New Spirit). Athens: Sakellariou, 1906.

——————————. *Ekklesis pros to Panellenion Koinon* (Appeal to the Panhellenic Public). Athens: Kollaros, 1907.

——————————. *E Ellenike Gramme* (The Greek Line). Athens: Galaxia, 1961. Ta Nea Grammata. *Perikles Giannopoulos* (in Greek). Athens, Jan.-March, 1938.

Articles

Giannopoulos, Perikles (Lotos). "Ponos" (Pain). *To Asty*, August 3, 1894, poem.

_____ (Xerotagaros). "Mesaionike Panagia" (Medieval Virgin Mary). *Estia*, December 26, 1898, poem

_____ (Neoellen). "Poios einai o protos ton zonton poieton" (Who is the First Among the Living Poets). *To Asty*, December 31, 1898.

_____ (Neoellen). "Entyposeis apo ten architektoniken ton Athenon" (Impressions of the Architecture of Athens). *Akropolis*, March 21, 1899.

_____ (Neoellen). "Ethnikoi euergetai" (National Benefactors). *Akropolis*, July 18, 1899.

_____ (Neoellen). "O Vasileus" (The King). *Akropolis*, August 8, 1899.

_____ (Neoellen). "Filologia kai patriotismos" (Literature and Patriotism). *Estia*, pt. 1, August 13, 1899, pp. 3, 4.

_____ (Neoellen). "Poietai kai patris" (Poets and the Motherland). *Akropolis*, August 15, 1899.

_____ (Neoellen). "O Diadochos" (The Crown Prince). *Akropolis*, December 4, 1899.

_____ (Neoellen). "Ellenika paradoxa: E agnostos chora" (Greek Paradoxes: The Unknown Land). *To Asty*, December 10, 1899.

_____. "To kathekon mas" (Our Duty). *O Noumas*, January 12, 1903, p. 4.

_____. "E xenomania" (Obsession with Foreign Things). *O Noumas*, January 16, 1903, p. 4.

_____. "Ochi xena" (Nothing Foreign). *O Noumas*, January 30, 1903, pp. 1-2.

_____. "Ta dyo idanika: Dyo medenika" (The Two Ideals: Two Naughts). *Akropolis*, February 9, 10, 11, 12, 13, 18, 19, 1903.

_____. "Ti na kamomen?" (What Should We Do?). *Protevousa*, March 19, 1903.

_____. "Ta pantalonia tes filologias" (The Trousers of Literature). *O Noumas*, March 23, 1903, p. 2.

_____. "O chalasmenos kathreptes" (The Shattered Mirror). *O Noumas*, April 3, 1903, p. 2.

_____. "Pros ten ethniken zoen: I. O dynatos pothos" (Towards A National Life: I. The Strong Desire). *To Asty*, April 18, 1903, p. 2.

_____. "Pros ten ethniken zoen: II. E aoristia tou pothou" (Towards A National Life: II. The Uncertainity of Desire). *To Asty*, April 19, 1903, pp. 2, 3.

_____. "Pros ten ethniken zoen: III. E syndrome tou typou" (Towards A National Life: III. The Contribution of the Press). *To Asty*, April 22, 1903, p. 2.

_____. "Byzantine men, rinoklasia de" (Byzantine on the One Hand, Nosebreaking on the Other). *O Noumas*, April 24, 1903, p. 2.

_____. "Dia tous xenomaneis sofologious" (For the Foreign-minded Pedants). *O Noumas*, May 4, 1903, pp. 1-2.

_____ (Th. Thanatos). "Apo ta nea ereipia pros ten anagennesin: Salpismata" (From the New Ruins Towards Regeneration: Trumpet Calls). *To Asty*, Sept. 29, 30, 1904; October 1, 4, 5, 9, 11, 13, 15, 1904.

——————————. "Kai e Makedonia anthizei sten oran tes–O Megas Alexandros architekton tou kosmou" (Macedonia too Blossoms in its Time–Alexander the Great as Architect of the World). *Akropolis,* December 1, 1907.

Works by Ion Dragoumis

Books

Dragoumis, Ion. *To Monopati.* (The Footpath). Athens: Nea Zoe, 1925.

—————— (Idas). *Martyron kai Eroon Aima* (The Blood of Martyrs and Heroes). 2d ed., Athens: n.p., 1914.

—————— (Idas). Ellenikos Politismos (Hellenic Civilization). Alexandria: Grammata, 1913.

——————. *Deka Arthra sto Nouma* (Ten Articles in Nouma). Athens: Typos, 1920.

——————. *Stamatema* (Stopping). Athens: Nea Zoe, 1927.

——————. *O Ellenismos mou kai oi Ellenes* (My Hellenism and the Greeks). Athens: n.p., 1927.;

——————. *Osoi Zontanoi* (Those Who Are Alive). 2d ed. Athens: Nea Zoe, 1926.

——————. *Samothrake* (Samothrace). 2d ed. Athens: *Estia,* 1926.

Articles

Dragoumis, Ion. "Apospasmata apo ta teleutaia grammata tou Ionos St. Dragoume pros ton filo tou Petro Vlasto" (Excerpts from the Last Letters of Ion St. Dragoumis to his Friend Petros Vlastos). *Nea Estia,* August 1, 1960, pp. 976-78.

—————— (Ydragoras). "Epistolai ek Monasteriou" (Letters from Monastir). *Nea Emera,* Oct. 4, 1903.

—————— (Anon.). "Apostrofe ton vlemmaton" (Looking Away). *Neon Asty,* December 8, 1903, p. 1.

—————— (Anon.). "Metaxy Ellenon kai Boulgaron" (Between Greeks and Bulgarians). *Neon Asty,* Oct. 13, 1965, p. 1.

—————— (Ion o Skleros). "O nomos plakonei enan Ellenikotato antho" (The Law Crushes a Most Hellenic Flower). *O Noumas,* April 2, 1906.

—————— (Toxotes). "To eschaton dilemma eis mnemen ton kalos apothanonton" (The Last Dilemma in Memory of Those Who Died Well). *Nea Emera,* Sept. 2, 1906, p. 2.

——————. "Gia to vivlio tou Giannopoulou" (Concerning the Book of Giannopoulos). *O Noumas,* Oct. 15, 1906.

——————. "O dromos tes Makedonias" (The Road to Macedonia). *Neon Asty,* October 16, 1906.

—————— (Skorpios). "Ti erthe o Vasilias tes Italias" (Why did the King of Italy Come). *O Noumas,* April 1, 1907.

—————— (Idas). "To ethnos, oi taxeis kai o enas" (The Nation, the Classes and the Individual). *O Noumas,* November 25, 1907.

—————— (Idas). "O eugenikotera politismenos Laos" (The More Civilized People). *O Noumas,* Dec. 23, 1907.

_____ (Idas). "E these tes Tourkias I. (The Position of Turkey I.). *O Noumas,* Dec. 11, 1911, pp. 675-77.

_____ (Idas). "E these tes Tourkias II. (The Position of Turkey II.). *O Noumas,* Dec. 18, 1911, pp. 689-91.

_____ (Idas). "Ena Fylladio" (A Pamphlet), *Deltio tou Ekpaideutikou Omilou,* 1 (1911): 147-57.

_____ (Idas). *"Noumas* kai Demotikismos" (*Noumas* and Demoticism). *O Noumas,* Jan. 1, 1912, pp. 6-7.

_____ (Idas). "E these tes Tourkias III. (The Position of Turkey III.) *O Noumas,* Jan. 21, 1912, pp. 41-42.

_____ (Idas). "Ellenovoulgarika" I. (Greek-Bulgarian Affairs I.) *O Noumas,* Jan. 28, 1912, pp. 56-58.

_____ (Idas). "Ellenovoulgarika" II. (Greek-Bulgarian Affairs II.) *O Noumas,* Feb. 11, 1912, pp. 90-92.

_____ (Idas). "Arvanitia" (Albania). *O Noumas,* February 25, 1912, pp. 119-121.

_____ (Idas). "Nea politike sten Tourkia" (New Policies in Turkey). *O Noumas,* March 17, 1912, pp. 171-72.

_____ (Idas). "Dyo ekloges" (Two Elections). *O Noumas,* March 24, 1912, pp. 186-88.

_____. "Aytokratoria kai anatole" (Empire and the East). *Politike Epitheoresis,* Aug. 6, 1916, pp. 1083-91.

_____. "Ti einai o sosialismos?" (What is Socialism?). *Athenaike,* November 26, 1919.

_____. "Koinonika zetemata—E etairia politikon meleton" (Social Questions—The Society for Political Studies). *Kathemerine,* April 5, 1920.

_____. "To Ellenikon provlema" (The Greek Problem). *To Mellon,* Jan.-Feb., 1921, pp. 780-84.

Secondary and General Accounts

Akzin, Benjamin. *State and Nation.* London: Hutchinson and Co., 1964. *To Anatoliko Zetema kai e Megale Ellenike Idea os Lysis Aftou* (The Eastern Question and the Great Greek Idea as its Solution). Athens: n.p., 1878.

Arnakis, George. "Byzantium and Greece". *Balkan Studies* IV (1963): 379-400.

Aspreas, Georgios. *Politike Istoria tes Neoteras Ellados* (Political History of Modern Greece). 3 vols. Athens: n.p., 1922-30.

Augustinos, Jerry. "The Dynamics of Modern Greek Nationalism: The Great Idea and the Macedonian Problem." *East European Quarterly,* VI (Jan. 1973): 444-453.

Bien, Peter. *Kazantzakis and the Linguistic Revolution in Greek Literature.* Princeton: Princeton University Press, 1972.

Bikelas, Demetrios. *Le Rôle et les Aspirations de la Grèce dans la Question d'Orient.* Paris: Au Cercle Saint Simon, 1885.

Campbell, John & Sherrard, Philip. *Modern Greece.* London: Benn, 1968.

Delmouzos, Alex. "Gia to Zetema" (On the [Language] Question). *O Noumas,* September 16, 1907, p. 5.

_____ (Ntelos, A.), "Stous Demotikistas" (To the Demoticists). *O Noumas,* August 19, 1907, p. 1.

——————————. *Meletes kai Parerga* (Studies and Other Things). 2 vols. Athens: n.p., 1958.

Delta, Penelope. "Ta Anagnostika mas" (Our Primers). *Deltio tou Ekpaideutikou Omilou,* 3 (1913): 233-256.

——————————. "Stochasmoi peri tes anatrofes ton paidion mas" (Thoughts on the Upbringing of Our Children). *Deltio Tou Ekpaideutikou Omilou,* 1 (1911): 80-99.

Deutsch, Karl W. *Nationalism and Social Communication.* 2d ed. Cambridge, Mass.: MIT Press, 1966.

——————————. and William J. Foltz. *Nation-Building.* New York: Atherton Press, 1963.

Dillon, E.J. "The Fate of Greece". *Contemporary Review* July, 1897, pp. 1-34.

Dimaras, K. Th. "E Ellenike skepse kai to thema tou romantismou sta chronia 1829-39" (Greek Thought and the Theme of Romanticism During the Years 1829-39). *Grammata* VIII (1945): 77-88.

——————————. "Oi protes ekdoseis tes *Istorias* tou K. Paparrigopoulou" (The first Editions of K. Paparrigopoulos' *History).* O *Eranistes* (1967): 145-55.

——————————. *Kostes Palamas* (in Greek). Athens: Ikaros, 1948.

——————————. *Istoria tes Neoellenikes Logotechneias* (History of Modern Greek Literature). 4th ed. Athens: Ikaros, 1968.

Doob, Leonard W. *Patriotism and Nationalism.* New Haven: Yale Univ. Press., 1964.

Dragoumis, Philip S., ed. "Anekdota Keimena tou Ionos Dragoume" (Unpublished Documents of Ion Dragoumis). *Politike Epitheoresis,* May 29, 1921, pp. 817-30.

——————————. "Perikles Giannopoulos". *Ta Nea Grammata,* January, 1939.

——————————. "Viografiko semeioma tou demosiou viou tou Ionos Dragoume" (Biographical Note on the Public Life of Ion Dragoumis). *Ellenike Epitheoresis,* Aug.-Sept., 1929, pp. 1-4.

——————————. "O idios o Dragoumes" (The Same Dragoumis). *Ellenika Grammata,* Aug. 24, 1929, pp. 448-49.

Ta Eikosachrona tou Nouma 1903-1922 (The Twenty Years of Nouma 1903-1922). Athens: Typos, 1923.

Ekpaideutikos Omilos. *Katastatiko* (Statutes). Athens, 1915.

Ellenas [pseud]. "To Romaiiko mikrovio" (The Romaic Microbe). *O Noumas,* May 25, 1903.

"E epanastasis kai ai eklogai" (The Revolution and the Elections). *O Kallitechnes* A (1910): 163-69.

Eurygenes, D.I. *O Ion Dragoumis kai o Makedonikos Agon* (Ion Dragoumis and the Macedonian Struggle). Thessaloniki: n.p., 1961.

Finlay, George. *A History of Greece.* 7 vols. Oxford: Clarendon Press, 1877.

Fotiades, F.D. *To Glossikon Zetema k' e Ekpaideutike mas Anagennesis* (The Language Question and Our Educational Renaissance). Athens: Estia, 1902.

Fouriotes, A.D. *Pneumatike Poreia 1900-1950* (Spiritual Progress 1900-1950). Athens: Mourides, 1952.

Gavrilides, V. "Ekeinos!" (He!). *Akropolis,* April 12, 1910.

Golfe, Riga. "O Demotikistes" (The Demoticist). *Grammata,* 1943, pp. 283-90.

Hatzine, G. "Ai ideai kai o thanatos tou Perikle Giannopoulou" (The Ideas and the Death of Perikles Giannopoulos). *Kathemerine,* April 20, 1955.

Hatzepatera, Konst. *O Ion Dragoumis kai e Syneidese tes Ethnotetos* (Ion Dragoumis and National Consciousness). New York: n.p., 1948.

Haumant, E. "Les origines de la lutte pour la Macédoine 1855-1872". *Le Monde Slave* IV (1926): 52-66.

Hourmouzios, Aim. *O Palamas kai e Epoche tou* (Palamas and His Epoch). 3 vols. Athens: Dionysos, 1944-60.

Jenkins, Romilly J.H. "Samothrake" (Samothrace). *Aggloellenike Epitheorese* 3 (Sept.-Oct., 1948): 365-367.

_____. "Byzantium and Byzantinism". *Lectures in Memory of Louise Taft Semple.* Princeton, 1967.

_____. *Ion Dragoumis and Macedonia.* London, King's College, 1948.

Kaltchas, Nicholas. *Introduction to the Constitutional History of Modern Greece.* New York: Columbia Univ. Press., 1940.

Katsimbales, G. "O Palamas kai to Glossiko" (Palamas and the Language Question). *Ellenike Epitheoresis,* May-June 1931.

Kazazis, Neokles. *Hellenism and Macedonia.* London: Keith Thomas, 1904.

_____. *Greeks and Bulgarians in the Nineteenth and Twentieth Centuries.* London: Ballantyne & Co. Ltd., 1907.

Kaisar [pseud.]. "Kai sy Vroute?" (And You Brutus?). *O Noumas,* February 9, 1913, pp. 25-26.

Karolides, Pavlos. "E 25 Martiou tou 1821 kai tou 1908" (The 25th of March 1821 and 1908). *Akropolis,* March 25, 1908.

Konstantinidou, Stamatiou N. *E Fone ton Teknon tes Doules Ellados.* (The Voice of the Children of Enslaved Greece). (poem). Athens: n.p. 1864.

Konstantinopoulos, Ch. G. "Gyro ap' tous Palamades" (Concerning the Palamas'). *Nea Estia* (1961): 662-65.

Konstas, K.S. "Palamades". *Nea Estia* (1961): 303-21.

Kordatos, Giannes K. *Istoria tou Glossikou mas Zetematos.* (History of Our Language Question). Kallithea-Athens: G. Loukatos, 1943.

Koslin, Adamantia Pollis. "The Megali Idea—A Study in Greek Nationalism." Ph.D. dissertation, Johns Hopkins University, 1958.

Kougeas, S.V. "Konstantinos Paparrigopoulos". *Megale Ellenike Egkyklopaideia,* 19:573-74.

Kroeber, A.L. and Clyde Kluckhohn. *Culture.* New York: Random House, 1963.

Kyriakides, Epameinondas. *Istoria tou Sychronou Ellenismou 1832-1892* (History of Contemporary Hellenism 1832-1892). 2 vols. Athens: n.p., 1892.

Laourdas, Vasileios. *E Penelope Delta kai e Makedonia* (Penelope Delta and Macedonia). Thessalonike: Etairia Makedonikon Spoudon, 1958.

The Macedonian Syllogos in Athens. *Macedonia and the Reforms.* Athens: n.p., 1903.

"Makedonikon". *Skrip,* August 30, 1903.

Makropoulos, Theodoros. *To Mesologgi kai o Kostes Palamas* (Mesolonghi and Kostes Palamas). Athens: n.p., 1959.

Mango, Cyril. "Byzantinism and Romantic Hellenism". *Journal of the Warburg and Courtauld Institutes* 28 (1965): 29-43.

Massis, Henri. *La Pensée de Maurice Barrès.* Paris: n.p., 1909.

"Megale Idea" (The Great Idea). *Aion,* Sept. 10, 13, 17, 1847.

Mela, Natalia. *Pavlos Melas* (in Greek). 2d ed. Athens: Syllogos Pros Diadosin ton Ellenikon Grammaton, 1963.

[Melas, Leon]. *Hints on the Solution of the Eastern Question.* London: R. Clarke, 1853.

Melas, Spyros, ed. "Afieroma gia ton Giannopoulo" (Special Edition on Giannopoulos). *Ellenike Demiourgia,* Oct. 1, 1953.

Miller, William. *Travels and Politics in the Near East.* London: T. Fisher Unwin, 1898.

——————. *Greek Life in Town and Country.* London: George Newnes Ltd., 1905.

——————. *A History of the Greek People 1821-1921.* New York: E.P. Dutton, n.d.

Moskov, Kostes. *E Ethnike kai Koinonike Syneidese sten Ellada 1830-1909* (National and Social Consciousness in Greece 1830-1909). 2d ed. Athens: n.p., 1974.

Norman, Henry. "The Wreck of Greece". *Scribner's Magazine,* October, 1897, pp. 399-426.

Notare, Ioannes. *Pavlos Melas* (in Greek). Thessalonike: Etairia Makedonikon Spoudon, 1955.

——————. "Ethnikoi antiktypoi tou glossikou ste Makedonia" (National Repercussions of the Language [Question] in Macedonia). *Epoches,* October, 1964, pp. 52-56.

——————. ed. *Anekdota Eggrafa gia ten Epanastasi tou 1878 ste Makedonia* (Unpublished Documents on the Uprising of 1878 in Macedonia). Thessalonike: Etairia Makedonikon Spoudon, 1966.

Orologas, Petros. *Ion Dragoumis* (in Greek). Thessalonike: Neas Aletheias, 1938.

Palamas, Leandros. "Ion Dragoumis". *Deltio tou Ekpaideutikou Omilou* 9 (1921): 99-108.

Palles, Alexandros. "Grammata" (Letters). *O Noumas,* Oct. 15, 1906.

Papanoutsou, E.P. *Palamas, Kavafes, Sikelianos* (in Greek). Athens: Ikaros, 1955.

Paparrigopoulos, Konstantinos. "O archaios, o mesaionikos kai o neos Ellenismos" (Ancient, Medieval and Modern Hellenism). *Istorikai Pragmateiai.* Athens: G. Kasdones, 1889.

——————. *Epilogos tes Istorias tou Ellenikou Ethnous* (Conclusions on the History of the Hellenic Nation). Athens: S.K. Vlastou, 1877.

Paraschos, Kleon. *Ion Dragoumis* (in Greek). Athens: Pyrsos, 1936.

——————. "Pos antikrysei ton anthropon o I.D." (How I.D. Sees Man). *Kathemerine,* November 19, 1961.

To Periodikon mas, ed. "Ta Ellenika Ideode kai e Megale Idea: Gnomai ton Sygchronon" (Greek Ideals and the Great Idea: Opinions of Contemporaries). *To Periodikon Mas* 3 (May, 1901): 105-112, 137-142.

Prevelake, Eleutheriou. *E Megale Kretike Epanastase 1866-1869* (The Great Cretan Uprising 1866-1869). Athens: n.p., 1966.

Psicharis, Giannes. *The Language question in Greece.* Calcutta: Baptist Mission Press, 1902.

——————. "Enose tha pe Dyname". (Unity Means Strength). *O Noumas,* January 23, 1905, pp. 1-6.

——————. "O Argyres Eftaliotes". *O Noumas,* July-Sept., 1923, pp. 465-67.

Skliros, George. *Ta Sygchrona Prolemata tou Ellenismou* (The Contemporary Problems of Hellenism). Alexandria: n.p., 1919.

_____. *To Koinonikon mas Zetema* (Our Social Problem). Athens: A. Konstantinides, 1907.

Smith, Anthony D. *Theories of Nationalism*. London: Duckworth, 1971.

Souliotes-Nikolaides, Athanasios. *O Makedonikos Agon: E Organosis Thessalonikes, 1906-1908 Apomnemoneumata* (The Macedonian Struggle: The Thessalonike Organization, 1906-1908 Memoirs). Thessalonike: Etairia Makedonikon Spoudon, 1959.

_____. *E Megale Idea* (The Great Idea)., 1908.

_____. *Grammata apo ta Vouna—Semeiomatarion* (Letters from the Mountains-Notebook). Athens: Ikaros, 1971.

[_____] . "L'entente balkanique et l'Organosis de Constantinople 1908-1912". *Les Balkans*. March, 1931, pp. 1-6.

_____. (Ieromonachou Athanasiou Makedonos). *Profeteiai tou Megalou Alexandrou* (The Prophecies of Alexander the Great). Venice: n.p., 1907.

Tagopoulos, D.P. *Idas*. Alexandria: Grammata, 1916.

Tagopoulos, Panos. "Ta Istorika tou *Nouma:* E Prote Chronia tou" (The History of *Nouma:* Its First Year). *Ellenika Grammata* 3 (December, 1928): 553-561.

_____. "Selides apo to 1906: Tou Giannopoulou to *Neon Pneuma*" (Pages from 1906: *The Neon Pneuma* of Giannopoulos). *Ellenika Grammata* 4 (February, 1929): 177-181.

Theotokas, Giorgos. *Pneumatike Poreia* (Spiritual Development). Athens: Fexe, 1961.

Theotokas, Giorgos. *Eleuthero Pneuma* (Free Spirit). Athens: Ermes, 1973.

Theotokas, Giorgos *Argo*. Athens: Pyrsos, 1936.

_____. "Enas allos Dragoumis—Dragoumis kai Barrès" (Another Dragoumis—Dragoumis and Barrès). *Anagennese,* May-June, 1928, pp. 394-99.

_____. "Enas neos Dragoumis" (A New Dragoumis). Anagennese, July-August, 1928, pp. 473-81.

Toynbee, Arnold. *The Western Question in Greece and Turkey*. London: Constable & Co., 1922.

Triantafyllou, Kosta N. "O Perikles Giannopoulos kai o Theios tou Man. Chairetes" (Perikles Giannopoulos and his Uncle Man. Chairetes). *Nea Estia,* Sept. 15, 1961, pp. 1233-37.

_____. *E Byzantine Oikogeneia Chairete kai to en Patrais Archeion tes* (The Byzantine Family Chairetes and Its Archive in Patras). Patrai: n.p., 1962.

Triantaphyllides, Manoles. *Demotikismos kai Antidrase* (Demoticism and Reaction). Athens: n.p., 1960.

_____. (Kl. P.). "Apologia tes Demotikes" (Apology for Demoticism). *Deltio tou Ekpaideutikou Omilou* 4 (1914).

_____. *O Psicharis kai to glossiko zetema* (Psicharis and the Language Question). Athens: Serigade, 1929.

Tsatsou, Konstantinou. *Palamas* (in Greek). 3d ed. Athens: Estia, n.d.

Tsirimokos, Markos. *Istoria tou Ekpaideutikou Omilou* (History of the Educational Society). Athens: n.p., 1927.

Tuckerman, Charles K. *The Greeks of Today*. 2d ed. New York: G.P. Putnam's Sons, 1878.

Vacalopoulos, Ap. "Byzantinism and Hellenism: Remarks on the Racial Origin and the Intellectual Continuity of the Greek Nation." *Balkan Studies* IX (1968): 101-126.

Vasiliev, A.A. *History of the Byzantine Empire 324-1453.* 2 vols. Madison: Univ. of Wisconsin Press, 1958.

Venezes, Elias. "Sta ichne trion Ellenon: Germanou Karavagele, Pavlou Mela, kai Ionos Dragoume" (On the Trail of three Greeks: Germanos Karavageles, Pavlos Melas and Ion Dragoumis). *Vema,* June 2, 9, 16, 23, 30, 1964.

Voutierides, Elia. *Syntome Istoria tes Neoellenikes Logotechnias* (Concise History of Modern Greek Literature). 2d ed. Athens: Papadema, 1966.

Voyatzidis, J. "La Grande Idée". *L'Hellénisme Contemporain.* Athens, 1953, pp. 279-87.

Xanthopoulos-Palamas, Ch. *L'Idée de Paix dans l'Oeuvre de Costes Palamas,* Athens: n.p., 1936.

Xenopoulos, G. "Ena Systema" (A System). *O Noumas,* Sept. 24, 1906, pp. 1-3.

Xydis, Stephen. "Mediaeval Origins of Modern Greek Nationalism." *Balkan Studies* 9(1968):1-20.

——————. "Modern Greek Nationalism." *Nationalism in Eastern Europe* ed. by Peter Sugar & Ivo Lederer. Washington: Univ. of Washington Press, 1969.

Zakynthinos, Dion. *E Politike Istoria tes Neoteras Ellados* (The Political History of Modern Greece). Athens: Estia, 1965.

Zambeliou, S. *Byzantinai Meletai peri Pegon Neoellenikes Ethnotetos* (Byzantine Studies on the Sources of Modern Greek Nationality). Athens, 1857.

1. *Political Ideas and the Enlightenment in the Romanian Principalities, 1750-1831*. By Vlad Georgescu. 1971.

2. *America, Italy and the Birth of Yugoslavia, 1917-1919*. By Dragan R. Zivojinovic. 1972.

3. *Jewish Nobles and Geniuses in Modern Hungary*. By William O. McCagg, Jr. 1972.

4. *Mixail Soloxov in Yugoslavia: Reception and Literary Impact*. By Robert F. Price. 1973.

5. *The Historical and National Thought of Nicolae Iorga*. By William O. Oldson. 1973.

6. *Guide to Polish Libraries and Archives*. By Richard C. Lewanski. 1974.

7. *Vienna Broadcasts to Slovakia, 1938-1939: A Case Study in Subversion*. By Henry Delfiner. 1974.

8. *The 1917 Revolution in Latvia*. By Andrew Ezergailis. 1974.

9. *The Ukraine in the United Nations Organization: A Study in Soviet Foreign Policy. 1944-1950*. By Konstantin Sawczuk. 1975.

10. *The Bosnian Church: A New Interpretation*. By John V.A. Fine, Jr. 1975.

11. *Intellectual and Social Developments in the Habsburg Empire from Maria Theresa to World War I*. Edited by Stanley B. Winters and Joseph Held. 1975.

12. *Ljudevit Gaj and the Illyrian Movment*. By Elinor Murray Despalatovic. 1975.

13. *Tolerance and Movements of Religious Dissent in Eastern Europe*. Edited by Bela K. Kiraly. 1975.

14. *The Parish Republic: Hlinka's Slovak People's Party, 1939-1945*. By Yeshayahu Jelinek. 1976.

15. *The Russian Annexation of Bessarabia, 1774-1828*. By George F. Jewsbury. 1976.

16. *Modern Hungarian Historiography*. By Steven Bela Vardy. 1976.

17. *Values and Community in Multi-National Yugoslavia*. By Gary K. Bertsch. 1976.

18. *The Greek Socialist Movement and the First World War: the Road to Unity*. By George B. Leon. 1976.

19. *The Radical Left in the Hungarian Revolution of 1848*. By Laszlo Deme. 1976.

20. *Hungary between Wilson and Lenin: The Hungarian Revolution of 1918-1919 and the Big Three*. By Peter Pastor. 1976.

21. *The Crises of France's East-Central European Diplomacy, 1933-1938;*. By Anthony J. Komjathy. 1976.

22. *Polish Politics and National Reform, 1775-1788*; By Daniel Stone. 1976.

23. *The Habsburg Empire in World War I*. Robert A. Kann, Bela K. Kiraly, and Paula S. Fichtner, eds. 1977.

24. *The Slovenes and Yugoslavism, 1890-1914*. By Carole Rogel. 1977.

25. *German-Hungarian Relations and the Swabian Problem*. By Thomas Spira. 1977.

26. *The Metamorphosis of a Social Class in Hungary During the Reign of Young Franz Joseph*. By Peter I. Hidas. 1977.

27. *Tax Reform in Eighteenth Century Lombardy*. By Daniel M. Klang. 1977.

28. *Tradition versus Revolution: Russia and the Balkans in 1917*. By Robert H. Johnston. 1977.

29. *Winter into Spring: The Czechoslovak Press and the Reform Movement 1963-1968*. By Frank L. Kaplan. 1977.

30. *The Catholic Church and the Soviet Government, 1939-1949*. By Dennis J. Dunn. 1977.

31. *The Hungarian Labor Service System, 1939-1945*. By Randolph L. Braham. 1977.

32. *Consciousness and History: Nationalist Critics of Greek Society 1897-1914*. By Gerasimos Augustinos. 1977.

33. *Emigration in Polish Social and Political Thought, 1870-1914*. By Benjamin P. Murdzek. 1977.

34 *Serbian Poetry and Milutin Bojic*. By Mihailo Dordevic. 1977.